the algebra of infinite justice

arundhati roy

the algebra of infinite justice

With a foreword by John Berger

Flamingo
An Imprint of HarperCollinsPublishers

| *flamingo* | The term 'Original' signifies publication direct into paperback with no preceding British hardback edition. |
| **O**RIGINAL | The Flamingo Original series publishes fine writing at an affordable price at the point of first publication. |

Flamingo
An imprint of HarperCollins*Publishers*
77–85 Fulham Palace Road,
Hammersmith, London W6 8JB

Flamingo is a registered trademark of
HarperCollins*Publishers* Limited.

www.harpercollins.co.uk

Published by Flamingo 2002
5

First published in Viking by Penguin Books India 2001

'democracy' and 'war talk' first published in
this Flamingo edition, 2002

Publisher's Note (pages 303–305) is an extension of
the copyright page.

Copyright © Arundhati Roy 2001 and 2002

Arundhati Roy asserts the moral right to be
identified as the author of this work

ISBN 0 00 714949 2

Set in Linotype Bembo by
Rowland Phototypesetting Ltd, Bury St Edmunds, Suffolk

Printed and bound in Great Britain by
Clays Ltd, St Ives plc

For Babi Krishen

contents

acknowledgements

N. Ram and Vinod Mehta, editors of *Frontline* and *Outlook*, who have always made space for my writing.

Himanshu Thakker, who first revealed to me—brilliantly, meticulously, almost shyly—the horrors of the Narmada Valley Development Projects. To him I owe my first (belated) conspectus of this intricate method of pulverizing a people.

Shripad Dharmadhikary, Nandini Oza, Alok Aggarwal, who honed this understanding and sharpened my way of seeing.

Medha Patkar and Baba Amte, whose resilience and commitment cannot be described in a one-line acknowledgement.

Patrick McCully, whose book *Silenced Rivers* is the rock on which my understanding of the politics of Big Dams stands.

Prashant and Shanti Bhushan, who provide not just me but many of us with the rare comfort of having lawyers who are friends and who share our political views.

Anthony Arnove of South End Press who has endlessly checked and researched the facts in these essays.

David Godwin, without whom I would put all my writing into a drawer and hope that some day someone might find it and publish it.

Deepak Sarkar and Anurag Singh for their friendship and intricate understanding of all that I write about.

Silvy, whose mind gleams like a jewel that's caught the light. Whose affection and friendship are a constant source of comfort.

Jharana Jhaveri, most tenacious of fighters and gentlest of friends. Thank you for travelling with me.

Jojo, Raghu, Aradhana, Viveka, Pia, Mithva and Golak. Family. Philip and Veena for a home away from home.

Arjun Raina, my personal magician.

Sanjay Kak, whose wisdom and stillness I need like food and drink.

Mary Roy senior, the woman I admire most of all, Mary Roy junior, my sister, and LKC, who's always there, my brother, my friend, my refuge.

Thank you.

To Try and Understand

I wish to quote here, at the beginning of this illuminated and lucid book, a paragraph from the essay 'war is peace':

'Nothing can excuse or justify an act of terrorism, whether it is committed by religious fundamentalists, private militia, people's resistance movements—or whether it's dressed up as a war of retribution by a recognized government. The bombing of Afghanistan is not revenge for New York and Washington. It is yet another act of terror against the people of the world. Each innocent person that is killed must be *added to*, not set off against, the grisly toll of civilians who died in New York and Washington.'

On 11 September 2001, the pilots who attacked New York and Washington put an end for ever to a 'normalcy', and thus to a sense of security, which had prevailed in the

First World since the disintegration of the Soviet Union. (Let us note in passing how the rich are called the First.) This 'normalcy' lived hand in glove with extremities of humiliation, poverty and suffering which were—and still remain each day—comparable in their extremity to what happened that morning when the World Trade Center, the hub of the new world economic order, crumbled. All these extremities are interlinked.

Comparing degrees of horror is as futile and self-indulgent as comparing degrees of courage; neither can ever be assessed from the outside. Apart from the thousands of passive and innocent victims of the momentous attack, nineteen hijackers gave their lives (they were not cowards, as Bush immediately declared) as did three hundred and forty-three Manhattan firemen.

What it *is* legitimate to compare are the reactions to the different extremities. The tragedy in New York instantly mobilized the governments of the First World and provoked a war whose aims were unobtainable. I use the word 'tragedy' for first-hand reasons: what happened brought the tragic into the lives of many, many thousands of people. I also use it because, as in all tragedies, the precise vengeance and the carnage were foreseeable. Roy writes:

'It must be hard for ordinary Americans, so recently bereaved, to look up at the world with their eyes full of tears and encounter what might appear to them to be indifference. It isn't indifference. It's just augury. An absence of surprise. The tired wisdom of knowing that what goes around, eventually comes round.'

The extremities which preceded the New York tragedy were, by contrast, ignored, belittled or treated as irrelevant by those who at the moment believe they have the right to govern and dictate to the world. Every kind of appeal or warning concerning disaster after disaster fell upon deaf ears. (Read, from inside, where you can hear the breathing, Roy's intrepid essay 'the greater common good' about the Narmada Valley Dam Projects.)

Why this deafness? First and foremost, because the disasters were—and still are—the direct consequence of trying to impose everywhere the new world economic order (the abstract, soaring, groundless market) which insists that man's supreme task is to make profit. I use the word supreme for it may suggest how this insistence is the result of a new, secular fanaticism, originally developed in megalomaniac Chicago think tanks. The arrogance and ignorance which naturally accompany such fanaticism then proceed to make the deaf deafer.

Further, there is, I think, one more probable explanation for the deafness: a deep, never admitted, hidden fear of the excluded billions, an unadmitted nightmare-fear of all those whom the new order is in the process of eliminating, because they are not, and can never become, consumers. On 11 September, an equivalent nightmare turned into a reality—a fact which, in part, explains the ensuing hysteria.

In another essay, Roy personifies the forces behind corporate globalization and makes believe that they are a new kind of king:

'Powerful, pitiless and armed to the teeth. He's the kind of king the world has never known before. His realm is raw capital, his conquests emerging markets, his prayers profits, his borders limitless, his weapons nuclear. To even try and imagine him, to hold the whole of him in your field of vision, is to situate yourself at the very edge of sanity, to offer yourself up for ridicule.'

At the very edge of sanity, yes. Besides extending global poverties and displacements (the latter is the committee-word for homelessness), globalization has led, within the First World, to other extremities, this time of an eschato-logical nature. Don't laugh at the word. The effects are immediate.

For those living with some comfort in the First World, the future no longer exists as a common reference point. Yet for human beings, being sane depends on the acknowledgement of a continuity between the long since dead and those waiting to be born. The richer societies are being increasingly deprived of a temporal dimension essential to any spiritual life.

Individuals can find the missing dimension for themselves and, if they seek to share it, are drawn towards sects. But politics, which are a local or national procedure for choosing a future and working towards one, have been robbed of this perspective. Politicians mostly live from opinion poll to opinion poll. The more far-sighted project to the end of their term of office, no further. Nobody takes into account (except rhetorically) the generations to come. All times-to-come have been filched by the unpredictabilities of the market.

Meanwhile, the real decision-makers, operating the market, make their choices in the face of hourly or, at the most, daily fluctuations. Old-age pensions (the promise of small individual futures) are risked for immediate speculation. Since Bush's unilateral withdrawal—despite election promises to the contrary—from the Kyoto Agreements, the same goes for the planet. And this state of affairs is called Democracy.

Which brings us to the second eschatological extremity, one which concerns language.

'I witnessed,' writes Roy, 'the ritualistic slaughter of language as I know and understand it.' She was at the World Water Forum at The Hague in Holland, where several thousand experts were discussing the privatization of the world's water. 'God gave us the rivers,' declared one American expert, 'but he didn't put in the delivery systems. That's why we need private enterprise.' Roy continues:

'As a writer, one spends a lifetime journeying into the heart of language, trying to minimize, if not eliminate, the distance between thought and language . . . At The Hague I stumbled on a denomination, a sub-world, whose life's endeavour was to mask intent . . . They breed and prosper in the space that lies between what they say and what they sell.'

Today the Operation, by which the most powerful country in the world is bombing the rubble of one of the poorest into even smaller dust, was first named *Infinite Justice*. A meaningless term which has nothing to do with legal procedures, and is tragically, absurdly, only reminiscent of the hype in some promotional campaign for a new commodity.

Somebody in the Pentagon must have had doubts, since the name was changed. The same blind operation of vengeance is now called *Enduring Freedom*. Enduring refers to the capacity to last, but equally, it means suffering, perhaps surviving, an ordeal. Freedom, by its nature, is bound to be in a continual state of flux depending upon what it has to confront. So these two words slip, skid, because they were put together without the slightest awareness of the human effort of struggling towards clarity, which informs any language.

In a monstrous manner, *Enduring Freedom* describes exactly what the Afghanistan population among the rubble are now suffering. They (who are in the Last World) are *enduring* what the White House and the Pentagon call *Freedom*.

This loss of any sense of words (a collateral damage inflicted on language) inevitably leads to a diminution of the faculty of imagination, for imagination has to have solid, precise categories, so as to be able to leap across and between them. It is this which probably explains, in part, the colossal and continuous errors of US foreign policy. Ronald Reagan received a group of Afghan mujahideen at the White House in 1985 and announced that his guests were 'the moral equivalent of America's Founding Fathers'. That is to say George Washington and Thomas Jefferson!

A crucial question today is: What makes a terrorist and, in extremity, what makes a suicide 'martyr'? (I speak here of the anonymous volunteers: Terrorist Leaders are another story.) What makes a terrorist is, first, a form of despair. Or, to put it more accurately, it is a way of transcending, and by the gift of one's own life, making sense of a form of despair.

This is why the term 'suicide' is somewhat inappropriate, for the transcendence gives to the person a sense of triumph. A triumph over those he is supposed to hate? I doubt it. The triumph is over the passivity, the bitterness, the sense of absurdity which emanate from a certain depth of despair.

It is hard for the First World to imagine such despair. Not so much because of its relative wealth (wealth produces its own despairs), but because the First World is being continually distracted and its attention diverted. The despair to which I refer comes to those suffering conditions which oblige them to be single-minded. Decades lived in a refugee camp, for example.

This despair consists of what? The sense that your life and the lives of those close to you count for nothing. And this is felt on several different levels so that it becomes total. That is to say, as in totalitarianism, without appeal.

The search each morning
to find the scraps
with which to survive another day

The knowledge on waking
that in this legal wilderness
no rights exist

The experience over the years
of nothing getting better
only worse

The humiliation of being able
to change almost nothing,
and of seizing upon the almost
which then leads to another impasse.

The listening to a thousand promises
which pass inexorably
beside you and yours

The example of those who resist
being bombarded to dust

The weight of your own killed
a weight which closes
innocence for ever
because they are so many.

These are seven levels of despair—one for each day of the week—which lead, for some of the more courageous, to the revelation that to offer one's own life in contesting the forces which have pushed the world to where it is, is the only way of invoking an *all*, which is larger than that of the despair.

Let us now return to what Roy has said. 'To even try and imagine him (the new king), to hold the whole of him in your field of vision, is to situate yourself at the very edge of sanity . . .'

This is the confession of a wonderful writer but it is also a confession which many millions of people will instantly recognize as part of their own experience.

I'm tempted to say that the world has never been more confused. Yet this would be untrue. The world has never had to face such a global confusion. Only in facing it can we make sense of what we have to do. And this is precisely what Arundhati Roy does in the pages which follow. She makes sense of what we have to do. Thereby offering an example. An example of what? Of being fully alive in our world, such as it is, and of getting close to and listening to those for whom this world has become intolerable.

She answers the question herself perhaps better than I have just done:

'The only dream worth having . . . is to dream that you will live while you're alive and die only when you're dead . . .

'"Which means exactly what?"

'To love. To be loved. To never forget your own insignificance. To never get used to the unspeakable violence and vulgar disparity of life around you. To seek joy in the saddest places. To pursue beauty to its lair. To never simplify what is complicated or complicate what is simple. To respect strength, never power. Above all, to watch. To try and understand. To never look away. And never, never to forget.'

France
14 October 2001   *JOHN BERGER*

the end of imagination

For
marmots and voles
and everything else on earth
that is threatened and terrorized
by the human race

the end of imagination

'The desert shook,' the Government of India informed us (its people).

'The whole mountain turned white,' the Government of Pakistan replied.

By afternoon the wind had fallen silent over Pokhran. At 3.45 p.m. the timer detonated the three devices. Around 200 to 300 metres deep in the earth, the heat generated was equivalent to a million degrees centigrade—as hot as temperatures on the sun. Instantly, rocks weighing around a thousand tons, a mini mountain underground, vaporized . . . shockwaves from the blast began to lift a mound of earth the size of a football field by several metres. One scientist on seeing it said, 'I can now believe stories of Lord Krishna lifting a hill.'

—India Today[1]

May 1998. It'll go down in history books, provided, of course, we have history books to go down in. Provided, of course, we have a future. There's nothing new or original left to be said about nuclear weapons. There can be nothing more humiliating for a writer of fiction to have to do than restate a case that has, over the years, already been made by other people in other parts of the world, and made passionately, eloquently and knowledgeably.

I'm prepared to grovel. To humiliate myself abjectly, because, in the circumstances, silence would be indefensible. So those of you who are willing: let's pick our parts, put on these discarded costumes and speak our second-hand lines in this sad second-hand play. But let's not forget that the stakes we're playing for are huge. Our fatigue and our shame could mean the end of us. The end of our children and our children's children. Of everything we love. We have to reach within ourselves and find the strength to think. To fight.

Once again we are pitifully behind the times—not just scientifically and technologically (ignore the hollow claims), but more pertinently in our ability to grasp the true nature of nuclear weapons. Our Comprehension of the Horror Department is hopelessly obsolete. Here we are, all of us in India and in Pakistan, discussing the finer points of politics and foreign policy, behaving for all the world as though our governments have just devised a newer, bigger bomb, a sort of immense hand grenade with which they will annihilate the enemy (each other) and protect us from all harm. How desperately we want to believe that. What wonderful, willing, well-behaved, gullible subjects we have turned out to be. The rest of humanity (yes, yes, I know, I *know*, but let's ignore Them for the moment; They forfeited their votes a long time ago), the rest of the rest of humanity may not forgive us, but then the rest of humanity, depending on who fashions its views, may not know what a tired, dejected, heart-broken people we are. Perhaps it doesn't realize how urgently we need a miracle. How deeply we yearn for magic.

If only, if *only*, nuclear war was just another kind of war. If only it was about the usual things—nations and terri-tories, gods and histories. If only those of us who dread it were just worthless moral cowards who are not prepared to die in defence of our beliefs. If only nuclear war was the kind of war in which countries battle countries and men battle men. But it isn't. If there is a nuclear war, our foes will not be China or America or even each other. Our foe will be the earth herself. The very elements—the sky, the air, the land, the wind and water—will all turn against us. Their wrath will be terrible.

Our cities and forests, our fields and villages will burn for days. Rivers will turn to poison. The air will become fire. The wind will spread the flames. When everything there is to burn has burned and the fires die, smoke will rise and shut out the sun. The earth will be enveloped in darkness. There will be no day. Only interminable night. Temperatures will drop to far below freezing and nuclear winter will set in. Water will turn into toxic ice. Radioactive fallout will seep through the earth and contaminate groundwater. Most living things, animal and vegetable, fish and fowl, will die. Only rats and cockroaches will breed and multiply and compete with foraging, relict humans for what little food there is.

What shall we do then, those of us who are still alive? Burned and blind and bald and ill, carrying the cancerous carcasses of our children in our arms, where shall we go? What shall we eat? What shall we drink? What shall we breathe?

The Head of the Health, Environment and Safety Group of the Bhabha Atomic Research Centre in Bombay has a plan. He declared in an interview that India could survive nuclear war.[2] His advice is that if there is a nuclear war, we should adopt the same safety measures as the ones scientists recommend in the event of accidents at nuclear plants.

Take iodine pills, he suggests. And other steps such as remaining indoors, consuming only stored water and food and avoiding milk. Infants should be given powdered milk. 'People in the danger zone should immediately go to the ground floor and if possible to the basement.'

What do you do with these levels of lunacy? What do you do if you're trapped in an asylum and the doctors are all dangerously deranged?

Ignore it, it's just a novelist's naïveté, they'll tell you, Doomsday Prophet hyperbole. It'll never come to that. There will *be* no war. Nuclear weapons are about peace, not war. 'Deterrence' is the buzzword of the people who like to think of themselves as hawks. (Nice birds, those. Cool. Stylish. Predatory. Pity there won't be many of them around after the war. Extinction is a word we must try and get used to.) Deterrence is an old thesis that has been resurrected and is being recycled with added local flavour. The Theory of Deterrence cornered the credit for having prevented the Cold War from turning into a Third World War. The only immutable fact about the Third World War is that if there's going to be one, it will be fought after the Second World War. In other words, there's no fixed schedule. In other words, we still have time. And perhaps the pun (the *Third World* War) is prescient. True, the Cold War is over, but let's not be hoodwinked by the ten-year lull in nuclear posturing. It was just a cruel joke. It was only in remission. It wasn't cured. It proves no theories. After all, what is ten years in the history of the world? Here it is again, the disease. More widespread and less amenable to any sort of treatment than ever. No, the Theory of Deterrence has some fundamental flaws.

Flaw Number One is that it presumes a complete, sophisticated understanding of the psychology of your enemy. It assumes that what deters you (the fear of annihilation) will deter them. What about those who are *not* deterred by that? The suicide-bomber psyche—the 'We'll take you with us' school—is that an outlandish thought?

In any case, who's the 'you' and who's the 'enemy'? Both are only governments. Governments change. They wear masks within masks. They moult and reinvent themselves all the time. The one we have at the moment, for instance, does not even have enough seats to last a full term in office, but demands that we trust it to do pirouettes and party tricks with nuclear bombs even as it scrabbles around for a foothold to maintain a simple majority in Parliament.

Flaw Number Two is that Deterrence is premised on fear. But fear is premised on knowledge. On an understanding of the true extent and scale of the devastation that nuclear war will wreak. It is not some inherent, mystical attribute of nuclear bombs that they automatically inspire thoughts of peace. On the contrary, it is the endless, tireless, confrontational work of people who have had the courage to openly denounce them: their marches and demonstrations, their films, their outrage—*that* is what has averted, or perhaps only postponed, nuclear war. Deterrence will not and cannot work given the levels of ignorance and illiteracy that hang over our two countries like dense, impenetrable veils. (Witness the VHP wanting to distribute radioactive sand from the Pokhran desert as *prasad* all across India. A cancer yatra?) The Theory of Deterrence is nothing but a perilous joke in a world where iodine pills are prescribed as a prophylactic for nuclear irradiation.

India and Pakistan have nuclear bombs now and feel entirely justified in having them. Soon others will too. Iran, Iraq, Saudi Arabia, Norway, Nepal (I'm trying to be eclectic here), Denmark, Germany, Bhutan, Mexico, Lebanon, Sri Lanka, Burma, Bosnia, Singapore, North Korea, Sweden, South Korea, Vietnam, Cuba, Afghanistan, Uzbekistan . . . And why not? Every country in the world has a special case to make. Everybody has borders and beliefs. And when all our larders are bursting with shiny bombs and our bellies are empty (deterrence is an exorbitant beast), we can trade bombs for food. And when nuclear technology goes on the market, when it gets truly competitive and prices fall, not just governments, but anybody who can afford it, can have their own private arsenal—businessmen, terrorists, perhaps even the occasional rich writer (like myself). Our planet will bristle with beautiful missiles. There will be a new world order. The dictatorship of the pro-nuke elite. We can get our kicks by threatening each other. It'll be like bungee-jumping when you can't rely on the bungee cord, or playing Russian roulette all day long. An additional perk will be the thrill of Not Knowing What to Believe. We can be victims of the predatory imagination of every green-card-seeking charlatan who surfaces in the West with concocted stories of imminent missile attacks. We can delight at the prospect of being held to ransom by every petty trouble-maker and rumour-monger, the more the merrier, if truth be told, anything for an excuse to make more bombs. So you see, even without a war, we have a lot to look forward to.

But let us pause to give credit where it's due. Whom must we thank for all this?

The Men who made it happen. The Master of the Universe. Ladies and gentlemen, the United States of America! Come on up here folks, stand up and take a bow. Thank you for doing this to the world. Thank you for making a difference. Thank you for showing us the way. Thank you for altering the very meaning of life.

From now on it is not dying we must fear, but living.

It is such supreme folly to believe that nuclear weapons are deadly only if they're used. The fact that they exist at all, their very presence in our lives, will wreak more havoc than we can begin to fathom. Nuclear weapons pervade our thinking. Control our behaviour. Administer our societies. Inform our dreams. They bury themselves like meat hooks deep in the base of our brains. They are purveyors of madness. They are the ultimate colonizer. Whiter than any white man who ever lived. The very heart of whiteness.

All I can say to every man, woman and sentient child here in India, and over there, just a little way away in Pakistan, is: take it personally. Whoever you are—Hindu, Muslim, urban, agrarian—it doesn't matter. The only good thing about nuclear war is that it is the single most egalitarian idea that man has ever had. On the day of reckoning, you will not be asked to present your credentials. The devastation will be undiscriminating. The bomb isn't in your back yard. It's in your body. And mine. *Nobody*, no nation, no government, no man, no god, has the right to put it there. We're radioactive already, and the war hasn't even begun. So stand up and say something. Never mind if it's been said before. Speak up on your own behalf. Take it very personally.

The Bomb and I

In early May 1998 (before the bomb), I left home for three weeks.

While I was away, I met a friend of mine whom I have always loved for, among other things, her ability to combine deep affection with a frankness bordering on savagery.

'I've been thinking about you,' she said, 'about *The God of Small Things*—what's in it, what's over it, under it, around it, above it . . .'

She fell silent for a while. I was uneasy and not at all sure that I wanted to hear the rest of what she had to say. She, however, was sure that she was going to say it. 'In this last year—less than a year actually—you've had too much of everything—fame, money, prizes, adulation, criticism, condemnation, ridicule, love, hate, anger, envy, generosity—everything. In some ways it's a perfect story. Perfectly baroque in its excess. The trouble is that it has, or can have, only one perfect ending.' Her eyes were on me, bright with a slanting, probing brilliance. She knew that I knew what she was going to say. She was insane.

She was going to say that nothing that happened to me in the future could ever match the buzz of this. That the whole of the rest of my life was going to be vaguely dissatisfying. And, therefore, the only perfect ending to the story would be death. My death.

The thought had occurred to me too. Of course it had. The fact that all this, this global dazzle—the lights in my eyes, the applause, the flowers, the photographers, the journalists feigning a deep interest in my life (yet struggling to get a single fact straight), the men in suits fawning over me, the shiny hotel bathrooms with endless towels—none of it was likely to happen again. Would I miss it? Had I grown to need it? Was I a fame-junkie? Would I have withdrawal symptoms?

The more I thought about it, the clearer it became to me that if fame was going to be my permanent condition, it would kill me. Club me to death with its good manners and hygiene. I'll admit that I've enjoyed my own five minutes of it immensely, but primarily *because* it was just five minutes. Because I knew (or thought I knew) that I could go home when I was bored and giggle about it. Grow old and irresponsible. Eat mangoes in the moonlight. Maybe write a couple of failed books—worstsellers—to see what it felt like. For a whole year I'd cartwheeled across the world, anchored always to thoughts of home and the life I would go back to. Contrary to all the enquiries and predictions about my impending emigration, that was the well I dipped into. That was my sustenance. My strength. I told my friend there was no such thing as a perfect story. I said in any case hers was an external view of things, this assumption that the trajectory of a person's happiness, or let's say fulfilment, had peaked (and now must trough) because she had accidentally stumbled upon 'success'. It was premised on the unimaginative belief that wealth and fame were the mandatory stuff of everybody's dreams.

You've lived too long in New York, I told her. There are other worlds. Other kinds of dreams. Dreams in which failure is feasible. Honourable. Sometimes even worth striving for. Worlds in which recognition is not the only barometer of brilliance or human worth. There are plenty of warriors that I know and love, people far more valuable than myself, who go to war each day, knowing in advance that they will fail. True, they are less 'successful' in the most vulgar sense of the word, but by no means less fulfilled.

The only dream worth having, I told her, is to dream that you will live while you're alive and die only when you're dead. (Prescience? Perhaps.)

'Which means exactly what?' (Arched eyebrows, a little annoyed.)

I tried to explain, but didn't do a very good job of it. Sometimes I need to write to think. So I wrote it down for her on a paper napkin. This is what I wrote: *To love. To be loved. To never forget your own insignificance. To never get used to the unspeakable violence and the vulgar disparity of life around you. To seek joy in the saddest places. To pursue beauty to its lair. To never simplify what is complicated or complicate what is simple. To respect strength, never power. Above all, to watch. To try and understand. To never look away. And never, never, to forget.*

I've known her for many years, this friend of mine. She's an architect too.

She looked dubious, somewhat unconvinced by my paper napkin speech. I could tell that structurally, just in terms of the sleek, narrative symmetry of things, and because she loved me, her thrill at my 'success' was so keen, so generous, that it weighed in evenly with her (anticipated) horror at the idea of my death. I understood that it was nothing personal. Just a design thing.

Anyhow, two weeks after that conversation, I returned to India. To what I think/thought of as home. Something had died but it wasn't me. It was infinitely more precious. It was a world that had been ailing for a while, and had finally breathed its last. It's been cremated now. The air is thick with ugliness and there's the unmistakable stench of fascism on the breeze.

Day after day, in newspaper editorials, on the radio, on TV chat shows, on MTV for heaven's sake, people whose instincts one thought one could trust—writers, painters, journalists—make the crossing. The chill seeps into my bones as it becomes painfully apparent from the lessons of everyday life that what you read in history books is true. That fascism is indeed as much about people as about governments. That it begins at home. In drawing rooms. In bedrooms. In beds. 'Explosion of Self-esteem', 'Road to Resurgence', 'A Moment of Pride', these were headlines in the papers in the days following the nuclear tests.[3] 'We have proved that we are not eunuchs any more,' said Mr Thackeray of the Shiv Sena.[4] (Whoever said we were? True, a good number of us are women, but that, as far as I know, isn't the same thing.) Reading the papers, it was often hard to tell when people were referring to Viagra (which was competing for second place on the front pages) and when they were talking about the bomb—'We have superior strength and potency.' (This was our Minister for Defence after Pakistan completed its tests.)[5]

'These are not just nuclear tests, they are nationalism tests,' we were repeatedly told.

This has been hammered home, over and over again. The bomb is India, India is the bomb. Not just India, Hindu India. Therefore, be warned, any criticism of it is not just anti-national, but anti-Hindu. (Of course, in Pakistan the bomb is Islamic. Other than that, politically, the same physics applies.) This is one of the unexpected perks of having a nuclear bomb. Not only can the Government use it to threaten the Enemy, it can use it to declare war on its own people. Us.

In 1975, one year after India first dipped her toe into the nuclear sea, Mrs Gandhi declared the Emergency. What will the future bring? There's talk of cells being set up to monitor anti-national activity. Talk of amending cable laws to ban networks 'harming national culture'.[6] Of churches being struck off the list of religious places because 'wine is served' (announced and retracted).[7] Artists, writers, actors and singers are being harassed, threatened (and are succumbing to the threats). Not just by goon squads, but by instruments of the government. And in courts of law. There are letters and articles circulating on the Net—creative interpretations of Nostradamus' predictions claiming that a mighty, all-conquering Hindu nation is about to emerge—a resurgent India that will 'burst forth upon its former oppressors and destroy them completely'. This may well be the work of some lone nut, or a bunch of arcane god-squadders. The trouble is that having a nuclear bomb makes thoughts like these seem feasible. It *creates* thoughts like these. It bestows on people these utterly misplaced, utterly deadly, notions of their own power. It's happening. It's all happening. I wish I could say 'slowly but surely'—but I can't. Things are moving at a pretty fair clip.

Why does it all seem so familiar? Is it because, even as you watch, reality dissolves and seamlessly rushes forward into the silent, black-and-white images from old films—scenes of people being hounded out of their lives, rounded up and herded into camps? Of massacre, of mayhem, of endless columns of broken people making their way to nowhere? Why is there no soundtrack? Why is the hall so quiet? Have I been seeing too many films? Am I mad? Or am I right? Could those images be the inescapable culmination of what we have set into motion? Could our future be rushing forward into our past? I think so. Unless, of course, nuclear war settles it once and for all.

When I told my friends that I was writing this piece, they cautioned me. 'Go ahead,' they said, 'but first make sure you're not vulnerable. Make sure your taxes are paid.'

My papers are in order. My taxes are paid. But how can one *not* be vulnerable in a climate like this? Everyone is vulnerable. Accidents happen. There's safety only in acquiescence. As I write, I am filled with foreboding. In this country, I have truly known what it means for a writer to feel loved (and, to some degree, hated too). In 1997, I was one of the items being paraded in the media's end-of-the-year National Pride Parade. Among the others, much to my mortification, were a bomb-maker and an international beauty queen. Each time a beaming person stopped me on the street and said 'You have made India proud' (referring to the prize I won, not the book I wrote), I felt a little uneasy. It frightened me then and it terrifies me now, because I know how easily that swell, that tide of emotion, can turn against me. Perhaps the time for that has come. I'm going to step out from under the fairy lights and say what's on my mind.

It's this:

If protesting against having a nuclear bomb implanted in my brain is anti-Hindu and anti-national, then I secede. I hereby declare myself an independent, mobile republic. I am a citizen of the earth. I own no territory. I have no flag. I'm female, and have nothing against eunuchs. My policies are simple. I'm willing to sign any nuclear non-proliferation treaty or nuclear test ban treaty that's going. Immigrants are welcome.

My world has died. And I write to mourn its passing.

Admittedly, it was a flawed world. An unviable world. A scarred and wounded world. It was a world that I myself have criticized unsparingly, but only because I loved it. It didn't deserve to die. It didn't deserve to be dismembered. Forgive me, I realize that sentimentality is uncool —but what shall I do with my desolation?

I loved it simply because it offered humanity a choice. It was a rock out at sea. A stubborn chink of light that insisted that there was a different way of living. It was a functioning possibility. A real option. All that's gone now. India's nuclear tests, the manner in which they were conducted, the euphoria with which they have been greeted (by us) is indefensible. To me, it signifies dreadful things. The end of imagination. The end of freedom actually, because, after all, that's what freedom is. Choice.

On 15 August 1997 we celebrated the fiftieth anniversary of India's independence. From now on we can celebrate a future of nuclear bondage.

Why did they do it?

Political expediency is the obvious, cynical answer, except that it only raises another, more basic question: why should it have been politically expedient?

The three Official Reasons given are: China, Pakistan and Exposing Western Hypocrisy.

Taken at face value, and examined individually, they're somewhat baffling. I'm not for a moment suggesting that these are not real issues. Merely that they aren't new. The only new thing on the old horizon is the Indian Government. In his appallingly cavalier letter to the US President (why bother to write at all if you're going to write like this?) our Prime Minister says India's decision to go ahead with the nuclear tests was due to a 'deteriorating security environment'. He goes on to mention the war with China in 1962 and the 'three aggressions we have suffered in the last fifty years (from Pakistan). And for the last ten years we have been the victim of unremitting terrorism and militancy sponsored by it . . . especially in Jammu and Kashmir.'8

The war with China is several decades old. Unless there's some vital state secret that we don't know, it certainly seemed as though matters had improved slightly between us. Just a few days before the nuclear tests, General Fu Quanyou, Chief of General Staff of the Chinese People's Liberation Army, was the guest of our Chief of Army Staff. We heard no words of war.

The most recent war with Pakistan was fought twenty-seven years ago. Admittedly Kashmir continues to be a deeply troubled region and no doubt Pakistan is gleefully fanning the flames. But surely there must be flames to fan in the first place? Surely the kindling is crackling and ready to burn? Can the Indian State with even a modicum of honesty absolve itself completely of having a hand in Kashmir's troubles? Kashmir, and for that matter, Assam, Tripura, Nagaland—virtually the whole of the northeast—Jharkhand, Uttarakhand and all the trouble that's still to come—these are symptoms of a deeper malaise. It cannot and will not be solved by pointing nuclear missiles at Pakistan.

Even Pakistan can't be solved by pointing nuclear missiles at Pakistan. Though we are separate countries, we share skies, we share winds, we share water. Where radioactive fallout will land on any given day depends on the direction of the wind and rain. Lahore and Amritsar are thirty miles apart. If we bomb Lahore, Punjab will burn. If we bomb Karachi, then Gujarat and Rajasthan, perhaps even Bombay, will burn. Any nuclear war with Pakistan will be a war against ourselves.

As for the third Official Reason: Exposing Western Hypocrisy—how much more exposed can it be? Which decent human being on earth harbours any illusions about it? These are people whose histories are spongy with the blood of others. Colonialism, apartheid, slavery, ethnic cleansing, germ warfare, chemical weapons—they virtually invented it all. They have plundered nations, snuffed out civilizations, exterminated entire populations. They stand on the world's stage stark naked but entirely unembarrassed, because they know that they have more money, more food and bigger bombs than anyone else. They know they can wipe us out in the course of an ordinary working day. Personally, I'd say it is more arrogance than hypocrisy.

We have less money, less food and smaller bombs. However, we have—or had—all kinds of other wealth. Delightful, unquantifiable. What we have done with it is the opposite of what we think we've done. We've pawned it all. We've traded it in. For what? In order to enter into a contract with the very people we claim to despise. In the larger scheme of things, we've agreed to play their game and play it their way. We've accepted their terms and conditions unquestioningly. The CTBT ain't nothin' compared to this.

All in all, I think it is fair to say that *we're* the hypocrites. We're the ones who've abandoned what was arguably a moral position, i.e. *We have the technology, we can make bombs if we want to, but we won't. We don't believe in them.*

We're the ones who have now set up this craven clamouring to be admitted into the club of Superpowers. (If we are, we will no doubt gladly slam the door after us, and say to hell with principles about fighting Discriminatory World Orders.) For India to demand the status of a Superpower is as ridiculous as demanding to play in the

World Cup finals simply because we have a ball. Never mind that we haven't qualified, or that we don't play much soccer and haven't got a team.

Since we've chosen to enter the arena, it might be an idea to begin by learning the rules of the game. Rule number one is Acknowledge the Masters. Who are the best players? The ones with more money, more food, more bombs.

Rule number two is Locate Yourself in Relation to Them, i.e. make an honest assessment of your position and abilities. The honest assessment of ourselves (in quantifiable terms) reads as follows:

We are a nation of a billion people. In development terms we rank No. 138 out of the 175 countries listed in the UNDP's 1997 Human Development Index.[9] More than 400 million of our people are illiterate and live in absolute poverty, over 600 million lack even basic sanitation and over 200 million have no drinking water.

So the three Official Reasons, taken individually, don't add up to much. However, if you link them, a kind of twisted logic reveals itself. It has more to do with us than them.

The key words in our Prime Minister's letter to the US President were 'suffered' and 'victim'. That's the substance of it. That's our meat and drink. We need enemies. We have so little sense of ourselves as a nation, we cast about for targets to define ourselves against. To prevent the state from crumbling, we need a national cause, and other than our currency (and, of course, poverty, illiteracy and elections), we have none. This is the heart of the matter. This is the road that has led us to the bomb. This search for selfhood. If we are looking for a way out, we need some honest answers to some uncomfortable questions. Once again, it isn't as though these questions haven't been asked before. It's just that we prefer to mumble the answers and hope that no one's heard.

Is there such a thing as an Indian identity?

Do we really need one?

Who is an authentic Indian and who isn't?

Is India Indian?

Does it matter?

Whether or not there has ever been a single civilization that could call itself 'Indian', whether or not India was, is, or ever will become a cohesive cultural entity, depends on whether you dwell on the differences or the similarities in the cultures of the people who have inhabited the sub-continent for centuries. India, as a modern nation state, was marked out with precise geographical boundaries by a British Act of Parliament in 1899. Our country, as we know it, was forged on the anvil of the British Empire for the entirely unsentimental reasons of commerce and administration. But even as she was born, she began her struggle against her creators. So is India Indian? It's a tough question. Let's just say that we're an ancient people learning to live in a recent nation.

The majority of India's citizens will not (to this day) be able to identify its boundaries on a map, or say which language is spoken where or which god is worshipped in what region. To them the idea of India is, at best, a noisy slogan that comes around during wars and elections. Or a montage of people on government TV programmes wearing regional costumes and saying *Mera Bharat Mahaan*.

The people who have a vital stake (or, more to the point, a business interest) in India having a single, lucid, cohesive national identity are the politicians who constitute our national political parties. The reason isn't far to seek, it's simply because their struggle, their career goal, is—and must necessarily be—to *become* that identity. To be identi-fied with that identity. If there isn't one, they have to manufacture one and persuade people to vote for it. It isn't their fault. It comes with the territory. It is inherent in the nature of our system of centralized government. A congenital defect in our particular brand of democracy. The more morally bankrupt the politicians, the cruder the ideas of what that identity should be. However, to be fair, cobbling together a viable pre-digested 'National Identity' for India would be a formidable challenge even for the wise and the visionary. Every single Indian citizen could, if he or she wants to, claim to belong to some minority or the other. The fissures, if you look for them, run vertically, horizontally, and are layered, whorled, circular, spiral, inside out and outside in. Fires, when they're lit, race along any one of these schisms, and in the process, release tremendous bursts of political energy. Not unlike what happens when you split an atom.

It is this energy that Gandhi sought to harness when he rubbed the magic lamp and invited Ram and Rahim to partake of human politics and India's war of independence against the British. It was a sophisticated, magnificent, imaginative struggle, but its objective was simple and lucid, the target highly visible, easy to identify and succulent with political sin. In the circumstances, the energy found easy focus. The trouble is that the circumstances are entirely changed now, but the genie is out of its lamp and won't go back in. (It *could* be sent back, but nobody wants it to go, it's proved itself too useful.) Yes, it won us freedom. But it also won us the carnage of Partition. And now, in the hands of lesser statesmen, it has won us the Hindu Nuclear Bomb.

To be fair to Gandhi and to other leaders of the National Movement, they did not have the benefit of hindsight, and could not possibly have known what the eventual, long-term consequences of their strategy would be. They could not have predicted how quickly the situation would career out of control. They could not have foreseen what would happen when they passed their flaming torches into the hands of their successors, or how venal those hands could be.

It was Indira Gandhi who started the real slide. It is she who made the genie a permanent State Guest. She injected the venom into our political veins. She invented our particularly vile local brand of political expediency. She showed us how to conjure enemies out of thin air, to fire at phantoms that she had carefully fashioned for that very purpose. It was she who discovered the benefits of never burying the dead, but preserving their putrid carcasses and trundling them out to worry old wounds when it suited her. Between herself and her sons she managed to bring the country to its knees. Our new Government has just kicked us over and arranged our heads on the chopping block.

The BJP is, in some senses, a spectre that Indira Gandhi and the Congress created. Or, if you want to be less harsh, a spectre that fed and reared itself in the political spaces and communal suspicion that the Congress nourished and cultivated. It has put a new complexion on the politics of governance. While Mrs Gandhi played hidden games with politicians and their parties, she reserved a shrill convent school rhetoric, replete with tired platitudes, to address the general public. The BJP, on the other hand, has chosen to light its fires directly on the streets and in the homes and hearts of people. It is prepared to do by day what the Congress would do only by night. To legitimize what was previously considered unacceptable (but done anyway). There is perhaps a fragile case to be made here in favour of hypocrisy. Could the hypocrisy of the Congress Party, the fact that it conducted its wretched affairs surreptitiously instead of openly, could that possibly mean there is a tiny glimmer of guilt some-where? Some small fragment of remembered decency?

Actually, no.

No.

What am I doing? Why am I foraging for scraps of hope?

The way it has worked—in the case of the demolition of the Babri Masjid as well as in the making of the nuclear bomb—is that the Congress sowed the seeds, tended the crop, then the BJP stepped in and reaped the hideous harvest. They waltz together, locked in each other's arms. They're inseparable, despite their professed differences. Between them they have brought us here, to this dreadful, dreadful place.

The jeering, hooting young men who battered down the Babri Masjid are the same ones whose pictures appeared in the papers in the days that followed the nuclear tests. They were on the streets, celebrating India's nuclear bomb and simultaneously 'condemning Western Culture' by emptying crates of Coke and Pepsi into public drains. I'm a little baffled by their logic: Coke is Western Culture, but the nuclear bomb is an old Indian tradition?

Yes, I've heard—the bomb is in the Vedas. It might be, but if you look hard enough, you'll find Coke in the Vedas too. That's the great thing about all religious texts. You can find anything you want in them—as long as you know what you're looking for.

But returning to the subject of the non-Vedic 1990s: we storm the heart of whiteness, we embrace the most diabolic creation of Western science and call it our own. But we protest against their music, their food, their clothes, their cinema and their literature. That's not hypocrisy. That's humour.

It's funny enough to make a skull smile.

We're back on the old ship. The *SS Authenticity and Indianness*.

If there is going to be a pro-authenticity/anti-national drive, perhaps the Government ought to get its history straight and its facts right. If they're going to do it, they may as well do it properly.

First of all, the original inhabitants of this land were not Hindu. Ancient though it is, there were human beings on earth before there was Hinduism. India's Adivasi people have a greater claim to being indigenous to this land than anybody else, and how are they treated by the State and its minions? Oppressed, cheated, robbed of their lands, shunted around like surplus goods. Perhaps a good place to start would be to restore to them the dignity that was once theirs. Perhaps the Government could make a public undertaking that more dams like the Sardar Sarovar on the Narmada will not be built, that more people will not be displaced.

But, of course, that would be inconceivable, wouldn't it? Why? Because it's impractical. Because Adivasis don't really matter. Their histories, their customs, their deities are dispensable. They must learn to sacrifice these things for the greater good of the Nation (that has snatched from them everything they ever had).

Okay, so that's out.

For the rest, I could compile a practical list of things to ban and buildings to break. It'll need some research, but off the top of my head, here are a few suggestions.

They could begin by banning a number of ingredients from our cuisine: chillies (Mexico), tomatoes (Peru), potatoes (Bolivia), coffee (Morocco), tea, white sugar, cinnamon (China) . . . They could then move into recipes. Tea with milk and sugar, for instance (Britain).

Smoking will be out of the question. Tobacco came from North America.

Cricket, English and Democracy should be forbidden. Either kabaddi or kho-kho could replace cricket. I don't want to start a riot, so I hesitate to suggest a replacement for English (Italian . . .? It has found its way to us via a kinder route: marriage, not imperialism). We have already discussed (earlier in this essay) the emerging, apparently acceptable, alternative to democracy.

All hospitals in which Western medicine is practised or prescribed should be shut down. All national newspapers discontinued. The railways dismantled. Airports closed. And what about our newest toy—the mobile phone? Can we live without it, or shall I suggest that they make an exception there? They could put it down in the column marked 'Universal'? (Only essential commodities will be included here. No music, art or literature.)

Needless to say, sending your children to university in the US, and rushing there yourself to have your prostate operated upon, will be a cognizable offence.

The building demolition drive could begin with the Rashtrapati Bhavan and gradually spread from cities to the countryside, culminating in the destruction of all monuments (mosques, churches, temples) that were built on what was once Adivasi or forest land.

It will be a long, long list. It would take years of work. I couldn't use a computer because that wouldn't be very authentic of me, would it?

I don't mean to be facetious, merely to point out that this surely is the shortcut to hell. There's no such thing as an Authentic India or a Real Indian. There is no Divine Committee that has the right to sanction one single, authorized version of what India is or should be. There is no one religion or language or caste or region or person or story or book that can claim to be its sole representative. There are, and can only be, visions of India, various ways of seeing it—honest, dishonest, wonderful, absurd, modern, traditional, male, female. They can be argued over, criticized, praised, scorned, but not banned or broken. Not hunted down.

Railing against the past will not heal us. History has *happened*. It's over and done with. All we can do is to change its course by encouraging what we love instead of destroying what we don't. There is beauty yet in this brutal, damaged world of ours. Hidden, fierce, immense. Beauty that is uniquely ours and beauty that we have received with grace from others, enhanced, reinvented and made our own. We have to seek it out, nurture it, love it. Making bombs will only destroy us. It doesn't *matter* whether or not we use them. Bombs will destroy us either way.

India's nuclear bomb is the final act of betrayal by a ruling class that has failed its people.

However many garlands we heap on our scientists, however many medals we pin to their chests, the truth is that it is far easier to make a bomb than to educate four hundred million people.

According to opinion polls, we're expected to believe that there's a national consensus on the issue. It's official now. Everybody loves the bomb. (Therefore the bomb is good.)

■

Is it possible for people who cannot write their own names to understand even the basic, elementary facts about the nature of nuclear weapons? Has anybody told them that nuclear war has nothing at all to do with their received notions of war? Nothing to do with honour, nothing to do with pride? Has anybody bothered to explain to them about thermal blasts, radioactive fallout and the nuclear winter? Are there even words in their language to describe the concepts of enriched uranium, fissile material and critical mass? Or has their language itself become obsolete? Are they trapped in a time capsule, watching the world pass by, unable to understand or communicate with it because their language never took into account the horrors that the human race would dream up? Do they not matter at all? Shall we just treat them as though they're cretins? If they ask any questions, ply them with iodine pills and parables about how Lord Krishna lifted a hill or how the destruction of Lanka by Hanuman was unavoidable in order to preserve Sita's virtue and Ram's reputation? Use their own stories as weapons against them? Shall we release them from their capsule only during elections, and once they've voted, shake them by the hand, flatter them with some bullshit about the Wisdom of the Common Man, and send them right back in?

I'm not talking about just a handful of people, I'm talking about millions and millions who live in this country. This is their land too, you know. They have the right to make an informed decision about its fate and, as far as I can tell, nobody informed them about anything. The tragedy is that nobody could, even if they wanted to. Truly, literally, there's no language to do it in. This is the real horror of India. The orbits of the powerful and the powerless spinning further and further apart from each other, never intersecting, sharing nothing. Not a language. Not even a country.

Who the hell conducted those opinion polls? Who the hell is the Prime Minister to decide whose finger will be on the nuclear button that could turn everything we love—our earth, our skies, our mountains, our plains, our rivers, our cities and villages—to ash in an instant? Who the hell is he to reassure us that there will be no accidents? How does he know? Why should we trust him? What has he ever done to make us trust him? What have any of them ever done to make us trust them?

The nuclear bomb is the most anti-democratic, anti-national, anti-human, outright evil thing that man has ever made.

If you are religious, then remember that this bomb is Man's challenge to God.

It's worded quite simply: *We have the power to destroy everything that You have created.*

If you're not (religious), then look at it this way. This world of ours is 4,600 million years old.

It could end in an afternoon.

August 1998

the greater common good

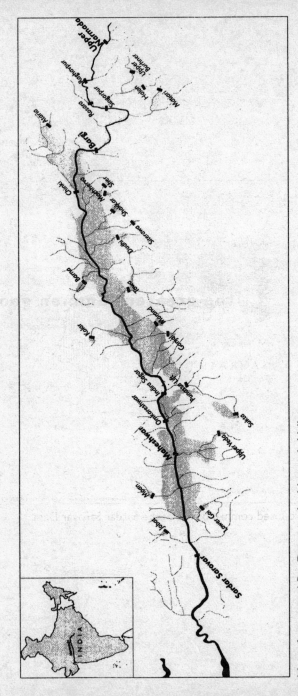

Map of proposed Big Dams in the Narmada Valley

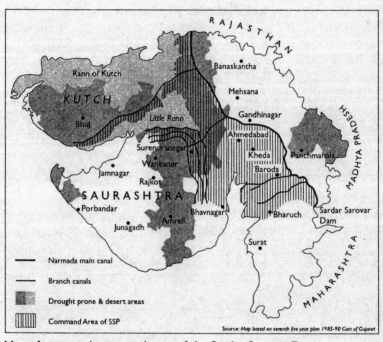

Map of proposed command area of the Sardar Sarovar Dam

To
the Narmada,
and all the life she sustains

the greater common good

If you are to suffer, you should suffer in the interest of the country . . .

> Jawaharlal Nehru, speaking to villagers who were to be displaced by the Hirakud dam, 1948[1]

I stood on a hill and laughed out loud.

I had crossed the Narmada by boat from Jalsindhi and climbed the headland on the opposite bank from where I could see, ranged across the crowns of low, bald hills, the Adivasi hamlets of Sikka, Surung, Neemgavan and Domkhedi. I could see their airy, fragile homes. I could see their fields and the forests behind them. I could see little children with littler goats scuttling across the landscape like motorized peanuts. I knew I was looking at a civilization older than Hinduism, slated—*sanctioned* (by the highest court in the land)—to be drowned this monsoon when the waters of the Sardar Sarovar reservoir will rise to submerge it.

Why did I laugh?

Because I suddenly remembered the tender concern with which the Supreme Court judges in Delhi (before vacating the legal stay on further construction of the Sardar Sarovar dam) had enquired whether Adivasi children in the re-settlement colonies would have children's parks to play in. The lawyers representing the Government had hastened to assure them that indeed they would, and what's more, that there were see-saws and slides and swings in every park. I looked up at the endless sky and down at the river rushing past and for a brief, brief moment the absurdity of it all reversed my rage and I laughed. I meant no disrespect.

Let me say at the outset that I'm not a city-basher. I've done my time in a village. I've had first-hand experience of the isolation, the inequity and the potential savagery of it. I'm not an anti-development junkie, nor a proselyt-iser for the eternal upholding of custom and tradition. What I *am*, however, is curious. Curiosity took me to the Narmada valley. Instinct told me that this was the big one. The one in which the battle lines were clearly drawn, the warring armies massed along them. The one in which it would be possible to wade through the congealed morass of hope, anger, information, disinformation, political artifice, engineering ambition, disingenuous socialism, radical activism, bureaucratic subterfuge, misinformed emotionalism and of course the pervasive, unerringly dubious, politics of International Aid.

Instinct led me to set aside Joyce and Nabokov, to postpone reading Don DeLillo's big book and substitute it with reports on drainage and irrigation, with journals and books and documentary films about dams and why they're built and what they do. My first tentative questions revealed that few people know what is really going on in the Narmada valley. Those who know, know a lot. Most know nothing at all. And yet, almost everyone has a passionate opinion. Nobody's neutral. I realized very quickly that I was straying into mined territory.

In India over the last ten years, the fight against the Sardar Sarovar dam has come to represent far more than the fight for one river. This has been its strength as well as its weakness. Some years ago, it became a debate that captured the popular imagination. That's what raised the stakes and changed the complexion of the battle. From being a fight over the fate of a river valley, it began to raise doubts about an entire political system. What is at issue now is the very nature of our democracy. Who owns this land? Who owns its rivers? Its forests? Its fish? These are huge questions. They are being taken hugely seriously by the state. They are being answered in one voice by every institution at its command—the army, the police, the bureaucracy, the courts. And not just answered, but answered unambiguously, in bitter, brutal ways.

For the people of the valley, the fact that the stakes were raised to this degree has meant that their most effective weapon—*specific* facts about *specific* issues in this *specific* valley—has been blunted by the debate on the big issues. The basic premise of the argument has been inflated until it has burst into bits that have, over time, bobbed away. Occasionally a disconnected piece of the puzzle floats by—an emotionally charged account of the Government's callous treatment of displaced people; an outburst at how the Narmada Bachao Andolan (NBA), 'a handful of activists', is holding the nation to ransom; a legal correspondent reporting on the progress of the NBA's writ petition in the Supreme Court.

Though there has been a fair amount of writing on the subject, most of it is for a 'special interest' readership. News reports tend to be about isolated aspects of the project. Government documents are classified as secret. Experts and consultants have hijacked various aspects of the issue—displacement, rehabilitation, hydrology, drainage, water-logging, catchment area treatment, passion, politics—and carried them off to their lairs where they guard them fiercely against the unauthorized curiosity of interested laypersons. Social anthropologists conduct acrimonious debates with economists about whose jurisdiction R&R falls in. Engineers refuse to discuss politics when they present their proposals. Disconnecting the politics from the economics from the emotion and human tragedy of uprootment is like breaking up a band. The individual musicians don't rock in quite the same way. You keep the noise but lose the music.

I think it's fair to say that public perception of the issue is pretty crude and is divided, crudely, into two categories:

On the one hand, it is seen as a war between modern, rational, progressive forces of 'Development' versus a sort of neo-Luddite impulse—an irrational, emotional 'Anti-Development' resistance, fuelled by an arcadian, pre-industrial dream.

On the other, as a Nehru versus Gandhi contest. This lifts the whole sorry business out of the bog of deceit, lies, false promises and increasingly successful propaganda (which is what it's *really* about) and confers on it a false legitimacy. It makes out that both sides have the Greater Good of the Nation in mind—but merely disagree about the means by which to achieve it.

Both interpretations put a tired spin on the dispute. Both stir up emotions that cloud the particular facts of this particular story. Both are indications of how urgently we need new heroes—new *kinds* of heroes—and how we've overused our old ones (like we overbowl our bowlers).

The Nehru versus Gandhi argument pushes this very contemporary issue back into an old bottle. Nehru and Gandhi were generous men. Their paradigms for development were based on assumptions of inherent morality. Nehru's on the paternal, protective morality of the Soviet-style centralized state. Gandhi's on the nurturing, maternal morality of romanticized village Republics. Both would probably work, if only we were better human beings. If we all wore khadi and suppressed our base urges. Fifty years down the line, it's safe to say that we haven't made the cut. We haven't even come close. We need an updated insurance plan against our own basic natures.

It's possible that as a nation we've exhausted our quota of heroes for this century, but while we wait for shiny new ones to come along, we have to limit the damage. We have to support our small heroes. (Of these we have many. Many.) We have to fight specific wars in specific ways. Who knows, perhaps that's what the twenty-first century has in store for us. The dismantling of the Big. Big bombs, big dams, big ideologies, big contradictions, big countries, big wars, big heroes, big mistakes. Perhaps right now, this very minute, there's a small god up in heaven readying herself for us. Could it be? Could it *possibly* be? It sounds finger-licking good to me.

I was drawn to the valley because I sensed that the fight for the Narmada had entered a newer, sadder phase. I went because writers are drawn to stories the way vultures are drawn to a kill. My motive was not compassion. It was sheer greed. I was right. I found a story there.

And what a story it is . . .

People say that the Sardar Sarovar dam is an expensive project. But it is bringing drinking water to millions. This is our lifeline. Can you put a price on this? Does the air we breathe have a price? We will live. We will drink. We will bring glory to the state of Gujarat.

Urmilaben Patel, wife of Gujarat Chief Minister Chimanbhai Patel, speaking at a public rally in Delhi in 1993

We will request you to move from your houses after the dam comes up. If you move it will be good. Otherwise we shall release the waters and drown you all.

Morarji Desai, speaking at a public meeting in the submergence zone of the Pong dam in 1961[2]

Why didn't they just poison us? Then we wouldn't have to live in this shit-hole and the Government could have survived along with its precious dam all to itself.

Ram Bai, whose village was submerged when the Bargi dam was built on the Narmada. She now lives in a slum in Jabalpur[3]

In the fifty years since Independence, Nehru's famous 'Dams are the Temples of Modern India' speech (one that he grew to regret in his own lifetime)[4] has made its way into primary school textbooks in every Indian language. Every schoolchild is taught that Big Dams will deliver the people of India from hunger and poverty. Nehru's foot-soldiers threw themselves into the business of building dams with unnatural fervour. Dam building grew to be equated with Nation building. The enthusiasm of our Nation-builders alone should have been reason enough to make one suspicious. Not only did they build new dams and new irrigation systems, they took control of small, traditional systems that had been managed by village communities for thousands of years, and allowed them to atrophy.[5] To compensate the loss, the Government built more and more dams. Big ones, little ones, tall ones, short ones. The result of its exertions is that India now boasts of being the world's third largest dam builder. According to the Central Water Commission, we have 3,600 dams that qualify as Big Dams, 3,300 of them built after Independence. Six hundred and ninety-five more are under construction.[6] This means that forty per cent of all the Big Dams being built in the world are being built in India. Yet one-fifth of our population does not have safe drinking water and two-thirds lack basic sanitation.[7]

There was a time when everybody loved Big Dams. Everybody had them—Communists, Capitalists, Christians,

Muslims, Hindus, Buddhists. They did not start out as a cynical enterprise. They began as a dream. They've ended up being a nightmare. It's time to wake up.

All over the world there is a movement growing against Big Dams.

In the First World, they're being decommissioned, blown up.[8] The fact that they do more harm than good is no longer just conjecture. Big Dams are obsolete. They're uncool. They're undemocratic. They're a Government's way of accumulating authority (deciding who will get how much water and who will grow what where). They're a guaranteed way of taking a farmer's wisdom away from him. They're a brazen means of taking water, land and irrigation away from the poor and gifting it to the rich. Their reservoirs displace huge populations of people, leaving them homeless and destitute.

Ecologically, too, they're in the doghouse.[9] They lay the earth to waste. They cause floods, waterlogging, salinity, they spread disease. There is mounting evidence that links Big Dams to earthquakes.

Big Dams haven't really lived up to their role as the monuments of Modern Civilization, emblems of Man's ascendancy over Nature. Monuments are supposed to be timeless, but dams have an all too finite lifetime. They last only as long as it takes Nature to fill them with silt.[10] It's common knowledge now that Big Dams do the opposite of what their Publicity People say they do—the Local Pain for National Gain myth has been blown wide open.

For all these reasons, the dam-building industry in the First World is in trouble and out of work. So it's exported to the Third World in the name of Development Aid,[11] along with their other waste, like old weapons, super-annuated aircraft carriers and banned pesticides.

On the one hand, the Indian Government, *every* Indian Government, rails self-righteously against the First World, and on the other, actually *pays* to receive their gift-wrapped garbage. Aid is just another praetorian business enterprise. Like Colonialism was. It has destroyed most of Africa. Bangladesh is reeling from its ministrations. We *know* all this, in numbing detail. Yet in India our leaders welcome it with slavish smiles (and make nuclear bombs to shore up their flagging self-esteem).

Over the last fifty years, India has spent €18,270,000,000[12] on the irrigation sector alone.[13] Yet there are more drought-prone areas and more flood-prone areas today than there were in 1947.[14] Despite the disturbing evidence of irrigation disasters, dam-induced floods and rapid disenchantment with the Green Revolution[15] (declining yields, degraded land), the Government has not commissioned a post-project evaluation of a *single one* of its 3,600 dams to gauge whether or not it has achieved what it set out to achieve, whether or not the (always phenomenal) costs were justified, or even what the costs actually were.

The Government of India has detailed figures for how many million tonnes of foodgrain or edible oils the country produces and how much more we produce now than we did in 1947. It can tell you how much bauxite is mined in a year or what the total surface area of the National Highways adds up to. It's possible to access minute-to-minute information about the stock exchange or the value of the rupee in the world market. We know how many cricket matches we've lost on a Friday in Sharjah. It's not hard to find out how many graduates India produces, or how many men had vasectomies in any given year. But the Government of India does not have a figure for the number of people that have been displaced by dams or sacrificed in other ways at the altar of 'National Progress'. Isn't this *astounding*? How can you measure Progress if you don't know what it costs and who has paid for it? How can the 'market' put a price on things—food, clothes, electricity, running water—when it doesn't take into account the *real* cost of production?

According to a detailed study of fifty-four Large Dams done by the Indian Institute of Public Administration, the *average* number of people displaced by a Large Dam in

India is 44,182.[16] Admittedly, fifty-four dams out of 3,300 is not a big enough sample. But since it's all we have, let's try and do some rough arithmetic. A first draft.

To err on the side of caution, let's halve the number of people. Or, let's err on the side of *abundant* caution and take an average of just 10,000 people per Large Dam. It's an improbably low figure, I know, but . . . never mind. Whip out your calculators, 3,300 × 10,000 = 33,000,000.

That's what it works out to, thirty-three *million* people. Displaced by Big Dams *alone* in the last fifty years. What about those who have been displaced by the thousands of other Development Projects? At a private lecture, N.C. Saxena, Secretary to the Planning Commission, said he thought the number was in the region of fifty million (of whom forty million were displaced by dams).[17] We daren't say so, because it isn't official. It isn't official because we daren't say so.[18] You have to murmur it for fear of being accused of hyperbole. You have to whisper it to yourself, because it really does sound unbelievable. It *can't be*, I've been telling myself. I must have got the zeroes muddled. *It can't be true*. I barely have the courage to say it aloud. To run the risk of sounding like a 1960s hippie dropping acid ('It's the System, man!'), or a paranoid schizophrenic with a persecution complex. But it *is* the System, man. What else can it be?

Fifty million people.

Go on, Government, quibble. Bargain. Beat it down. Say *something*.

I feel like someone who's just stumbled on a mass grave.

Fifty million is more than the population of Gujarat. Almost three times the population of Australia. More than three times the number of refugees that Partition created in India. Ten times the number of Palestinian refugees. The Western world today is convulsed over the future of one million people who have fled from Kosovo.

A huge percentage of the displaced are Adivasis (57.6 per cent in the case of the Sardar Sarovar dam).[19] Include Dalits and the figure becomes obscene. According to the Commissioner for Scheduled Castes and Tribes, it's about sixty per cent.[20] If you consider that Adivasis account for only eight per cent and Dalits another fifteen per cent of India's population, it opens up a whole other dimension to the story. The ethnic 'otherness' of their victims takes some of the pressure off the Nation Builders. It's like having an expense account. Someone *else* pays the bills. People from another country. Another world. India's poorest people are subsidizing the lifestyles of her richest.

Did I hear someone say something about the world's biggest democracy?

What has happened to all these millions of people? Where are they now? How do they earn a living? Nobody really knows. (The *Indian Express* had an account of how Adivasis displaced from the Nagarjunasagar Dam Project are selling their babies to foreign adoption agencies.[21] The Government intervened and put the babies in two public hospitals, where six infants died of neglect.) When it comes to Rehabilitation, the Government's priorities are clear. India does not *have* a National Rehabilitation Policy. According to the Land Acquisition Act of 1894 (amended in 1984) the Government is not legally bound to provide a displaced person with anything but cash compensation. Imagine that. A cash compensation, to be paid by an Indian government official to an illiterate male Adivasi (the women get nothing) in a land where even the postman demands a tip for a delivery! Most Adivasis have no formal title to their land and therefore cannot claim compensation anyway. Most Adivasis—or let's say, most small farmers—have as much use for money as a Supreme Court judge has for a bag of fertilizer.

The millions of displaced people don't exist any more. When history is written, they won't be in it. Not even as statistics. Some of them have subsequently been displaced three and four times—a dam, an artillery range, another dam, a uranium mine, a power project. Once they start rolling there's no resting place. The great majority is eventually absorbed into slums on the periphery of our great cities, where it coalesces into an immense pool of cheap construction labour (that builds more projects that displace more people). True, they're not being annihilated or taken to gas chambers, but I can warrant that the quality of their accommodation is worse than in any concentration camp of the Third Reich. They're not captive, but they redefine the meaning of liberty.

And still the nightmare doesn't end. They continue to be uprooted even from their hellish hovels by government bulldozers that fan out on clean-up missions whenever elections are comfortingly far away and the urban rich get twitchy about hygiene. In cities like Delhi, they run the risk of being shot by the police for shitting in public places—like three slum-dwellers were, not too long ago.

In the French Canadian wars of the 1770s, Lord Amherst exterminated most of Canada's native Indians by offering them blankets infested with the smallpox virus. Two centuries on, we of the Real India have found less obvious ways of achieving similar ends.

The millions of displaced people in India are nothing but refugees in an unacknowledged war. And we, like the citizens of White America and French Canada and

Hitler's Germany, are condoning it by looking away. Why? Because we're told that it's being done for the sake of the Greater Common Good. That it's being done in the name of Progress, in the name of the National Interest (which, of course, is paramount). Therefore gladly, un-questioningly, almost gratefully, we believe what we're told. We believe what it benefits us to believe.

Allow me to shake your faith. Put your hand in mine and let me lead you through the maze. Do this, because it's important that you understand. If you find reason to dis-agree, by all means take the other side. But please don't ignore it, don't look away. It isn't an easy tale to tell. It's full of numbers and explanations. Numbers used to make my eyes glaze over. Not any more. Not since I began to follow the direction in which they point.

Trust me. There's a story here.

It's true that India has progressed. Today India has more irrigated land than any other country in the world. In the last fifty years, the area under irrigation increased by about 140 per cent. It's true that in 1947, when colonialism formally ended, India was food deficient. In 1951 we produced fifty-one million tonnes of foodgrain. Today we produce close to 200 million tonnes.[22] Certainly, this is a tremendous achievement. (Even though there are worrying signs that it may not be sustainable.)

The unspoken assumption is that the massive increase in foodgrain production is all thanks to Big Dams. That Big Dams are the key to India's food security.

Ninety per cent of India's Big Dams are irrigation dams. But *are* they the key to India's food security?

To even ask this question is to invite accusations of sedition, of being anti-national, anti-development, of being a foreign agent, of receiving 'foreign funds'. However, the question must be asked.

The extraordinary thing is that there is no answer. There are no official government figures for exactly what proportion of the total foodgrain production comes from the mechanized exploitation of groundwater, from the use of high-yielding hybrid seeds, from the use of chemical fertilizers and from irrigation from Big Dams.

What is this if not a state's unforgivable disregard for its citizens? Given that the people of the Narmada valley have been fighting for over fifteen years, surely the least the government could do is to actually substantiate its case that Big Dams are India's only option to provide food for her growing population.

The only study I know of was presented to the World Commission on Dams by Himanshu Thakker. It estimates that Big Dams account for only twelve per cent of India's total foodgrain production![23]

Twelve per cent of the total produce is twenty-four million tonnes. In 1995, the state granaries were overflowing with thirty million tonnes of foodgrain, while at the same time 350 million people lived below the poverty line.[24]

According to the Ministry of Food and Civil Supplies, ten per cent of India's total foodgrain production, that is twenty million tonnes, is lost to rodents and insects because of bad and inadequate storage facilities. We must be the only country in the world that builds dams, uproots communities and submerges forests, in order to feed rats. Clearly we need better storerooms more urgently than we need dams.

So, unfortunately, it appears that while India has progressed, the majority of her people have not.

Indians are too poor to buy the food their country produces. Indians are being forced to grow the kinds of food they can't afford to eat themselves. Look at what happened in Kalahandi district in western Orissa, best known for its starvation deaths. In the drought of 1996, people died of starvation (sixteen according to the state, over one hundred according to the press).[25] Yet that same year, rice production in Kalahandi was higher than the national average! Rice was exported from Kalahandi district to the Centre.[26]

Our leaders say that we must have nuclear missiles to protect us from the threat of China and Pakistan. But who will protect us from ourselves?

What kind of country is this? Who owns it? Who runs it? What's going on?

It's time to spill a few State Secrets. To puncture the myth about the inefficient, bumbling, corrupt, but ultimately genial, essentially democratic, Indian state. Carelessness cannot account for fifty million disappeared people. Nor can karma. Let's not delude ourselves. There is method here, precise, relentless and 100 per cent man-made.

The Indian state is not a state that has failed. It is a state that has succeeded impressively in what it set out to do. It has been ruthlessly efficient in the way it has appropriated India's resources—its land, its water, its forests, its fish, its meat, its eggs, its air—and redistributed it to a favoured few (in return, no doubt, for a few favours). It is superbly accomplished in the art of protecting its cadres of paid-up elite, consummate in its methods of pulverizing those who inconvenience its intentions. But its finest feat of all is the way it achieves all this and emerges smelling sweet. The way it manages to keep its secrets, to contain information—that vitally concerns the daily lives of one billion people—in government files, accessible only to the keepers of the flame: ministers, bureaucrats, state engineers, defence strategists. Of course we make it easy for them, we, its beneficiaries. We take care not to dig too deep. We don't really *want* to know the grisly details.

Thanks to us, Independence came (and went), elections come and go, but there has been no shuffling of the deck. On the contrary, the old order has been consecrated, the rift fortified. We, the Rulers, won't pause to look up from our groaning table. We don't seem to know that the resources we're feasting on are finite and rapidly depleting. There's cash in the bank, but soon there'll be nothing left to buy with it. The food's running out in the kitchen. And the servants haven't eaten yet. Actually, the servants stopped eating a long time ago.

India lives in her villages, we're told, in every other sanctimonious public speech. That's bullshit. It's just another fig leaf from the Government's bulging wardrobe. India doesn't live in her villages. India *dies* in her villages. India gets kicked around in her villages. India lives in her cities. India's villages live only to serve her cities. Her villagers are her citizens' vassals and for that reason must be controlled and kept alive, but only just.

This impression we have of an overstretched state, struggling to cope with the sheer weight and scale of its problems, is a dangerous one. The fact is that it's *creating* the problem. It's a giant poverty-producing machine, masterful in its methods of pitting the poor against the very poor, of flinging crumbs to the wretched so that they dissipate their energies fighting each other, while peace (and advertising) reigns in the Master's Lodge.

Until this process is recognized for what it is, until it is addressed and attacked, elections—however fiercely they're contested—will continue to be mock battles that serve only to further entrench unspeakable inequity. Democracy (our version of it) will continue to be the benevolent mask behind which a pestilence flourishes unchallenged. On a scale that will make old wars and past misfortunes look like controlled laboratory experiments. Already fifty million people have been fed into the Development Mill and have emerged as air-conditioners and popcorn and rayon suits—*subsidized* air-conditioners and popcorn and rayon suits. If we must have these nice things—and they *are* nice—at least we should be made to pay for them.

There's a hole in the flag and it's bleeding.

It's a sad thing to have to say, but as long as we have faith—we have no hope. To hope, we have to *break* the faith. We have to fight specific wars in specific ways and we have to fight to win. Listen then, to the story of the Narmada valley. Understand it. And, if you wish, enlist. Who knows, it may lead to magic.

■

The Narmada wells up on the plateau of Amarkantak in the Shahdol district of Madhya Pradesh, then winds its way through 1,300 kilometres of beautiful broadleaved forest and perhaps the most fertile agricultural land in India. Twenty-five million people live in the river valley, linked to the ecosystem and to each other by an ancient, intricate web of interdependence (and, no doubt, exploitation).

Though the Narmada has been targeted for 'water resource development' for more than fifty years now, the reason it has, until recently, evaded being captured and dismembered is that it flows through three states—Madhya Pradesh, Maharashtra and Gujarat.

Ninety per cent of the river flows through Madhya Pradesh; it merely skirts the northern border of Maharashtra, then flows through Gujarat for about 180 kilometres before emptying into the Arabian sea at Bharuch.

As early as 1946, plans had been afoot to dam the river at Gora in Gujarat. In 1961, Nehru laid the foundation stone for a 49.8-metre-high dam—the midget progenitor of the Sardar Sarovar.

Around the same time, the Survey of India drew up new topographical maps of the river basin. The dam planners in Gujarat studied the new maps and decided that it would be more profitable to build a much bigger dam. But this meant first hammering out an agreement with neighbouring states.

For years the three states bickered and balked but failed to agree on a water-sharing formula. Eventually, in 1969, the Central Government set up the Narmada Water Disputes Tribunal. It took the Tribunal another ten years to announce its Award. *The people whose lives were going to be devastated were neither informed nor consulted nor heard.*

To apportion shares in the waters, the first, most basic thing the Tribunal had to do was to find out how much water there was in the river. Usually this can only be reliably estimated if there are at least forty years of accumulated data on the volume of actual flow in the river. Since this was not available, they decided to extrapolate from rainfall data. They arrived at a figure of 27.22 million acre feet (MAF).[27]

This seminal figure is the statistical bedrock of the Narmada Valley Projects. We are still living with its legacy. It more or less determines the overall design of the Projects—the height, location and number of dams. By inference, it determines the cost of the Projects, how much area will be submerged, how many people will be displaced and what the benefits will be.

In 1992, actual observed flow data for the Narmada—which was now available for forty-five years (from 1948 to 1992)—showed that the yield from the river was only 22.69 MAF—eighteen per cent less![28] The Central Water Commission admits that there is less water in the Narmada than had previously been assumed.[29] The Government of India says:

> It may be noted that clause 11 (of the decision of the Tribunal) relating to determination of dependable flow as 28 MAF is non-reviewable (!)[30]

Never mind the data—the Narmada is legally bound by human decree to produce as much water as the Government of India commands.

Its proponents boast that the Narmada Valley Project is the most ambitious river valley project ever conceived in human history. They plan to build 3,200 dams that will reconstitute the Narmada and her forty-one tributaries into a series of step reservoirs—an immense staircase of amenable water. Of these, thirty will be major dams, 135 medium and the rest small. Two of the major dams will be multipurpose mega-dams. The Sardar Sarovar in Gujarat and the Narmada Sagar in Madhya Pradesh will, between them, hold more water than any other reservoir on the Indian subcontinent.

Whichever way you look at it, the Narmada Valley Development Project is Big. It will alter the ecology of the entire river basin of one of India's biggest rivers. For better or for worse, it will affect the lives of twenty-five million people who live in the valley. It will submerge and destroy 4,000 square kilometres of natural deciduous forest.[31] Yet, even before the Ministry of Environment cleared the project, the World Bank offered to finance the linchpin of the project—the Sardar Sarovar dam, whose reservoir displaces people in Madhya Pradesh and Maharashtra, but whose benefits go to Gujarat. The Bank was ready with its chequebook *before* any costs were computed, *before* any studies had been done, *before* anybody had any idea of what the human cost or the environmental impact of the dam would be! The $450 million loan for the Sardar Sarovar Projects was sanctioned and in place in 1985. The Ministry of Environment clearance for the project came only in 1987! Talk about enthusiasm. It fairly borders on evangelism. Can anybody care so much?

Why were they so keen?

Between 1947 and 1994, the World Bank's management submitted 6,000 projects to the Executive Board. The Board did not turn down a single one. *Not a single one*. Terms like 'Moving money' and 'Meeting loan targets' suddenly begin to make sense.

India is in a situation today where it pays back more money to the Bank in interest and repayment instalments than it receives from it. We are forced to incur new debts in order to be able to repay our old ones. According to the *World Bank Annual Report* (1998), after the arithmetic, India paid the Bank $478 million more than it borrowed. Between 1993 and 1998 India paid the Bank $1.475 billion more than it received.[32] The relationship between us is exactly like the relationship between a landless labourer steeped in debt and the village moneylender—it is an affectionate relationship, the poor man loves his moneylender because he's always there when he's needed. It's not for nothing that we call the world a Global Village. The only difference between the landless labourer and the Government of India is that one uses the money to survive. The other just funnels it into the private coffers of its officers and agents, pushing the country into an economic bondage that it may never escape.

The international Dam Industry is worth $20 billion a year.[33] If you follow the trails of Big Dams the world over, wherever you go—China, Japan, Malaysia, Thailand, Brazil, Guatemala—you'll rub up against the same story, encounter the same actors: the Iron Triangle (dam jargon for the nexus between politicians, bureaucrats and dam construction companies), the racketeers who call themselves International Environmental Consultants (who are usually directly employed by dam builders or their subsidiaries), and more often than not, the friendly neighbourhood World Bank. You'll grow to recognize the same inflated rhetoric, the same noble 'People's Dam' slogans, the same swift, brutal repression that follows the first sign of civil insubordination. (Of late, especially after its experience in the Narmada valley, the Bank is more cautious about choosing the countries in which it finances projects that involve mass displacement. At present, China is its Most Favoured client. It's the great irony of our times—American citizens protest the massacre in Tiananmen Square, but the Bank has used their money to fund studies for the Three Gorges dam in China which is going to displace 1.3 million people. The Bank is today the biggest foreign financier of large dams in China.)[34]

It's a skilful circus and the acrobats know each other well. Occasionally they'll swap parts—a bureaucrat will join the Bank, a Banker will surface as a Project Consultant. At the end of play, a huge percentage of what's called

'Development Aid' is re-channelled back to the countries it came from, masquerading as equipment cost or consultants' fees or salaries to the agencies' own staff. Often, Aid is openly 'tied' (as in the case of the Japanese loan for the Sardar Sarovar dam—to a contract for purchasing turbines from the Sumitomo Corporation).[35] Sometimes the connections are more murky. In 1993, Britain financed the Pergau dam in Malaysia with a subsidized loan of £234 million, despite an Overseas Development Administration report that said that the dam would be a 'bad buy' for Malaysia. It later emerged that the loan was offered to 'encourage' Malaysia to sign a £1.3 *billion* contract to buy British arms.[36]

In 1994, British consultants earned $2.5 billion on overseas contracts.[37] The second biggest sector of the market after Project Management was writing what are called EIAs (Environmental Impact Assessments). In the Development racket, the rules are pretty simple. If you get invited by a Government to write an EIA for a big dam project and you point out a problem (say, you quibble about the amount of water available in a river, or, God forbid, you suggest that the human costs are perhaps too high) then you're history. You're an OOWC—an Out of Work Consultant. And oops—there goes your Range Rover. There goes your holiday in Tuscany. There goes your children's private boarding school. There's good money in poverty. Plus Perks.

In keeping with Big Dam tradition, concurrent with the construction of the 138.68-metre-high Sardar Sarovar dam, began the elaborate Government pantomime of conducting studies to estimate the actual project costs and the impact it would have on people and the environment. The World Bank participated wholeheartedly in the charade—occasionally it beetled its brows and raised feeble requests for more information on issues like the resettlement and rehabilitation of what it calls 'PAPs'—Project Affected Persons. (They help, these acronyms—they manage to mutate muscle and blood into cold statistics. PAPs soon cease to be people.) The merest crumbs of information satisfied the Bank and it proceeded with the project. The implicit, unwritten but fairly obvious understanding between the concerned agencies was that whatever the costs—economic, environmental or human—the project would go ahead. They would justify it as they went along. They knew full well that eventually, in a courtroom or to a committee, no argument works as well as a fait accompli.

M' lord, the country is losing two crores a day due to the delay.

The Government refers to the Sardar Sarovar dam as the 'Most Studied Project in India', yet the game goes something like this: when the Tribunal first announced its Award and the Gujarat Government announced its plan of how it was going to use its share of water, *there was no mention of drinking water for villages in Kutch and Saurashtra,* the arid areas of Gujarat. When the project ran into political trouble, the Government suddenly discovered the emotive power of Thirst. Suddenly, quenching the thirst of parched throats in Kutch and Saurashtra became the whole *point* of the Sardar Sarovar Projects. (Never mind that water from two rivers—the Sabarmati and the Mahi, both of which are *miles* closer to Kutch and Saurashtra than the Narmada—have been dammed and diverted to Ahmedabad, Mehsana and Kheda. Neither Kutch nor Saurashtra has seen a drop of it.) Officially, the number of people who will be provided drinking water by the Sardar Sarovar canal fluctuates from twenty-eight million (1983) to 32.5 million (1989)—nice touch, the decimal point!—down to ten million (1992) and twenty-five million (1993).[38] In 1979 the number of villages that would receive drinking water was zero. In the early 1980s it was 4,719, in 1990 it was 7,234 and in 1991 it was 8,215.[39] When pressed, the Government admitted that the figures for 1991 mistakenly included 236 *uninhabited* villages.[40]

Every aspect of the project is approached in this almost playful manner, as if it's a family board game. Even when it concerns the lives and futures of vast numbers of people.

In 1979, the number of families that would be displaced by the Sardar Sarovar reservoir was estimated to be a little over 6,000. In 1987, it grew to 12,000. In 1991, it surged to 27,000. In 1992 the Government acknowledged that 40,000 families would be affected. Today, the official figure hovers between 40,000 and 41,500.[41] (Of course even this is an absurd figure, because the reservoir isn't the *only* thing that displaces people. According to the NBA, the actual figure is about 85,000 families—that's half a million people.)

The estimated cost of the project bounced up from under Rs 5,000 crore to Rs 20,000 crore (officially).[42] The NBA says that it will cost Rs 44,000 crore.[43]

The Government claims the Sardar Sarovar Projects will produce 1,450 megawatts of power.[44] The thing about multipurpose dams like the Sardar Sarovar is that their 'purposes' (irrigation, power production and flood-control) conflict with one another. Irrigation uses up the water you need to produce power. Flood control requires you to keep the reservoir empty during the monsoon months to deal with an anticipated surfeit of water. And if there's no surfeit, you're left with an empty dam. And this defeats the purpose of irrigation, which is to *store* the monsoon water. It's like the conundrum of trying to ford a river with a fox, a chicken and a bag of grain. The result of these mutually conflicting aims, studies say, is that when the Sardar Sarovar Projects are completed and the scheme is fully functional, it will end up producing only three per cent of the power that its planners say it will. About fifty megawatts. And if you take into account the power needed to pump water through its vast network of canals, the Sardar Sarovar Projects will end up *consuming* more electricity than they produce![45]

In an old war, everybody has an axe to grind. So how do you pick your way through these claims and counter-claims? How do you decide whose estimate is more reliable? One way is to take a look at the track record of Indian dams.

The Bargi dam near Jabalpur was the first dam on the Narmada to be completed (in 1990). It cost ten times more than was budgeted and submerged three times more land than the engineers said it would. About 70,000 people from 101 villages were supposed to be displaced, but when they filled the reservoir (without warning any-body), 162 villages were submerged. Some of the resettle-ment sites built by the Government were submerged as well. People were flushed out like rats from the land they had lived on for centuries. They salvaged what they could, and watched their houses being washed away. One hundred and fourteen thousand people were displaced.[46] There was no rehabilitation policy. Some were given meagre cash compensations. Many got absolutely noth-ing. A few were moved to government rehabilitation sites. The site at Gorakhpur is, according to Government publicity, an 'ideal village'. Between 1990 and 1992, five people died of starvation there. The rest either returned to live illegally in the forests near the reservoir, or moved to slums in Jabalpur.

The Bargi dam irrigates only as much land as it submerged in the first place—*and only five per cent of the area that its planners claimed it would irrigate.*[47] Even that is now water-logged.

Time and again, it's the same story. The Andhra Pradesh Irrigation II scheme claimed it would displace 63,000 people. When completed, it displaced 150,000 people.[48] The Gujarat Medium Irrigation II scheme displaced 140,000 people instead of 63,600.[49] The revised estimate of the number of people to be displaced by the Upper Krishna irrigation project in Karnataka is 240,000 against its initial claims of displacing only 20,000.[50]

These are World Bank figures. Not the NBA's. Imagine what this does to our conservative estimate of thirty-three million.

Construction work on the Sardar Sarovar dam site, which had continued sporadically since 1961, began in earnest in 1988. At the time, nobody, not the Government, nor the World Bank, were aware that a woman called Medha Patkar had been wandering through the villages slated to be submerged, asking people whether they had any idea of the plans that the Government had in store for them. When she arrived in the valley all those years ago, opposing the construction of the dam was the furthest thing from her mind. Her chief concern was that displaced villagers should be resettled in an equitable, humane way. It gradually became clear to her that the Government's intentions towards them were far from honourable. By 1986, word had spread and each state had a people's organization that questioned the promises about resettlement and rehabilitation that were being bandied about by Government officials. It was only some years later that the full extent of the horror—the impact that the dams would have, both on the people who were to be displaced and the people who were supposed to benefit—began to surface. The Narmada Valley Development Project came to be known as India's Greatest Planned Environmental Disaster. The various people's organizations coalesced into a single organization and the Narmada Bachao Andolan—the extraordinary NBA—was born.

In 1988, the NBA formally called for all work on the Narmada Valley Development Projects to be stopped. People declared that they would drown if they had to, but would not move from their homes. Within two years, the struggle had burgeoned and had won support from other resistance movements. In September 1989, more than 50,000 people gathered in the valley from all over India to pledge to fight Destructive Development. The dam site and its adjacent areas, already under the Indian Official Secrets Act, were clamped under Section 144 which prohibits the gathering of groups of more than five people. The whole area was turned into a police camp. Despite the barricades, one year later, on 28 September 1990, thousands of villagers made their way on foot and by boat to a little town called Badwani, in Madhya Pradesh, to reiterate their pledge to drown rather than agree to move from their homes.

News of the people's opposition to the Projects spread to other countries. The Japanese arm of Friends of the Earth mounted a campaign in Japan that succeeded in getting the Government of Japan to withdraw its twenty-seven billion yen loan to finance the Sardar Sarovar Projects. (The contract for the turbines still holds.) Once the Japanese withdrew, international pressure from various environmental activist groups who supported the struggle began to mount on the World Bank.

This of course led to an escalation of repression in the valley. Government policy, described by a particularly articulate minister, was to 'flood the valley with khaki'.

On Christmas Day in 1990, 6,000 men and women walked over a hundred kilometres, carrying their provisions and their bedding, accompanying a seven-member sacrificial squad that had resolved to lay down their lives for the river. They were stopped at Ferkuwa on the Gujarat border by battalions of armed police and crowds of people from the city of Baroda—some of whom perhaps genuinely believed that the Sardar Sarovar was 'Gujarat's lifeline', but many of whom were hired. It was a telling confrontation. Middle-Class Urban India versus a Rural, predominantly Adivasi, Army. The marching people demanded they be allowed to cross the border and walk to the dam site. The police refused them passage. To stress their commitment to non-violence, each villager had his or her hands bound together. One by one, they defied the battalions of police. They were beaten, arrested and dragged into waiting trucks in which they were driven off and dumped some miles away, in the wilderness. They just walked back and began all over again.

The face-off continued for almost two weeks. Finally, on 7 January 1991, the seven members of the sacrificial squad announced that they were going on an indefinite hunger strike. Tension rose to dangerous levels. The Indian and international press, TV camera crews and documentary film-makers were present in force. Reports appeared in the papers almost every day. Environmental activists stepped up the pressure in Washington. Eventually, acutely embarrassed by the glare of unfavourable media, the World Bank announced that it would commission an independent review of the Sardar Sarovar Projects—

unprecedented in the history of Bank behaviour. When the news reached the valley, it was received with distrust and uncertainty. The people had no reason to trust the World Bank. But still, it was a victory of sorts. The villagers, understandably upset by the frightening deterioration in the condition of their comrades who had not eaten for twenty-two days, pleaded with them to call off the fast. On 28 January, the fast at Ferkuwa was called off and the brave, ragged army returned to their homes shouting *'Hamare gaon mein hamara Raj!'* ('Our rule in our villages').

There has been no army quite like this one anywhere else in the world. In other countries—China (Chairman Mao got a Big Dam for his seventy-seventh birthday), Malaysia, Guatemala, Paraguay—every sign of revolt has been snuffed out almost before it began. Here in India, it goes on and on. Of course, the state would like to take credit for this too. It would like us to be grateful to it for not crushing the movement completely, for *allowing* it to exist. After all what *is* all this, if not a sign of a healthy functioning democracy in which the state has to intervene when its people have differences of opinion?

I suppose that's one way of looking at it. (Is this my cue to cringe and say 'Thank you, thank you, for *allowing* me to write the things I write?')

We don't need to be grateful to the state for permitting us to protest. We can thank ourselves for that. It is we who have insisted on these rights. It is we who have refused to surrender them. If we have anything to be truly proud of as a people, it is this.

The struggle in the Narmada valley lives, *despite* the state.

The Indian state makes war in devious ways. Apart from its apparent benevolence, its other big weapon is its ability to wait. To roll with the punches. To wear out the opposition. The state never tires, never ages, never needs a rest. It runs an endless relay.

But fighting people tire. They fall ill, they grow old. Even the young age prematurely. For twenty years now, since the Tribunal's Award, the ragged army in the valley has lived with the fear of eviction. For twenty years, in most areas there has been no sign of 'development'—no roads, no schools, no wells, no medical help. For twenty years, it has borne the stigma 'slated for submergence'—so it's isolated from the rest of society (no marriage proposals, no land transactions). The 'fruits of modern development', when they finally came, brought only horror. Roads brought surveyors. Surveyors brought trucks. Trucks brought policemen. Policemen brought bullets and beatings and rape and arrest and, in one case, murder. The only genuine 'fruit' of modern development that reached them, reached them inadvertently—the right to raise their voices, the right to be heard. But they have fought for twenty years now. How much longer can they last?

The struggle in the valley is tiring. It's no longer as fashionable as it used to be. The international camera crews and the radical reporters have moved (like the World Bank) to newer pastures. The documentary films have been screened and appreciated. Everybody's sympathy is all used up. But the dam goes on. It's getting higher and higher . . .

Now, more than ever before, the ragged army needs reinforcements. If we let it die, if we allow the struggle to be crushed, if we allow the people to be brutalized, we will lose the most precious thing we have: our spirit, or what's left of it.

'India will go on,' they'll tell you, the sage philosophers who don't want to be troubled by piddling Current Affairs. As though 'India' is somehow more valuable than her people.

Old Nazis probably soothe themselves in similar ways. It's too late, some people say. Too much time and money has gone into the project to revoke it now.

So far, the Sardar Sarovar reservoir has submerged only a fourth of the area that it will when *(if)* the dam reaches its full height. If we stop it now, we would save 325,000 people from certain destitution. As for the economics of it—it's true that the Government has already spent €15,750,000, but continuing with the project would mean throwing good money after bad. We would save something like €73,500,000 of public money. Enough to fund local water harvesting projects in every village in this vast country. What could possibly be a more worthwhile war?

The war for the Narmada valley is not just some exotic tribal war, or a remote rural war or even an exclusively Indian war. It's a war for the rivers and the mountains and the forests of the world. All sorts of warriors from all over the world, anyone who wishes to enlist, will be honoured and welcomed. Every kind of soldier will be needed. Doctors, lawyers, teachers, judges, journalists, students, sportsmen, painters, actors, singers, lovers . . . The borders are open, folks! Come on in.

◼

Anyway, back to the story.

In June 1991, the World Bank appointed Bradford Morse, a former head of the United Nations Development

Program, as Chairman of the Independent Review. His brief was to make a thorough assessment of the Sardar Sarovar Projects. He was guaranteed free access to all secret Bank documents relating to the Projects.

Morse and his team arrived in India in September 1991. The NBA, convinced that this was yet another set-up, at first refused to meet them. The Gujarat Government welcomed the team with a red carpet (and a nod and a wink) as covert allies. A year later, in June 1992, the historic Independent Review (known also as the 'Morse Report') was published.

The Independent Review unpeels the project delicately, layer by layer, like an onion. Nothing was too big, and nothing too small for the members of the Morse Committee to inquire into. They met ministers and bureaucrats, they met NGOs working in the area, went from village to village, from resettlement site to resettlement site. They visited the good ones. The bad ones. The temporary ones, the permanent ones. They spoke to hundreds of people. They travelled extensively in the submergence area and the command area. They went to Kutch and other drought-hit areas in Gujarat. They commissioned their own studies. They examined every aspect of the project: hydrology and water management, the upstream environment, sedimentation, catchment area treatment, the downstream environment, the anticipation of likely problems in the command area—waterlogging, salinity, drainage, health, the impact on wildlife.

What the Independent Review reveals in temperate, measured tones (which I admire, but cannot emulate) is scandalous. It is the most balanced, unbiased, yet damning indictment of the relationship between the Indian state and the World Bank. Without appearing to, perhaps even without intending to, the Report cuts through to the cosy core, to the space where they live together and love each other (somewhere between what they say and what they do).

The core recommendation of the 357-page Independent Review was unequivocal and wholly unexpected:

> We think the Sardar Sarovar Projects as they stand are flawed, that resettlement and rehabilitation of all those displaced by the Projects is not possible under prevailing circumstances, and that environmental impacts of the Projects have not been properly considered or adequately addressed. Moreover, we believe that the Bank shares responsibility with the borrower for the situation that has developed . . . it seems clear that engineering and economic imperatives have driven the Projects to the exclusion of human and environmental concerns . . . India and the states involved . . . have spent a great deal of money. No one wants to see this money wasted. But we

caution that it may be more wasteful to proceed without
full knowledge of the human and environmental costs
. . . As a result, we think that the wisest course would
be for the Bank to step back from the Projects and
consider them afresh . . .[51]

Four committed, knowledgeable, truly independent
men—they do a lot to make up for the faith eroded by
hundreds of other venal ones who are paid to do similar
jobs.

The World Bank, however, was still not prepared to give
up. It continued to fund the project. Two months after
the Independent Review, it sent out the Pamela Cox
Committee which did exactly what the Morse Review
had cautioned against ('. . . *it would be irresponsible for us*
to patch together a series of recommendations on implementation
when the flaws in the Projects are as obvious as they seem to
us')[52] and suggested a sort of patchwork remedy to try and
salvage the operation. In October 1992, on the recommendation of the Pamela Cox Committee, the Bank
asked the Indian Government to meet some minimum,
primary conditions within a period of six months.[53] Even
that much the Government couldn't do. Finally, on 30
March 1993, the World Bank pulled out of the Sardar
Sarovar Projects. (Actually, technically, on 29 March, one
day *before* the deadline, the Government of India asked the
World Bank to withdraw.[54] Details. Details.)

No one has ever managed to make the World Bank step back from a project before. Least of all a ragtag army of the poorest people in one of the world's poorest countries. A group of people whom Lewis Preston, then President of the Bank, never managed to fit into his busy schedule when he visited India.[55] Sacking the Bank was and is a huge moral victory for the people in the valley.

The euphoria didn't last. The Government of Gujarat announced that it was going to raise the $200 million shortfall on its own and push ahead with the project.

During the period of the Independent Review and after it was published, confrontation between people and the Authorities continued unabated in the valley—humiliation, arrests, baton charges. Indefinite fasts terminated by temporary promises and permanent betrayals. People who had agreed to leave the valley and be resettled had begun returning to their villages from their resettlement sites. In Manibeli, a village in Maharashtra and one of the nerve-centres of the resistance, hundreds of villagers participated in a Monsoon Satyagraha. In 1993, families in Manibeli remained in their homes as the waters rose. They clung to wooden posts with their children in their arms and refused to move. Eventually policemen prised them loose and dragged them away. The NBA declared that if the Government did not agree to review the project, on 6 August 1993 a band of activists would drown themselves in the rising waters of the reservoir. On 5 August, the Union Government constituted yet another committee called the Five Member Group (FMG) to review the Sardar Sarovar Projects. The Government of Gujarat refused it entry into Gujarat.[56]

The FMG report (a 'desk report') was submitted the following year.[57] It tacitly endorsed the grave concerns of the Independent Review. But it made no difference. Nothing changed. This is another of the state's tested strategies. It kills you with committees.

In February 1994, the Government of Gujarat ordered the permanent closure of the sluice gates of the dam.

In May 1994, the NBA filed a writ petition in the Supreme Court questioning the whole basis of the Sardar Sarovar dam and seeking a stay on its construction.[58]

That monsoon, when the level in the reservoir rose and the surging waters smashed down on the other side of the dam, 65,000 cubic metres of concrete and 35,000 cubic metres of rock were torn out of a stilling basin, leaving a crater 65 metres wide. The river bed powerhouse was flooded. The damage was kept secret for months.[59] Reports started appearing about it in the press only in January 1995.

In early 1995, on the grounds that the rehabilitation of displaced people had not been adequate, the Supreme Court ordered work on the dam to be suspended until further notice.[60] The height of the dam was 80 metres above mean sea level.

■

Meanwhile, work had begun on two more dams in Madhya Pradesh—the massive Narmada Sagar (without which the Sardar Sarovar loses seventeen to thirty per cent of its efficiency) and the Maheshwar dam.[61] The Maheshwar dam is next in line, upstream from the Sardar Sarovar. The Government of Madhya Pradesh has signed a power purchase contract with a private company— S. Kumars, one of India's leading textile magnates.

Tension in the Sardar Sarovar area abated temporarily and the battle moved upstream to Maheshwar, in the fertile plains of Nimad.

The case pending in the Supreme Court led to a palpable easing of repression in the valley. Construction work had stopped on the dam, but the rehabilitation charade continued. Forests (slated for submergence) continued to be cut and carted away in trucks, forcing people who depended on them for a livelihood to move out.

Even though the dam is nowhere near its eventual projected height, its impact on the environment and the people living along the river is already severe.

Around the dam site and in nearby villages, the number of cases of malaria has increased sixfold.[62]

Several kilometres upstream from the Sardar Sarovar dam, huge deposits of silt, hip-deep and over 200 metres wide, have cut off access to the river. Women carrying water pots now have to walk miles, literally *miles,* to find a negotiable entry point. Cows and goats get stranded in the mud and die. The little single-log boats that Adivasis use have become unsafe on the irrational circular currents caused by the barricade downstream.

Further upstream, where the silt deposits have not yet become a problem, there's another tragedy. Landless people (predominantly Adivasis and Dalits) have traditionally cultivated rice, melons, cucumbers and gourds on the rich, shallow silt banks the river leaves when it recedes in the dry months. Every now and then, the engineers manning the Bargi dam (way upstream, near Jabalpur) release water from the reservoir without warning. Downstream, the water level in the river suddenly rises. Hundreds of families have had their crops washed away several times, leaving them with no livelihood.

Suddenly they can't trust their river any more. It's like a loved one who has developed symptoms of psychosis. Anyone who has loved a river can tell you that the loss of a river is a terrible, aching thing. But I'll be rapped on the knuckles if I continue in this vein. When we're discussing the Greater Common Good, there's no place for sentiment. One must stick to facts. Forgive me for letting my heart wander.

■

The state Governments of Madhya Pradesh and Maharashtra continue to be completely cavalier in their dealings with displaced people. The Government of Gujarat has a rehabilitation policy (on paper) that makes the other two states look medieval. It boasts of being the best rehabilitation package in the world.[63] It offers land for land to displaced people from Maharashtra and Madhya Pradesh and recognizes the claims of 'encroachers' (usually Adivasis with no *pattas* or title deeds to their land). The deception, however, lies in its definition of who qualifies as 'Project Affected'.

In point of fact, the Government of Gujarat hasn't even managed to rehabilitate people from its own nineteen villages slated for submergence, let alone the rest of the 226 villages in the other two states. The inhabitants of these nineteen villages have been scattered to 175 separate rehabilitation sites. Social links have been smashed, communities broken up.

In practice, the resettlement story (with a few 'Ideal Village' exceptions) continues to be one of callousness and broken promises. Some people have been given land, others haven't. Some have land that is stony and uncultivable. Some have land that is irredeemably waterlogged. Some have been driven out by landowners who had sold their land to the Government but hadn't been paid.[64]

Some who were resettled on the periphery of other villages have been robbed, beaten and chased away by their host villagers. There have been instances when displaced people from two different dam projects have been allotted contiguous lands. In one case, displaced people from *three* dams—the Ukai dam, the Sardar Sarovar dam and the Karjan dam—were resettled in the *same* area.[65] In addition to fighting amongst themselves for resources—water, grazing land, jobs—they had to fight a group of landless labourers who had been sharecropping the land for absentee landlords who had subsequently sold it to the Government.

There's another category of displaced people—people whose lands have been acquired by the Government for resettlement sites. There's a pecking order even amongst the wretched—Sardar Sarovar 'oustees' are more glamorous than other 'oustees' because they're occasionally in the news and have a case in court. (In other Development Projects where there's no press, no NBA, no court case, there are no records. The displaced leave no trace at all.)

In several resettlement sites, people have been dumped in rows of corrugated tin sheds that are furnaces in summer and fridges in winter. Some of them are located in dry river beds that, during the monsoon, turn into fast-flowing drifts. I've been to some of these 'sites'. I've seen film footage[66] of others: shivering children, perched like birds on the edges of *charpais*, while swirling waters enter their tin homes. Frightened, fevered eyes watch pots and pans carried through the doorway by the current, floating out into the flooded fields, thin fathers swimming after them to retrieve what they can.

When the waters recede they leave ruin. Malaria, diarrhoea, sick cattle stranded in the slush. The ancient teak beams dismantled from their previous homes, carefully stacked away like postponed dreams, now spongy, rotten and unusable.

Forty households were moved from Manibeli to a resettlement site in Gujarat. In the first year, thirty-eight children died.[67] On 26 April 1999, the *Indian Express* reported nine deaths in a single rehabilitation site in

Gujarat. In the course of a single week. That's 21–42 cents a day, if you're counting.

Many of those who have been resettled are people who have lived all their lives deep in the forest with virtually no contact with money and the modern world. Suddenly they find themselves left with the option of starving to death or walking several kilometres to the nearest town, sitting in the marketplace (both men and women) offering themselves as wage labour, like goods on sale.

Instead of a forest from which they gathered everything they needed—food, fuel, fodder, rope, gum, tobacco, tooth powder, medicinal herbs, housing materials—they earn between ten and twenty rupees a day with which to feed and keep their families. Instead of a river, they have a hand pump. In their old villages, they had no money, but they were insured. If the rains failed, they had the forests to turn to. The river to fish in. Their livestock was their fixed deposit. Without all this, they're a heartbeat away from destitution.

In Vadaj, a resettlement site I visited near Baroda, the man who was talking to me rocked his sick baby in his arms, clumps of flies gathered on its sleeping eyelids. Children collected around us, taking care not to burn their bare skin on the scorching tin walls of the shed they call a home. The man's mind was far away from the troubles of his sick baby. He was making me a list of the fruit he used to pick in the forest. He counted forty-eight kinds. He told me that he didn't think he or his children would ever be able to afford to eat any fruit again. Not unless he stole it. I asked him what was wrong with his baby. He said it would be better for the baby to die than live like this. I asked what the baby's mother thought about that. She didn't reply. She just stared.

For the people who've been resettled, everything has to be re-learned. Every little thing, every big thing: from shitting and pissing (where d'you do it when there's no jungle to hide you?) to buying a bus ticket, to learning a new language, to understanding money. And worst of all, learning to be supplicants. Learning to take orders. Learning to have Masters. Learning to answer only when you're addressed. In addition to all this, they have to learn how to make written representations (in triplicate) to the Grievance Redressal Committee of the Sardar Sarovar Narmada Nigam for any particular problems they might have. Recently, 3,000 people came to Delhi to protest their situation—travelling overnight by train, living on the blazing streets.[68] The President wouldn't meet them because he had an eye infection. Maneka Gandhi, then Minister for Social Justice and Empowerment, wouldn't meet them but asked for a written representation. When the representation was handed to her she scolded the little delegation for not having written it in

English. *(Dear Maneka, Please don't build the dam, Love, The People).*

From being self-sufficient and free, to being impoverished and yoked to the whims of a world you know nothing, *nothing* about—what d'you suppose it must feel like?

It is just not possible for a state Administration, *any* state Administration, to carry out the rehabilitation of a people as fragile as this, on such an immense scale. It's like using a pair of hedge-shears to trim an infant's fingernails. You can't do it without shearing its fingers off.

Land for land sounds like a reasonable swap, but how do you implement it? How do you uproot 200,000 people (the official blinkered estimate)—of whom 117,000 are Adivasi—and relocate them in a humane fashion? How do you keep their communities intact in a country where every inch of land is fought over, where almost all litigation pending in courts has to do with land disputes? Where is all this fine, unoccupied but arable land that is waiting to receive these intact communities?

The simple answer is that there isn't any. Not even for the 'officially' displaced of this one dam.

What about the rest of the 3,199 dams?

What about the remaining thousands of PAPs earmarked for annihilation? Shall we just put the Star of David on their doors and get it over with?

◼

Resettling 200,000 people in order to take (or pretend to take) drinking water to forty million—there's something very wrong with the *scale* of operations here. This is Fascist Maths. It strangles stories. Bludgeons detail. And manages to blind perfectly reasonable people with its spurious, shining vision.

◼

When I arrived on the banks of the Narmada in late March 1999, it was a month after the Supreme Court had suddenly vacated the stay on construction work of the Sardar Sarovar dam. I had read pretty much everything I could lay my hands on (all those 'secret' Government documents). I had a clear idea of the lie of the land—of what had happened where and when and to whom. The story played itself out before my eyes like a tragic film whose actors I'd already met. Had I not known its history, nothing would have made sense. Because in the valley there are stories within stories and it's easy to lose the clarity of rage in the sludge of other people's sorrow.

I ended my journey in Kevadia Colony, where it all began.

Thirty-eight years ago, this is where the Government of Gujarat decided to locate the infrastructure it would need for starting work on the dam: guest houses, office blocks, accommodation for engineers and their staff, roads leading to the dam site, warehouses for construction material.

It is located on the cusp of what is now the Sardar Sarovar reservoir and the Wonder Canal, Gujarat's 'lifeline', that is going to quench the thirst of millions.

Nobody knows this, but Kevadia Colony is the key to the World. Go there, and secrets will be revealed to you.

■

In the winter of 1961, a government officer arrived in a village called Kothie and told the villagers that some of their land would be needed to construct a helipad because someone terribly important was going to come visiting. In a few days, a bulldozer arrived and flattened standing crops. The villagers were made to sign papers and were paid a sum of money, which they assumed was payment for their destroyed crops. When the helipad was ready, a helicopter landed on it, and out came Prime Minister Nehru. Most of the villagers couldn't see him because he was surrounded by policemen. Nehru made a speech.

Then he pressed a button and there was an explosion on the other side of the river. After the explosion he flew away.[69] That was the genesis of what was to become the Sardar Sarovar dam.

Could Nehru have known when he pressed that button that he had unleashed an incubus?

After Nehru left, the Government of Gujarat arrived in strength. It acquired 1,600 acres of land from 950 families from six villages.[70] The people were Tadvi Adivasis who, because of their proximity to the city of Baroda, were not entirely unversed in the ways of a market economy. They were sent notices and told that they would be paid cash compensations and given jobs on the dam site. Then the nightmare began.

Trucks and bulldozers rolled in. Forests were felled, standing crops destroyed. Everything turned into a whirl of jeeps and engineers and cement and steel. Mohan Bhai Tadvi watched 8 acres of his land with standing crops of jowar, toovar and cotton being levelled. Overnight he became a landless labourer. *Three years later* he received his cash compensation of €5.25 an acre in three separate instalments.

Dersukh Bhai, Vesa Bhai's father, was given €73.50 for his house and 5 acres of land with its standing crops and all the trees on it. He remembers walking all the way to Rajpipla (the district headquarters) as a little boy, holding his father's hand.

He remembers how terrified they were when they were called in to the Tehsildar's office. They were made to surrender their compensation notices and sign a receipt. They were illiterate, so they didn't know how much the receipt was made out for.

Everybody had to go to Rajpipla but they were always summoned on different days, one by one. So they couldn't exchange information or compare stories.

Gradually, out of the dust and bulldozers, an offensive, diffuse configuration emerged. Kevadia Colony. Row upon row of ugly cement flats, offices, guest houses, roads. All the graceless infrastructure of Big Dam construction. The villagers' houses were dismantled and moved to the periphery of the colony where they remain today, squatters on their own land. Those that caused trouble were intimidated by the police and the construction company. The villagers told me that in the contractor's headquarters they have a 'lock-up' like a police lock-up, where recalcitrant villagers are incarcerated and beaten.

The people who were evicted to build Kevadia Colony do not qualify as 'Project Affected' in Gujarat's Rehabilitation package.

Some of them work as servants in the officers' bungalows and waiters in the guest house built on the land where their own houses once stood. Can there be anything more poignant?

Those who had some land left, tried to cultivate it, but Kevadia municipality introduced a scheme in which they brought in pigs to eat uncollected refuse on the streets. The pigs stray into the villagers' fields and destroy their crops.

In 1992, thirty years later, each family has been offered a sum of €252 per acre, up to a maximum of €756, *provided* they agree to leave their homes and go away! Yet forty per cent of the land that was acquired is lying unused. The Government refuses to return it. Eleven acres acquired from Deviben, who is a widow now, have been given over to the Swami Narayan Trust (a big religious sect). On a small portion of it, the Trust runs a little school. The rest it cultivates, while Deviben watches through the barbed-wire fence. On 200 acres acquired in the village of Gora, villagers were evicted and blocks of flats were built. They lay empty for years. Eventually the Government hired it for a nominal fee to Jai Prakash Associates, the dam contractors, who, the villagers say, sublet it privately for €672 a month. (Jai Prakash Associates, the biggest dam contractors in the country, the *real* nation builders, own the Siddharth Continental and the Vasant Continental Hotels in Delhi.)

On an area of about 30 acres there is an absurd cement Public Works Department replica of the ancient Shoolpaneshwar temple that was submerged in the reservoir. The same political formation that plunged a whole nation into a bloody, medieval nightmare because it insisted on destroying an old mosque to dig up a non-existent temple thinks nothing of submerging a hallowed pilgrimage route and hundreds of temples that have been worshipped in for centuries.

It thinks nothing of destroying the sacred hills and groves, the places of worship, the ancient homes of the gods and demons of the Adivasi.

It thinks nothing of submerging a valley that has yielded fossils, microliths and rock paintings, the only valley in India, according to archaeologists, that contains an uninterrupted record of human occupation from the Old Stone Age.

What can one say?

In Kevadia Colony, the most barbaric joke of all is the wildlife museum. The Shoolpaneshwar Sanctuary Interpretation Centre gives you quick, comprehensive evidence of the Government's sincere commitment to Conservation.

The Sardar Sarovar reservoir, when the dam reaches its full height, is going to submerge about 13,000 hectares of prime forest land. (In anticipation of submergence, the forest began to be felled many greedy years ago.) Between the Narmada Sagar dam and the Sardar Sarovar dam, 50,000 hectares of old-growth broadleaved forest will be submerged. Madhya Pradesh has the highest rate of forest cover loss in the whole of India. This is partly responsible for the reduced flow in the Narmada and the increase in siltation. Have engineers made the connection between forest, rivers and rain? Unlikely. It isn't part of their brief. Environmentalists and conservationists were quite rightly alarmed at the extent of loss of biodiversity and wildlife habitat that submergence would cause. To mitigate this loss, the Government decided to expand the Shoolpanesh-war Wildlife Sanctuary near the dam, south of the river. There is a harebrained scheme that envisages drowning animals from the submerged forests swimming their way to 'wildlife corridors' that will be created for them, and setting up home in the (New! Improved!) Shoolpaneshwar Sanctuary.

Presumably wildlife and biodiversity can be protected and maintained only if human activity is restricted and tra-ditional rights to use forest resources curtailed. Forty thousand Adivasis from 101 villages within the boundaries of the Shoolpaneshwar Sanctuary depend on the forest for a livelihood. They will be 'persuaded' to leave. They are not included in the definition of 'Project Affected'.

Where will they go? I imagine you know by now.

Whatever their troubles in the real world, in the Shoolpaneshwar Sanctuary Interpretation Centre (where an old stuffed leopard and a mouldy sloth bear have to make do with a shared corner) the Adivasis have a whole room to themselves. On the walls there are clumsy wooden carvings, Government-approved Adivasi art, with signs that say 'TRIBAL ART'. In the centre, there is a life-sized thatched hut with the door open. The pot's on the fire, the dog is asleep on the floor and all's well with the world. Outside, to welcome you, are Mr and Mrs Adivasi. A lumpy papier-mâché couple, smiling.

Smiling. They're not even permitted the grace of rage. That's what I can't get over.

Oh, but have I got it wrong? What if they're smiling with National Pride? Brimming with the joy of having sacrificed their lives to bring drinking water to thirsty millions in Gujarat?

For twenty years now, the people of Gujarat have waited for the water they believe the Wonder Canal will bring them. For years the Government of Gujarat has invested eighty-five per cent of the state's irrigation budget in the Sardar Sarovar Projects. Every smaller, quicker, local, more feasible scheme has been set aside for the sake of this. Election after election has been contested and won on the 'water ticket'. Everyone's hopes are pinned to the Wonder Canal. Will she fulfil Gujarat's dreams?

From the Sardar Sarovar dam, the Narmada flows through 180 kilometres of rich lowland into the Arabian sea in Bharuch. What the Wonder Canal does, more or less, is to re-route most of the river, bending it almost ninety degrees northward. It's a pretty drastic thing to do to a river. The Narmada estuary in Bharuch is one of the last known breeding places of the hilsa, probably the hottest contender for India's favourite fish.

The Stanley dam wiped out hilsa from the Cauvery River in south India, and Pakistan's Ghulam Mohammed dam destroyed its spawning area on the Indus. Hilsa, like the salmon, is an anadromous fish—born in fresh water, migrating to the ocean as a smolt and returning to the river to spawn. The drastic reduction in water flow, the change in the chemistry of the water because of all the sediment trapped *behind* the dam, will radically alter the ecology of the estuary and modify the delicate balance of freshwater and seawater which is bound to affect the spawning. At present, the Narmada estuary produces 13,000 tonnes of hilsa and freshwater prawn (which also breeds in brackish water). Ten thousand fisher-families depend on it for a living.[71]

The Morse Committee was appalled to discover that no studies had been done of the downstream environment[72] —no documentation of the riverine ecosystem, its seasonal changes, biological species or the pattern of how its resources are used. The dam builders had no idea what the impact of the dam would be on the people and the environment downstream, let alone any ideas on what steps to take to mitigate it.

The Government simply says that it will alleviate the loss of hilsa fisheries by stocking the reservoir with hatchery-bred fish. (Who'll control the reservoir? Who'll grant the commercial fishing to its favourite paying customers?) The only hitch is that so far scientists have not managed to breed hilsa artificially. The rearing of hilsa depends on getting spawn from wild adults, which will in all likelihood be eliminated by the dam. Dams have either eliminated or endangered one-fifth of the world's freshwater fish.[73]

So! Quiz question—where will the 40,000 fisherfolk go?

Email your answers to the Government That Cares dot com.

At the risk of losing readers—I've been warned several times—'How can you write about *irrigation?* Who the *hell* is interested?'—let me tell you what the Wonder Canal is and what she's meant to achieve. *Be* interested, if you want to snatch your future back from the sweaty palms of the Iron Triangle.

Most rivers in India are monsoon-fed. Between eighty and eighty-five per cent of the flow takes place during the rainy months—usually between June and September. The purpose of a dam, an irrigation dam, is to store monsoon water in its reservoir and then use it judiciously for the rest of the year, distributing it across dry land through a system of canals. The extent of land irrigated by the canal network is called the 'command area'.

How will the command area, accustomed only to seasonal irrigation, its entire ecology designed for that single pulse of monsoon rain, react to being irrigated the whole year round? Perennial irrigation does to soil roughly what anabolic steroids do to the human body. Steroids can turn an ordinary athlete into an Olympic medal-winner; perennial irrigation can convert soil which produced only a single crop a year into soil that yields *several* crops a year. Lands on which farmers traditionally grew crops that don't need a great deal of water (maize, millet, barley, and a whole range of pulses) will suddenly yield water-guzzling cash crops—cotton, rice, soya bean and, the biggest guzzler of all (like those finned 1950s behemoth cars), sugarcane. This completely alters traditional crop patterns in the command area. People stop growing things that they can afford to *eat*, and start growing things that they can only afford to *sell*. By linking themselves to the 'market' they lose control over their lives.

Ecologically, too, this is a poisonous payoff. Even if the markets hold out, the soil doesn't. Over time it becomes too poor to support the extra demands made on it. Gradually, in the way a steroid-using athlete becomes an invalid, the soil becomes depleted and degraded, and agricultural yields begin to decrease.[74]

In India, land irrigated by well water is today almost twice as productive as land irrigated by canals.[75] Certain kinds of soil are less suitable for perennial irrigation than others. Perennial canal irrigation raises the level of the water table. As the water moves up through the soil, it absorbs salts. Saline water is drawn to the surface by capillary action, and the land becomes waterlogged. The 'logged' water (to coin a phrase) is then breathed into the atmosphere by plants, causing an even greater concentration of salts in the soil. When the concentration of salts in the soil reaches one per cent, that soil becomes toxic to plant life. This is what's called salinization.

A study by the Centre for Resource and Environmental Studies at the Australian National University says that one-fifth of the world's irrigated land is salt-affected.[76]

By the mid-1980s, twenty-five million of the thirty-seven million hectares under irrigation in Pakistan were estimated to be either salinized or waterlogged or both.[77] In India the estimates vary between six and ten million hectares.[78] According to 'secret' government studies, more than fifty-two per cent of the Sardar Sarovar command area is prone to waterlogging and salinization.[79]

And that's not the end of the bad news.

The 160-kilometre-long, concrete-lined Sardar Sarovar Wonder Canal and its 75,000-kilometre network of branch canals and sub-branch canals is designed to irrigate a total of two million hectares of land spread over twelve districts. The districts of Kutch and Saurashtra (the billboards of Gujarat's Thirst campaign) are at the very tail-end of this network.

The system of canals superimposes an arbitrary concrete grid on the existing pattern of natural drainage in the command area. It's a little like reorganizing the pattern of reticulate veins on the surface of a leaf. When a canal cuts across the path of a natural drain, it blocks the flow of the natural, seasonal water and leads to waterlogging. The engineering solution to this is to map the pattern of natural drainage in the area and replace it with an alternate, artificial drainage system that is built in conjunction with the canals. The problem, as you can imagine, is that this is enormously expensive. The cost of drainage is not included as part of the Sardar Sarovar Projects. It usually isn't, in most irrigation projects.

David Hopper, the World Bank's vice-president for South Asia, admitted that the Bank does not usually include the cost of drainage in its irrigation projects in South Asia because irrigation projects *with* adequate drainage are just too expensive.[80] It costs five times as much to provide adequate drainage as it does to irrigate the same amount of land. It makes the cost of a complete Project appear unviable.

The Bank's solution to the problem is to put in the irrigation system and wait—for salinity and waterlogging to set in. When all the money's spent and the land is devastated and the people are in despair, who should pop by? Why, the friendly neighbourhood banker! And what's that bulge in his pocket? Could it be a loan for a drainage project?

In Pakistan, the World Bank financed the Tarbela (1977) and Mangla dam (1967) projects on the Indus. The command areas are waterlogged.[81] Now the Bank has given

Pakistan a $785 million loan for a drainage project. In India, in Punjab and Haryana, it's doing the same.

Irrigation without drainage is like having a system of arteries and no veins. Pretty damn pointless.

Since the World Bank stepped back from the Sardar Sarovar Projects, it's a little unclear where the money for the drainage is going to come from. This hasn't deterred the Government from going ahead with the canal work. The result is that even before the dam is ready, before the Wonder Canal has been commissioned, before a single drop of irrigation water has been delivered, water-logging has set in. Among the worst affected areas are the resettlement colonies.

There is a difference between the planners of the Sardar Sarovar irrigation scheme and the planners of previous projects. At least they acknowledge that waterlogging and salinization are *real* problems and need to be addressed.

Their solutions, however, are corny enough to send a Hoolock Gibbon to a hooting hospital.

They plan to have a series of electronic groundwater sensors placed in every 100 square kilometres of the command area. (That works out to about 1,800 ground sensors.) These will be linked to a central computer that will analyse the data and send out commands to the canal heads to stop water flowing into areas that show early signs of waterlogging. A network of 'Only-irrigation', 'Only-drainage' and 'Irrigation-cum-drainage' tubewells will be sunk, and electronically synchronized by the central computer. The saline water will be pumped out, mixed with mathematically computed quantities of fresh water and then recirculated into a network of surface and sub-surface drains (for which more land will be acquired).[82]

To achieve the irrigation efficiency that they claim they'll achieve, according to a study done by Dr Rahul Ram for Kalpavriksh, eighty-two per cent of the water that goes into the Wonder Canal network will have to be pumped out again![83]

They've never implemented an electronic irrigation scheme before, not even as a pilot project. It hasn't occurred to them to experiment with some already degraded land, just to see if it works. No, they'll use our money to install it over the whole of the two million hectares and *then* see if it works. What if it doesn't? If it doesn't, it won't matter to the planners. They'll still draw the same salaries. They'll still get their pensions and their gratuity and whatever else you get when you retire from a career of inflicting mayhem on a people.

How can it *possibly* work? How can they manage a gigantic electronic irrigation system when they can't even line the walls of the canals without having them collapse and cause untold damage to crops and people?

When they can't even prevent the Big Dam itself from breaking off in bits when it rains?

To quote from one of their own studies, '*The design, the implementation and management of the integration of groundwater and surface water in the above circumstance is complex.*'[84]

Agreed. To say the least.

Their recommendation of how to deal with the complexity: '*It will only be possible to implement such a system if all groundwater and surface water supplies are managed by a single authority.*'[85]

Aha!

It's beginning to make sense now. Who will own the water?

The Single Authority.

Who will sell the water? The Single Authority.

Who will profit from the sales? The Single Authority.

The Single Authority has a scheme whereby it will sell water by the litre, not to individuals but to farmers' cooperatives (which don't exist just yet but no doubt the Single Authority can create cooperatives and force farmers to cooperate). Computer water, unlike ordinary river water, is expensive. Only those who can afford it will get it. Gradually, small farmers will be edged out by big farmers, and the whole cycle of uprootment will begin all over again.

The Single Authority, because it owns the computer water, will also decide who will grow what. It says that farmers getting computer water will not be allowed to grow sugarcane because they'll use up the share of the thirsty millions who live at the tail-end of the canal. But the Single Authority has *already* given licences to ten large sugar mills right near the head of the canal.[86] The chief promoter of one of them is Sanat Mehta, who was chairman of the Sardar Sarovar Narmada Nigam for several years. The chief promoter of another sugar mill was Chimanbhai Patel, former chief minister of Gujarat. He (along with his wife) was the most vocal, ardent proponent of the Sardar Sarovar dam. When he died, his ashes were scattered over the dam site.

In Maharashtra, thanks to a different branch of the Single Authority, the politically powerful sugar lobby that occupies one-tenth of the state's irrigated land uses *half* the state's irrigation water.

In addition to the sugar growers, the Single Authority has recently announced a scheme[87] that envisages a series of five-star hotels, golf courses and water parks that will come up along the Wonder Canal. What earthly reason could possibly justify this? The Single Authority says it's the only way to raise money to complete the project!

I really worry about those millions of good people in Kutch and Saurashtra.

Will the water *ever* reach them?

When the Government of Gujarat was negotiating for its share of the Narmada waters, it asked for (and received) more than what it would have received in the normal calculation of riparian rights, which in Gujarat's case is about two per cent of the total projected figure of 27.22 MAF. Gujarat argued that it needed water to irrigate eleven lakh hectares of land in the drought-prone regions of Kutch and Saurashtra. In view of this, the Tribunal allocated 9.5 MAF of water to Gujarat. It did not specify how the water should be used.

When the project started and the irrigation plans were drawn up, the Gujarat Government then reduced the eleven lakh hectares to less than a tenth of that. To one lakh hectares! That's 1.8 per cent of the cultivable area in Kutch and nine per cent of the cultivable land in Saurashtra. And that's on paper. (If you ask the government what they're going to do about the rest of the drought-prone regions, they talk of 'alternatives'. Watershed management. Rainwater harvesting. Well-recharging. The point is that if there are alternatives which are good enough for 98.2 per cent of Kutch and 91 per cent of Saurashtra, why won't they work for the whole 100 per cent?)

What are the chances that the people of Kutch and Saurashtra will get even this reduced amount of water?

First of all, we know that there's a lot less water in the river than the Single Authority claims there is.

Second of all, in the absence of the Narmada Sagar dam, the irrigation benefits of the Sardar Sarovar drop by a further seventeen to thirty per cent.

Third of all, the irrigation efficiency of the Wonder Canal (the *actual* amount of water delivered by the system) has been arbitrarily fixed at sixty per cent. The *highest* irrigation efficiency in India, taking into account system leaks and surface evaporation, is thirty-five per cent.[88] This means it's likely that only *half* of the command area will be irrigated.

Which half? The first half.

Fourth, to get to Kutch and Saurashtra, the Wonder Canal has to negotiate its way past the ten sugar mills, the golf courses, the five-star hotels, the water parks and the cash-crop-growing, politically powerful, Patel-rich districts of Baroda, Kheda, Ahmedabad, Gandhinagar and Mehsana. (Already, in complete contravention of its own directives, the Single Authority has allotted the city of Baroda a sizeable quantity of water.[89] When Baroda gets, can Ahmedabad be left behind? The political clout of powerful urban centres in Gujarat will ensure that they secure their share.)

Fifth, even in the (100 per cent) unlikely event that water gets there, it has to be piped and distributed to those 8,000 waiting villages.

It's worth knowing that of the one billion people in the world who have no access to safe drinking water, 855 million live in rural areas.[90] This is because the cost of installing an energy-intensive network of thousands of kilometres of pipelines, aqueducts, pumps and treatment plants that would be needed to provide drinking water to scattered rural populations is prohibitive. Nobody builds Big Dams to provide drinking water to rural people. Nobody can afford to.

When the Morse Committee first arrived in Gujarat, it was impressed by the Gujarat Government's commitment to taking drinking water to such distant, rural districts.[91] The members of the Committee asked to see the detailed drinking water plans. There weren't any. (There still aren't any.)

They asked if any costs had been worked out. 'A few thousand crores,' was the breezy answer.[92] A billion dollars is an expert's calculated guess. It's not included as part of the project cost. So where is the money going to come from?

Never mind. Jus' askin'.

It's interesting that the Farakka Barrage that diverts water from the Ganga to Calcutta Port has reduced the drinking water availability for forty million people who live down-stream in Bangladesh.[93]

At times there's something so precise and mathematically chilling about nationalism.

Build a dam to take water *away* from forty million people. Build a dam to pretend to *bring* water to forty million people.

Who are these gods that govern us? Is there no limit to their powers?

■

The last person I met in the valley was Bhaiji Bhai. He is a Tadvi Advisi from Undava, one of the first villages where the government began to acquire land for the Wonder Canal and its 75,000-kilometre network. Bhaiji Bhai lost 17 of his 19 acres to the Wonder Canal. It crashes through his land, 700 feet wide including its walkways and steep, sloping embankments, like a velodrome for giant bicyclists.

The canal network affects more than 200,000 families. People have lost wells and trees, people have had their houses separated from their farms by the canal, forcing them to walk two or three kilometres to the nearest bridge and then two or three kilometres back along the other side. Twenty-three thousand families, let's say 100,000 people, will be, like Bhaiji Bhai, seriously affected. They don't count as 'Project Affected' and are not entitled to rehabilitation.

Like his neighbours in Kevadia Colony, Bhaiji Bhai became a pauper overnight.

Bhaiji Bhai and his people, forced to smile for photographs on government calendars. Bhaiji Bhai and his people, denied the grace of rage. Bhaiji Bhai and his people, squashed like bugs by this country they're supposed to call their own.

It was late evening when I arrived at his house. We sat down on the floor and drank over-sweet tea in the dying light. As he spoke, a memory stirred in me, a sense of déjà vu. I couldn't imagine why. I knew I hadn't met him before. Then I realized what it was. I hadn't recognized him, but I remembered his story. I'd seen him in an old documentary film, shot more than ten years ago in the valley. He was frailer now, his beard softened with age. But his story hadn't aged. It was still young and full of passion. It broke my heart, the patience with which he told it. I could tell he had told it over and over and over again, hoping, praying that one day one of the strangers passing through Undava would turn out to be Good Luck. Or God.

Bhaiji Bhai, Bhaiji Bhai, when will you get angry? When will you stop waiting? When will you say 'That's enough!' and reach for your weapons, whatever they may be? When will you show us the whole of your resonant, terrifying, invincible strength?

When will you break the faith? *Will* you break the faith? Or will you let it break you?

■

To slow a beast, you break its limbs. To slow a nation, you break its people. You rob them of volition. You demonstrate your absolute command over their destiny. You make it clear that ultimately it falls to you to decide who lives, who dies, who prospers, who doesn't. To exhibit your capability you show off all that you can do, and how easily you can do it. How easily you could press a button and annihilate the earth. How you can start a war, or sue for peace. How you can snatch a river away from one and gift it to another. How you can green a desert, or fell a forest and plant one somewhere else. You use caprice to fracture a people's faith in ancient things— earth, forest, water, air.

Once that's done, what do they have left? Only you. They will turn to you, because you're all they have. They will love you even while they despise you. They will trust you even though they know you well. They will vote for you even as you squeeze the very breath from their bodies. They will drink what you give them to drink. They will breathe what you give them to breathe. They will live where you dump their belongings. They have to. What else can they do? There's no higher court of redress.

You are their mother and their father. You are the judge and the jury. You are the World. You are God.

Power is fortified not just by what it destroys, but also by what it creates. Not just by what it takes, but also by what it gives. And Powerlessness is reaffirmed not just by the helplessness of those who have lost, but also by the gratitude of those who have (or *think* they have) gained.

This cold, contemporary cast of power is couched between the lines of noble-sounding clauses in democratic-sounding constitutions. It's wielded by the elected representatives of an ostensibly free people. Yet no monarch, no despot, no dictator in any other century in the history of human civilization has had access to weapons like these.

Day by day, river by river, forest by forest, mountain by mountain, missile by missile, bomb by bomb—almost without our knowing it—we are being broken.

Big Dams are to a Nation's 'Development' what Nuclear Bombs are to its Military Arsenal. They're both weapons of mass destruction. They're both weapons governments use to control their own people. Both twentieth-century emblems that mark a point in time when human intelligence has outstripped its own instinct for survival. They're both malignant indications of a civilization turning upon itself. They represent the severing of the link, not just the link—the *understanding*—between human beings and the planet they live on. They scramble the intelligence that connects eggs to hens, milk to cows, food to forests, water to rivers, air to life and the earth to human existence.

Can we unscramble it?

Maybe. Inch by inch. Bomb by bomb. Dam by dam. Maybe by fighting specific wars in specific ways. We could begin in the Narmada valley.

July 1999 will bring the last monsoon of the twentieth century. The ragged army in the Narmada valley has declared that it will not move when the waters of the Sardar Sarovar reservoir rise to claim its lands and homes. Whether you love the dam or hate it, whether you want it or you don't, it is in the fitness of things that you understand the price that's being paid for it. That you have the courage to watch while the dues are cleared and the books are squared.

Our dues. Our books. Not theirs.

Be there.

May 1999

Postscript

On 18 October 2000, a three-judge bench of the Supreme Court of India delivered its final verdict on the public interest litigation filed by the Narmada Bachao Andolan against the Union of India, and the Governments of Gujarat, Maharashtra and Madhya Pradesh. The primary imperative of 'the majority judgment' by Chief Justice A.S. Anand and Justice B.N. Kirpal was that the construction of the Sardar Sarovar dam be completed as 'expeditiously' as possible.

After expressly disallowing the NBA from making any submission on the performance of Big Dams in general, the 183-page judgment contains a veritable eulogy on the virtues of Dams, which is not based on any evidence produced before the Court. After six and a half years of litigation, the judgment also said that the Court ought to have no role in deciding such matters.

Justice S.P. Bharucha, the only one of the three judges to have heard the case through from the time it was filed, wrote a dissenting judgment in which he said that construction of the Sardar Sarovar dam should be stopped immediately. He made it clear that not only did he have a different point of view, he disagreed with everything contained in the majority opinion—'*I should not be deemed to have agreed with anything stated in Brother Kirpal's judgment . . .'*

Justice Bharucha went on to detail the reasons why construction should be suspended: *'An environment clearance based on next to no data in regard to the environmental impact of the Project was contrary to the terms of the then policy of the Union of India in regard to environmental clearances and, therefore, no clearance at all.'* His minority judgment says that it was mandatory under the guidelines of the Narmada Water Disputes Tribunal that catchment area treatment and the full rehabilitation of all displaced people be completed *before* any water is impounded in the reservoir. According to Justice Bharucha, the fact that this had not happened constituted a clear violation of the conditions of clearance.

The majority judgment swept this aside, calling environmental clearance *'only an administrative requirement'*. It also decreed that the project should be completed according to the guidelines of the Tribunal Award under the independent authority of the Narmada Control Authority (NCA). (The Chairman of the NCA is Secretary, Ministry of Water Resources; the Chairman of the NCA Review Committee is the Minister of Water Resources. There is not a single non-government member in the NCA.)

For thirteen years, the NCA has turned a blind eye to violations of the Tribunal Award. However, the majority judgment said that there was no reason to '*assume that the authorities will not function properly*'. It asked the NCA to produce within four weeks a Rehabilitation Master Plan, which it hadn't managed to produce in thirteen years. (A *plan*—not actual rehabilitation.) The weeks and months have gone by. There has been no sign of a Master Plan.

The majority judgment allowed the dam wall to be immediately raised despite the Madhya Pradesh Government's sworn affidavit stating that it had not readied a single rehabilitation site and had not been able to allot agricultural land to even one of the hundreds of oustee families that would be affected. In effect, the Court ordered a violation of the Tribunal Award while simultaneously maintaining that the Award was sacrosanct.

On 29 March 2001, the NBA's review petition was dismissed in the judges' chambers without a hearing. Justice Bharucha continued to stand by his dissenting judgment.

October 2001

power politics

The Reincarnation of Rumpelstiltskin

Remember him? The gnome who could turn straw into gold? Well he's back now, but you wouldn't recognize him. To begin with, he's not an individual gnome anymore. I'm not sure how best to describe him. Let's just say he's metamorphosed into an accretion, a cabal, an assemblage, a malevolent, incorporeal, transnational multignome. Rumpelstiltskin is a notion (gnotion), a piece of deviant, insidious, white logic that will eventually self-annihilate. But for now he's more than okay. He's cock of the walk. King of All That Really Counts (Cash). He's decimated the competition, killed all the other kings, the other kinds of kings. He's persuaded us that he's all we have left. Our only salvation.

What king or potentate is Rumpelstiltskin? Powerful, pitiless and armed to the teeth. He's the kind of king the world has never known before. His realm is raw capital, his conquests emerging markets, his prayers profits, his borders limitless, his weapons nuclear. To even try and imagine him, to hold the whole of him in your field of vision, is to situate yourself at the very edge of sanity, to offer yourself up for ridicule. King Rumpel reveals only part of himself at a time. He has a bank account heart. He has television eyes and a newspaper nose in which you see only what he wants you to see and read only what he wants you to read. (See what I mean about the edge of sanity?) There's more: a Surround Sound stereo mouth which amplifies his voice and filters out the sound of the rest of the world, so that you can't hear it even when it's shouting (or starving or dying) and King Rumpel is only whispering, rolling his r's in his North American way.

Listen carefully. This is most of the rest of his story. (It hasn't ended yet, but it will. It must.) It ranges across seas and continents, sometimes majestic and universal, some-times confining and local. Now and then I'll peg it down with disparate bits of history and geography that could mar the gentle art of storytelling. So, please bear with me.

In March 2000, the President of the US (H.E. the most exalted plenipotentiary of Rumpeldom) visited India. He brought his own bed, the feather pillow he hugs at night, and a merry band of businessmen. He was courted and fawned over by the genuflecting representatives of this ancient civilization with a fervour that can only be described as indecent. Whole cities were superficially spruced up. The poor were herded away, hidden from the presidential gaze. Streets were soaped and scrubbed and festooned with balloons and welcome banners.

In Delhi's dirty sky, vindicated nuclear hawks banked and whistled: *Dekho ji dekho!* Bill is here because we have the Bomb!

Those Indian citizens with even a modicum of self-respect were so ashamed they stayed in bed for days. Some of us had puzzled furrows on our brows. Since everybody behaved like a craven, happy slave when Master visited, we wondered why we hadn't gone the whole distance. Why hadn't we crawled under Master's nuclear umbrella in the first place? Then we could spend our pocket money on other things (instead of bombs) and still be all safe and slavey. No?

Just before The Visit, the Government of India lifted import restrictions on 1,400 commodities including milk, grain, sugar and cotton (even though there was a glut of sugar and cotton in the market, even though forty-two million tonnes of grain was rotting in government store-houses).[1] During The Visit, contracts worth about three (some say four) billion dollars were signed.[2]

For reasons of my own, I was particularly interested in a Memorandum of Intent signed between the Ogden Energy Group, a company that specializes in operating garbage incinerators in the United States, and the S. Kumars, an Indian textile company that manufactures what it calls 'suiting blends'.[3] Now what might garbage incineration and suiting blends possibly have in common? Suit incineration? Guess again. Garbage-blends? Nope.

A big hydroelectric dam on the river Narmada in central India. Neither Ogden nor the S. Kumars has ever built or operated a large dam before.

The 400-megawatt Shri Maheshwar Hydel Project being promoted by the S. Kumars is part of the Narmada Valley Development Project, which boasts of being the most ambitious river valley project in the world. It envisages building 3,200 dams (thirty big dams, 135 medium dams, and the rest small) that will reconstitute the Narmada and her forty-one tributaries into a series of stepped reservoirs.[4]

The dams that have been built on the river so far are all government projects. The Maheshwar dam is slated to be India's first major private hydro-electric power project.

What is interesting about this is not only that it's part of the most bitterly opposed river valley project in India, but also that it is a strand in the skein of a mammoth global enterprise. Understanding what is happening in Mahesh-war, decoding the nature of the deals that are being struck between two of the world's great democracies, will go a long way towards gaining a rudimentary grasp of what is being done to us, while we, poor fools, stand by and clap and cheer and hasten things along. (When I say 'us', I mean people, human beings. Not countries, not govern-ments.)

Personally, I took the first step towards this understanding when, over a few days in March 2000, I lived through a writer's bad dream. I witnessed the ritualistic slaughter of language as I know and understand it. Let me explain.

On the very days that President Clinton was in India, in far-away Holland, the World Water Forum was con-vened.[5] Three thousand five hundred bankers, business-men, government ministers, policy writers, engineers, economists (and—in order to pretend that the 'other side' was also represented—a handful of activists, indigenous dance troupes, impoverished street theatre groups, and half a dozen young girls dressed as inflatable silver faucets) gathered at the Hague to discuss the future of the world's water. Every speech was percussive with phrases like 'women's empowerment', 'people's participation' and 'deepening democracy'. Yet it turned out that the whole purpose of the forum was to press for the privatization of the world's water. There was righteous talk of making access to drinking water a Basic Human Right. How would this be implemented, you might ask. Simple. By putting a market value on water. By selling it at its 'true' price. (It's common knowledge that water is becoming a scarce resource. As we know, about a billion people in the world have no access to safe drinking water.)[6] The 'market' decrees that the scarcer something is, the more expensive it becomes. But there is a difference between valuing water and putting a market value on water. No one values water more than a village woman who has to walk miles to fetch it. No one values it less than urban folk who pay for it to flow endlessly at the turn of a tap.

So the talk of connecting human rights to a 'true price' was more than a little baffling. At first I didn't quite get their drift—did they believe in human rights for the rich, that only the rich are human, or that all humans are rich? But I see it now. A shiny, climate-controlled human rights supermarket with a clearance sale on Christmas Day.

One marrowy American panellist put it rather nicely— 'God gave us the rivers,' he drawled, 'but he didn't put in the delivery systems. That's why we need private enterprise.' No doubt with a little Structural Adjustment to the rest of the things God gave us, we could all live in a simpler world. (If all the seas were one sea, what a big sea it would be . . .) Evian could own the water, Rand the earth, Enron the air. Old Rumpelstiltskin could be the handsomely paid supreme CEO.

When all the rivers and valleys and forests and hills of the world have been priced, packaged, bar-coded and stacked in the local supermarket, when all the hay and coal and earth and wood and water has been turned to gold, what then shall we do with all the gold? Make nuclear bombs to obliterate what's left of the ravaged landscapes and the notional nations in our ruined world?

As a writer, one spends a lifetime journeying into the heart of language, trying to minimize, if not eliminate, the distance between language and thought. 'Language is the skin on my thought,' I remember saying to someone who once asked what language meant to me. At The Hague I stumbled on a denomination, a sub-world, whose life's endeavour was to mask intent. They earn their abundant livings by converting bar graphs that plot their companies' profits into consummately written, politically exemplary, socially just policy documents that are impossible to implement and designed to remain forever on paper, secret even (especially) from the people they're written for. They breed and prosper in the space that lies between what they say and what they sell. What they're lobbying for is not simply the privatization of natural resources and essential infrastructure, but the privatization of policy making itself.

Dam builders want to control public water policies. Power utility companies want to supervise government disinvestments.

Let's begin at the beginning. What does privatization really mean? Essentially, it is the transfer of productive public assets from the state to private companies. Productive assets include natural resources. Earth, forest, water, air. These are assets that the state holds in trust for the people. In a country like India, seventy per cent of the population lives in rural areas. That's seven hundred million people.[7] Their lives depend directly on access to natural resources. To snatch these away and sell them as stock to private companies is a process of barbaric dispossession on a scale that has no parallel in history.

What happens when you 'privatize' something as essential to human survival as water? What happens when you commodify water and say that only those who can come up with the cash to pay the 'market price' can have it? In 1999, the Government of Bolivia privatized the public water supply system in the city of Cochabamba, and signed a forty-year lease with Bechtel, a giant US engineering firm. The first thing Bechtel did was to triple the price of water. Hundreds of thousands of people simply couldn't afford it any more. Citizens took to the streets in protest. A transport strike brought the entire city to a standstill. Hugo Banzer, the former Bolivian dictator (now the president), ordered the police to fire at the crowds. Six people were killed, 175 injured and two children blinded. The protest continued because people had no option— what's the option to thirst? In April 2000, Banzer declared martial law. The protest continued. Eventually Bechtel was forced to flee its offices.[8] Now it's trying to extort a $12 million exit payment from the Bolivian government.

Cochabamba has a population of half a million people. Think of what would happen in an Indian city. Even a small one.

Rumpelstiltskin thinks big. Today he's stalking mega-game: dams, mines, armaments, power plants, public water supply, telecommunication, the management and dissemination of knowledge, biodiversity, seeds (he wants to own life and the very process of reproduction), and the industrial infrastructure that supports all this. His minions arrive in Third World countries masquerading as missionaries come to redeem the wretched. They have a completely different dossier in their briefcases. To understand what they're really saying (selling), you have to teach yourself to unscramble their vernacular.

Recently, Jack Welch, then CEO of General Electric (GE), visited India and was on national news.[9] 'I beg and pray to the Indian government to improve infrastructure,' he said, and added touchingly, 'Don't do it for GE's sake, do it for yourselves.' He went on to say that privatizing the power sector was the only way to bring India's one billion people into the digital network. 'You can talk about information and intellectual capital, but without the power to drive it, you will miss the next revolution.'

What he meant, of course, was: 'You are a market of one billion customers. If you don't buy our equipment, *we* will miss the next revolution.'

The story behind the story is as follows: there are four corporations that dominate the production of power generation equipment in the world. GE is one of them. Together, each year they manufacture (and therefore need to sell) equipment that can generate 20,000 megawatts of power.[10] For a variety of reasons, there is little (read almost zero) additional demand for power equipment in the First World. This leaves these mammoth multinationals with a redundant capacity that they desperately need to offload. India and China are their big target markets because between these two countries the demand for power-generating equipment is 10,000 megawatts per year.[11]

The First World needs to sell, the Third World needs to buy—it ought to be a reasonable business proposition. But it isn't. For many years, India has been more or less self-sufficient in power equipment. The Indian public

sector company, Bharat Heavy Electricals (BHEL), manu-
factured and even exported world-class power equipment.
All that's changed now. Over the years, our own government has starved it of orders, cut off funds for research and
development, and more or less edged it out of a dignified
existence. Today BHEL is no more than a sweatshop. It
is being forced into 'joint ventures' (one with GE and
one with Siemens) in which its only role is to provide
cheap labour while they provide the equipment and the
technology.[12]

Why? Why does more expensive, imported foreign
equipment suit our bureaucrats and politicians better? We
all know why. Because graft is factored into the deal.
Buying equipment from your local store is just not the
same thing. It's not surprising that almost half the officials
named in the major corruption scandal that came to be
known as the Jain Hawala case were officials from the
power sector involved with the selection and purchase of
power equipment.[13]

The privatization of power (felicitous phrase!) is at the top
of the Indian government's agenda. The United States is
the single largest foreign investor in the power sector
(which, to some extent, explains The Visit).[14] The argument being advanced (both by the government and by the
private sector) in favour of privatization is that over the
last fifty years the government has bungled its brief. It has

failed to deliver. The State Electricity Boards (SEBs) are insolvent. Inefficiency, corruption, theft and heavy subsidies have run them into the ground.

In the push for privatization, the customary depiction of the corrupt, oily Third World government official selling his country's interests for personal profit fits perfectly into the scheme of things. The private sector bristles accusingly. The government coyly acknowledges its culpability and pleads its inability to reform itself. In fact, it goes out of its way to exaggerate its own inefficiencies. This is meant to come across as refreshing candour.

In a speech he made just before he died, P.R. Kumaramangalam, Minister for Power, said that the overall figure of loss and deficit in the power sector was €77,700,000. He went on to say that India's transmission and distribution (T&D) losses were between thirty-five and forty per cent. Of the remaining sixty per cent, according to the minister, billing is restricted to only forty per cent. His conclusion: that only about a quarter of the electricity that is produced in India is metered.[15] Official sources say that this is a somewhat exaggerated account. The situation is bad enough. It doesn't need to be exaggerated. According to figures put out by the Power Ministry, the national average for T&D losses are twenty-three per cent. In 1947, it was 14.39 per cent. Even without the minister's hyperbole, this puts India in the same league as countries with the worst T&D losses in the world, like the Dominican Republic, Myanmar and Bangladesh.[16]

The solution to this malaise, we discover, is not to improve our housekeeping skills, not to try and minimize our losses, not to force the state to be more accountable, but to permit it to abdicate its responsibility altogether and privatize the power sector. Then magic will happen. Economic viability and Swiss-style efficiency will kick in like clockwork.

But there's a sub-plot missing. Over the years, the SEBs have been bankrupted by massive power thefts. Who's stealing the power? Some of it, no doubt, is stolen by the poor—slum dwellers, people who live in unauthorized colonies on the fringes of big cities. But they don't use the heavy-duty electrical gadgetry to consume the quantum of electricity we're talking about. The big stuff, the megawatt thievery, is orchestrated by the industrial sector in connivance with politicians and government officers.

Consider as an example the state of Madhya Pradesh, in which the Maheshwar dam is being built. Seven years ago it was a power surplus state. Today it finds itself in an intriguing situation. Industrial demand has declined by thirty per cent. Power production has increased from 3,813 megawatts to 4,025 megawatts. And the SEB is showing a loss of €25,200,000. An inspection drive solved the puzzle. It found that seventy per cent of the industrialists in the state steal electricity.[17] The theft adds up to a loss of nearly €105,000,000. That's forty-one per cent of the total deficit. Madhya Pradesh is by no means an unusual example. States like Orissa, Andhra Pradesh and Delhi have T&D losses of between thirty and fifty per cent (way over the national average), which indicates massive power theft.[18]

No one talks very much about this. It's so much nicer to blame the poor. The average economist, planner or drawing-room intellectual will tell you that the SEBs have gone belly up for two reasons: (a) because 'political compulsions' ensure that domestic power tariffs are kept unviably low, and (b) because subsidies given to the farm sector result in enormous hidden losses.

The first step that a 'reformed', privatized power sector is expected to take is to cut agricultural subsidies and put a 'realistic' tariff (market value) on power.

What are 'political compulsions'? Why are they considered such a bad thing? Basically, it seems to me, 'political compulsions' is a phrase that describes the fancy footwork that governments perform in order to strike a balance between redeeming a sinking economy and serving an impoverished electorate. Striking a balance between what the market demands and what people can afford is, or certainly ought to be, the primary, fundamental responsibility of any democratic government. Privatization seeks to disengage politics from the market. To do that would be to blunt the very last weapon that India's poor still have— their vote. Once that's gone, elections will become even more of a charade than they already are and democracy will just become the name of a new rock band. The poor will be absent from the negotiating table. They will simply cease to matter.

But the cry has already gone up. The demand to cut subsidies has almost become a blood sport. It's a small world. Bolivia's only a short walk down the road from here.

When it recommends privatizing the power sector, does the government mean that it is going to permit just anybody who wishes to generate power to come in and compete in a free market? Of course not. There's nothing free about the market in the power sector. Reforming the power sector in India means that the concerned state government underwrites preposterously one-sided Power Purchase Agreements with select companies, preferably huge multinationals. Essentially, it is the transfer of assets and infrastructure from bribe-taker to bribe-giver, which involves more bribery than ever. Once the agreements are signed, they are free to produce power at exorbitant rates that no one can afford. Not even, ironically enough, the Indian industrialists who have been rooting for them all along. They, poor chaps, end up like the vultures on a carcass who get chased off by a visiting hyena.

The fishbowl of the drive to privatize power, its truly star turn, is the story of Enron, the Houston-based natural gas company.[19] The Enron project was the first private power project in India. The Power Purchase Agreement between Enron and the Congress-Party-ruled state government of Maharashtra for a 695-megawatt power plant was signed in 1993. The opposition parties, the BJP and the Shiv Sena, set up a howl of swadeshi protest, and filed legal proceedings against Enron and the state government. They alleged malfeasance and corruption at the highest level. A year later, when state elections were announced, it was the only campaign issue of the BJP–Shiv Sena alliance.

In February 1995, this combine won the elections. True to their word, they 'scrapped' the project. In a savage, fiery statement, Mr Advani, who was at the time a leader of the Opposition in Parliament, attacked the phenomenon of what he called 'loot-through-liberalization'.[20] He more or less directly accused the Congress government of having taken a €14,595,000 bribe from Enron. Enron had made no secret of the fact that in order to secure the contract it had paid out millions of dollars to 'educate' the politicians and bureaucrats involved in the deal.[21]

Following the annulling of the contract, the US government began to pressure the Maharashtra government. US Ambassador Frank Wisner made several statements deploring the cancellation. (The day he completed his term as ambassador he joined Enron as director.)[22] In November 1995, the BJP–Shiv Sena Government of Maharashtra appointed a 're-negotiation' committee. In May 1996, a minority government headed by the BJP was sworn in at the Centre. It lasted for exactly thirteen days, then resigned before facing a vote of no-confidence in the Lok Sabha. On its last day in office, even as the no-confidence motion was in progress, the Cabinet met for a hurried 'lunch' and re-ratified the national government's counter-guarantee for the Enron project (which had become void because of the earlier 'cancelled' contract with Enron). In August 1996, the Government of Maharashtra signed a fresh contract with Enron on terms that would astound the most hard-boiled cynic.[23]

The impugned contract had involved annual payments to Enron of $430 million for Phase I (695 megawatts) of the project, with Phase II (2,015 megawatts) being optional. The 're-negotiated' Power Purchase Agreement made Phase II of the project mandatory and legally binds the Maharashtra State Electricity Board (MSEB) to pay Enron a sum of $30 billion. It constitutes the largest contract ever signed in the history of India. Experts who have studied the project have called it the most massive fraud in the county's history. The project's gross profits work out to between $12 billion and $14 billion dollars. The official return on equity is more than thirty per cent.[24] That's almost double what Indian law and statute permits in power projects.

In effect, for an increase in installed capacity of eighteen per cent, the MSEB has to set aside seventy per cent of its revenue to be able to pay Enron. There is, of course, no record of what mathematical formula was used to 're-educate' the new government. Nor any trace of how much trickled up or down or sideways and to whom.

But there's more: in an extraordinary decision, in May 1997, the Supreme Court of India refused to entertain an appeal against Enron.[25]

Today, four years later, everything that critics of the project predicted has come true with an eerie vengeance. The power that the Enron plant produces is twice as expensive as its nearest competitor and seven times as expensive as the cheapest electricity available in Maharashtra.[26] In May 2000, the Maharashtra Electricity Regulatory Committee (MERC) ruled that temporarily, until as long as was absolutely necessary, no power should be bought from Enron.[27] It was based on a calculation that it would be cheaper to just pay Enron the mandatory fixed charges for the maintenance and administration of the plant that it is contractually obliged to pay, than to actually buy and utilize any of its exorbitant power. The fixed charges alone work out to €21,000,000 a year for Phase I of the project. Phase II will be nearly twice the size.

A thousand crore a year for the next forty years.

Meanwhile, industrialists in Maharashtra have begun to generate their own power at a much cheaper rate, with private generators. The demand for power from the industrial sector has begun to decline rapidly. The MSEB, strapped for cash, with Enron hanging like an albatross around its neck, will now have no choice but to make private generators illegal. That's the only way that industrialists can be coerced into buying Enron's exorbitant electricity.

According to the MSEB's calculations, from January 2002 onwards, even if it were to buy ninety per cent of Enron's output, its losses will amount to $1.2 billion a year.

That's more than sixty per cent of Indian's annual rural development budget.[28]

In contravention of the MERC ruling, the MSEB is cutting back on production from its own cheaper plants in order to buy electricity from Enron. Hundreds of small industrial units have closed down because they cannot afford such expensive electricity.

In January 2001, the Maharashtra Government (the Congress Party now back in power with a new Chief Minister) announced that it did not have the money to pay Enron's bills. On 6 February, only ten days after the earthquake in the neighbouring state of Gujarat, at a time when the country was still reeling from the disaster, the newspapers announced that Enron had decided to invoke the counterguarantee and that if the government did not come up with the cash it would have to auction the government properties pledged as collateral security in the contract.[29]

At the time of writing this essay, Enron and the Government of Maharashtra are locked in a legal battle in the Mumbai High Court. But Enron has friends in high places.[30] It was one of the biggest corporate contributors to President George Bush Jr's election campaign. President Bush has helped Enron with its global business from as far back as 1998. So the old circus has started up all over again. The former US Ambassador (Richard Celeste, this time) publicly chastised the Maharashtra Chief Minister for reneging on payments.[31] US government officials have warned India about vitiating the 'investment climate' and running the risk of frightening away future investors. In other words: allow us to rob you blind or else we'll pull out.

The pressure is on for a re-negotiation. (Who knows, perhaps Phase III is on the anvil.)

In business circles, the Enron contract is called 'the sweet-heart deal'. A euphemism for rape without redress. There are several Enron clones in the pipeline. Indian citizens have a lot to look forward to.

Here's to the 'free' market.

Having said all this, there's no doubt that there *is* a power-shortage crisis in India. But there's another, more serious crisis on hand.

Planners boast that India consumes twenty times more electricity today than it did fifty years ago. They use it as an index of progress. They usually omit to mention that seventy per cent of rural households still have no electricity. In the poorest states, Bihar, Uttar Pradesh, Orissa and Rajasthan, more than eighty-five per cent of the poorest people, mostly Dalit and Adivasi households, have no electricity.[32] What a shameful, shocking record for the world's biggest democracy.

Unless this crisis is acknowledged and honestly addressed, generating 'lots and lots of power' (as Mr Welch put it) will only mean that it will be siphoned off by the rich with their endless appetites. It will require a very imaginative, very radical form of 'structural adjustment' to right this.

'Privatization' is presented as being the only alternative to an inefficient, corrupt state. In fact, it's not a choice at all. It's only made to look like one. Essentially, privatization is a mutually profitable business contract between the private (preferably foreign) company or financial institution and the ruling elite of the Third World. (One of the fall-outs is that even corruption becomes an elitist affair. Your average small-fry government official is in grave danger of losing his or her bit on the side.)

Of late, institutions like the World Bank and the International Monetary Fund, which have bled the Third World all these years, look like benevolent saints compared to the new mutants in the market. These are known as ECAs— Export Credit Agencies. If the World Bank is a lumbering colonizing army hamstrung by red tape and bureaucracy, the ECAs are freewheeling, marauding mercenaries.

Basically, ECAs insure private companies operating in foreign countries against commercial and political risks. The device is called an export credit guarantee. It's quite simple, really. No First World private company wants to export capital or goods or services to a politically and/or economically unstable country without insuring itself against unforeseen contingency. So the private company covers itself with an export credit guarantee. The ECA, in turn, has an agreement with the government of its own country. The government of its own country then signs an agreement with the government of the importing country. The upshot of this fine imbrication is that if a situation does arise in which the ECA has to pay its client, its own government pays the ECA and recovers the money by adding it to the bilateral debt owed by the importing country. (So the real guarantors are actually once again the poorest people in the poorest countries.) Complicated, but cool. And foolproof.

The quadrangular private company–ECA–government–government formation neatly circumvents political accountability. Though they're all actually business associates, flak from noisy, tiresome non-governmental organizations can be diverted and funnelled to the ECA, where, like noxious industrial effluent, it lies in cooling ponds before being disposed of. The attraction of the ECAs (for both governments and private companies) is that they are secretive and don't need to bother with tedious details like human rights violations and environmental guidelines. (The rare ones that do, like the US Export-Import Bank, are under pressure to change.) It short-circuits the lumbering World-Bank-style bureaucracy. It makes politically risky projects like Big Dams (involving as they do the displacement and impoverishment of large numbers of people) that much easier to finance. With an

ECA guarantee, 'developers' can go ahead and dig and quarry and mine and dam the hell out of people's lives without having to even address, never mind answer, embarrassing questions.

Now, coming back to the story of the Maheshwar Dam . . .

What the Maheshwar experience illustrates, in relentless detail, is that in a private project, the only thing that's more efficient and better managed is the corruption, the lies, and the swiftness and brutality of repression. And, of course, the escalating costs.

In 1994, the project cost of the Maheshwar dam was estimated at €97,650,000.[33] In 1996, following the contract with the S. Kumars, it rose to €32,490,000. Today it stands at €46,200,000. Initially, eighty per cent of this money was to be raised from foreign investors. There has been a procession of them—Pacgen of the United States, Bayernwerk, VEW, Siemens, and the Hypovereinsbank of Germany. And now, the latest in the line of ardent suitors, Ogden of the US.

According to the NBA's calculations, the cost of the electricity at the factory gate will be .13755 cent per unit, which is twenty-six times more expensive than existing hydel power in the state, five and a half times more expensive than thermal power, and four times more expensive than power from the central grid. (It's worth mentioning here that Madhya Pradesh today generates 1,500 megawatts more power than it can transmit and distribute.)

Though the installed capacity of the Maheshwar project is supposed to be 480 megawatts, studies using twenty-eight years of actual river flow data show that eighty per cent of the electricity will be generated only during the monsoon months, when the river is full. What this means is that most of the supply will be generated when it's least needed.[34]

The S. Kumars have no worries on this count. They have Enron as a precedent. They have an escrow clause in their contract, which guarantees them first call on government funds. This means that however much (or however little) electricity they produce, whether anybody buys it or not, for the next thirty-five years they are guaranteed a minimum payment from the government of approximately €12,600,000 a year. This money will be paid to them even before the employees of the bankrupt State Electricity Board get their salaries.

What did the S. Kumars do to deserve this largesse? It isn't hard to guess.

So who's actually paying for this dam that nobody needs?

According to government surveys, the reservoir of the Maheshwar dam will submerge sixty-one villages. Thirteen, they say, will be wholly submerged, the rest will lose their farmlands.[35] (The agency in charge of the survey is the same one that was in charge of the surveys for the Bargi reservoir. We know what happened there.) As usual, the villagers were not informed about the dam or their impending eviction. Of course, if they go to court now they'll be told it's too late since construction has already begun. The first surveys were done under a ruse that a railway line was being constructed. It was only in 1997, when blasting began at the dam site, that realization dawned on people, and the NBA became active in Maheshwar.

People in the submergence zone of the Maheshwar dam say that the surveys are completely wrong. Some villages marked for submergence are at a higher level than villages that are not counted as Project Affected. Since the Maheshwar dam is located in the broad plains of Nimad, even a small miscalculation in the surveys will lead to huge discrepancies between what is marked for submergence and what is actually submerged. The consequences of these errors will be far worse than what happened at Bargi.

There are other egregious assumptions in the 'survey'. Annexure Six of the resettlement plan states that there are thirty-eight wells and 176 trees in all the affected sixty-one villages combined. The villagers point out that in just a single village—Pathrad—there are forty wells and more than 4,000 trees.

As with trees and wells, so with people. There is no accurate estimate of how many people will be affected by the dam. Even the project authorities admit that new surveys must be done. So far, they've managed to survey only one out of the sixty-one villages. The number of affected households rose from 190 (in the preliminary survey) to 300 (in the new one).

In circumstances like these, it's impossible for even the NBA to have an accurate idea of the numbers of Project Affected people. Their rough guess is about 50,000. More than half of them are Dalits, Kevats and Kahars—ancient communities of ferrymen, fisherfolk, sand quarriers and cultivators of the river bed. Most of them own no land, but the river sustains them and means more to them than anyone else. If the dam is built, thousands of them will lose their only source of livelihood. Yet simply because they are landless, they do not qualify as Project Affected and will not be eligible for rehabilitation.

Jalud is the first of the sixty-one villages slated for submergence in the reservoir of the dam.[36] As early as 1985, twelve families, mostly Dalit, who had small holdings near the dam site had their land acquired. When they protested, cement was poured into their water pipes, their standing crops were bulldozed, and the police occupied their land by force. All twelve families are now landless and work as wage labourers. The new 'private' initiative has made no effort to help them.

According to the environmental clearance from the Central government, the people affected by the project ought to have been resettled in 1997. To date, the S. Kumars haven't even managed to produce a list of Project Affected people, let alone land on which they are to be resettled. Yet construction continues. The S. Kumars are so well entrenched with the state government that they don't even need to pretend to cover their tracks.

The Rajputs of Jalud are slated to be moved to a new village—a 'model resettlement village'—a few kilometres inland, away from the river, adjoining a predominantly Dalit and Adivasi precinct in a village called Samraj. A huge tract of land has been marked off for them. It's a hard, stony hillock with stubbly grass and scrub, on which truckloads of silt have been unloaded and spread out in a thin layer to make it look like rich, black humus.

On behalf of the S. Kumars, the District Magistrate acquired the hillock, which was actually village common grazing land that belonged to the people of Samraj. In addition to this, the land of thirty-four Dalit and Adivasi villagers was acquired. No compensation was paid.

The villagers, whose main source of income was their live-stock, had to sell their goats and buffaloes because they no longer had anywhere to graze them. Their only remaining source of income lies (lay) on the banks of a small pond on the edge of the village. In summer, when the water level recedes, it leaves a shallow ring of rich silt on which the villagers grow (grew) rice and melons and cucumber. The S. Kumars excavated this silt to cosmetically cover the stony grazing ground (that the Rajputs of Jalud don't want). The banks of the pond are now steep and uncultivable.

The already impoverished people of Samraj have been left to starve, while this photo opportunity is being readied for German and Swiss funders, Indian courts and anybody else who cares to pass that way.

This is the legacy that the Ogden Energy Group of the US was so keen to inherit. What it didn't realize is that the fight is on. Over the last three years, the struggle against the Maheshwar dam has grown into a veritable civil dis-obedience movement, though you wouldn't know it if you read the papers. (The S. Kumars sponsor massive advertisements for their blended suitings. After their James Bond campaign with Pierce Brosnan, they've signed India's biggest film star—Hrithik Roshan—as their star campaigner.[37] It's extraordinary how much silent admiration and support a hunk in a blended suit can evoke.)

Over the years, tens of thousands of villagers have captured
the dam site several times and halted construction work.[38]
Protests in the region forced two companies, Bayernwerk
and VEW of Germany, to withdraw from the project.[39]
The German company Siemens remained in the fray
(angling for an export credit guarantee from Hermes, the
German ECA). In the summer of 2000, the German
Ministry of Economic Cooperation and Development
sent in a team of experts headed by Richard Bissell (former
chairman of the Inspection Panel of the World Bank) to
do an independent review of the Resettlement and
Rehabilitation aspects of the project. The report, published on 15 June 2000, was unambiguous that resettlement and rehabilitation of people displaced by the
Maheshwar dam was simply not possible.[40]

At the end of August, Siemens withdrew its application
for a Hermes guarantee.[41]

The people of the valley don't get much time to recover
between bouts of fighting. In September 2000, the S.
Kumars were part of the Indian Prime Minister's business
entourage when he visited the US.[42] Desperate to find a
replacement for Siemens, they were hoping to convert
their Memorandum of Understanding with Ogden into a
final contract. That, fortunately (for Ogden as much as the
people of Maheshwar), hasn't happened yet.

The only time I have ever felt anything close to national pride was when I walked one night with 4,000 people towards the Maheshwar dam site, where we knew hundreds of armed policemen were waiting for us. From the previous evening, people from all over the valley had begun to gather in a village called Sulgaon. They came in tractors, in bullock carts, and on foot. They came prepared to be beaten, humiliated and taken to prison.

We set out at three in the morning. We walked for three hours—farmers, fisherfolk, sand-miners, writers, painters, film-makers, lawyers, journalists. All of India was represented. Urban, rural, touchable, untouchable. This alliance is what gives the movement its raw power, its intellectual rigour and its phenomenal tenacity. As we crossed fields and forded streams, I remember thinking—this is my land, this is the dream to which the whole of me belongs, this is worth more to me than anything else in the world. We were not just fighting against a dam. We were fighting for a philosophy. For a world view.

We walked in utter silence. Not a throat was cleared. Not a beedi lit. We arrived at the dam site at dawn. Though the police were expecting us, they didn't know exactly where we would come from. We captured the dam site. People were beaten, humiliated and arrested.

I was arrested and pushed into a private car that belonged to the S. Kumars. I remember feeling a hot stab of shame —as quick and sharp as my earlier sense of pride. This was my land too. My feudal land. Where even the police have been privatized. (On the way to the police station, they complained that the S. Kumars had given them nothing to eat all day.) That evening, there were so many arrests, the jail could not contain the people. The administration broke down and abandoned the jail. The people locked themselves in and demanded answers to their questions. So far, none have been forthcoming.

A Dutch documentary film-maker recently asked me a very simple question: What can India teach the world?

A documentary film-maker needs to see to understand. I thought of three places I could take him to.

First, to a 'Call Centre College' in Gurgaon on the out-skirts of Delhi. I thought it would be interesting for a film-maker to see how easily an ancient civilization can be humiliated and made to abase itself completely. In a Call Centre College, hundreds of young English-speaking Indians are being groomed to man the backroom opera-tions of giant transnational companies.[43] They are trained to answer telephone queries from the US and the UK (on subjects ranging from a credit card enquiry to advice about a malfunctioning washing machine or the availability of cinema tickets). On no account must the caller know that his or her enquiry is being attended to by an Indian, sitting at a desk on the outskirts of Delhi. The Call Centre Colleges train their students to speak in American and British accents. They have to read foreign papers so they can chitchat about the news or the weather. On duty they have to change their given names. Sushma becomes Susie, Govind becomes Jerry, Advani becomes Andy. (Hi! I'm Andy. Gee, hot day, innit? Shoot, how can I help ya?) Actually it's worse: Sushma becomes Mary. Govind becomes David. Perhaps Advani becomes Ulysses.

Call Centre workers are paid exactly one-tenth of the salaries of their counterparts abroad. From all accounts, Call Centres in India are billed to become a multi-million dollar industry.[44] Imagine that—a multi-million dollar industry built on a bedrock of lies, false identities and racism.

Recently the giant Tata industrial group announced their plans to redeploy 20,000 of their retrenched workers in Call Centres after a brief 'period of training' for the business, such as 'picking up the American accent and slang'.[45] The news report said that the older employees may find it difficult to work at night—a requirement for US-based companies, given the time difference between India and the US.

The second place I thought I'd take the film-maker to is another kind of training centre: a Rashtriya Swayam Sewak (RSS) *shakha*, where the terrible backlash to this enforced abasement is being nurtured and groomed. Where ordinary people march around in khaki shorts and learn that amassing nuclear weapons, religious bigotry, misogyny, homophobia, book burning and outright hatred are the ways in which to retrieve a nation's lost dignity. Here he might see for himself how the two arms of government work in synergy. How they have evolved and pretty near perfected an extraordinary pincer action— while one arm is busy selling the nation off in chunks, the other, to divert attention, is orchestrating a baying, howling, deranged chorus of cultural chauvinism. It would be fascinating to actually see how the inexorable ruthlessness of one process results in the naked, vulgar terrorism perpetrated by the other. They're Siamese twins—Advani and Andy. They share organs. They have the ability to say two entirely contradictory things simultaneously, to hold all positions at all times. There's no separating them.

The third place I thought I'd take him to is the Narmada valley. To witness the ferocious, magical, magnificent, tenacious and above all non-violent resistance that has grown on the banks of that beautiful river.

What is happening to our world is almost too colossal for human comprehension to contain. But it is a terrible,

terrible thing. To contemplate its girth and circumference, to attempt to define it, to try and fight it all at once, is impossible. The only way to combat it is by fighting specific wars in specific ways. A good place to begin would be the Narmada valley.

The borders are open. Come on in. Let's bury Rumpelstiltskin.

November 2000

the ladies have feelings, so . . .

Shall We Leave It to the Experts?

India lives in several centuries at the same time. Somehow we manage to progress and regress simultaneously.

As a nation we age by pushing outwards from the middle—adding a few centuries on to either end of our extraordinary cv. We greaten like the maturing head of a hammer-headed shark with eyes looking in diametrically opposite directions. On the one hand, we hear that European countries are considering changing their immigration laws in order to import Indian software engineers.[1] On the other, that a Naga Sadhu at the Kumbh Mela towed the District Collector's car with his penis while the officer sat in it solemnly with his wife and children.[2]

As Indian citizens, we subsist on a regular diet of caste massacres and nuclear tests, mosque breaking and fashion shows, church burning and expanding cellphone networks, bonded labour and the digital revolution, female infanticide and the Nasdaq crash, husbands who continue to burn their wives for dowry, and our delectable stockpile of Miss Worlds. I don't mean to put a simplistic value judgement on this peculiar form of 'progress' by suggesting that Modern is Good and Traditional is Bad—or vice versa. What's hard to reconcile oneself to, both personally and politically, is the schizophrenic nature of it. That applies not just to the ancient/modern conundrum, but to the utter illogic of what appears to be the current national enterprise. In the lane behind my house, every night I walk past road-gangs of emaciated labourers digging a trench to lay fibre-optic cables to speed up our digital revolution. In the bitter winter cold, they work by the light of a few candles.

It's as though the people of India have been rounded up and loaded onto two convoys of trucks (a huge big one and a tiny little one) that have set off resolutely in opposite directions. The tiny convoy is on its way to a glittering destination somewhere near the top of the world. The other convoy just melts into the darkness and disappears. A cursory survey that tallies the caste, class and religion of who gets to be in which convoy would make a good Lazy Person's Concise Guide to the History of India. For some of us, life in India is like being suspended between two of the trucks, one in each convoy, and being neatly dismembered as they move apart, not bodily, but emotionally and intellectually.

Of *course* India is a microcosm of the world. Of *course* versions of what happens here happen everywhere. Of *course*, if you're willing to look, the parallels are easy to find. The difference in India is only in the scale, the magnitude, and the sheer proximity of the disparity. In India, your face is slammed right up against it. To address it, to deal with it, to not deal with it, to try and understand it, to insist on not understanding it, to simply survive it—on a daily, hourly basis—is a fine art in itself. Either an art or a form of insular, inward-looking insanity. Or both.

To be a writer—a supposedly 'famous' writer—in a country where millions of people are illiterate[3] is a dubious honour. To be a writer in a country that gave the world Mahatma Gandhi, that invented the concept of non-violent resistance, and then, half a century later, followed that up with nuclear tests is a ferocious burden. (Though no more ferocious a burden, it has to be said, than being a writer in the United States, a country that has amassed enough nuclear weapons to destroy the earth several times over.) To be a writer in a country where something akin to an undeclared civil war is being waged on its citizens in the name of 'development' is an onerous responsibility. When it comes to writers and writing, I use words like 'onerous' and 'responsibility' with a heavy heart and not a small degree of sadness.

What is the role of writers and artists in society? Do they have a definable role? Can it be fixed, described, characterized in any definite way? *Should* it be?

Personally, I can think of few things more terrifying than if writers and artists were charged with an immutable charter of duties and responsibilities that they had to live and work by. Imagine if there was this little black book—a sort of Approved Guide to Good Writing—that said: All writers shall be politically conscious and sexually moral, or, All writers should believe in god, globalization, and the joys of family life . . .

Rule One for a writer, as far as I'm concerned, is that There Are No Rules. And Rule Two (since Rule One was made to be broken) is that There Are No Excuses for Bad Art. Painters, writers, singers, actors, dancers, filmmakers, musicians—they are meant to fly, to push at the frontiers, to worry the edges of the human imagination, to conjure beauty from the most unexpected things, to find magic in places where others never thought to look. If you limit the trajectory of their flight, if you weight their wings with society's existing notions of morality and responsibility, if you truss them up with preconceived values, you subvert their endeavour.

A good or great writer may refuse to accept any responsibility or morality that society wishes to impose on her. Yet the best and greatest of them know that if they abuse this hard-won freedom, it can only lead to bad art. There is an intricate web of morality, rigour and responsibility that art, that writing itself, imposes on a writer. It is singular, individual, but nevertheless it's there. At its best, it's an exquisite bond between the artist and the medium. At its acceptable end, a sort of sensible cooperation. At its worst, it's a relationship of disrespect and exploitation.

The absence of external rules complicates things. There's a very thin line that separates the strong, true, bright bird of the imagination from the synthetic, noisy bauble. Where is that line? How do you recognize it? How do you know you've crossed it? At the risk of sounding esoteric and arcane, I'm tempted to say that you just *know*. The fact is that nobody—no reader, no reviewer, agent, publisher, colleague, friend or enemy—can tell for sure. A writer just has to ask herself that question and answer it as honestly as possible. The thing about this 'line' is that once you learn to recognize it, once you see it, it's impossible to ignore. You have no choice but to live with it, to follow it through. You have to bear with all its complexities, contradictions and demands. And that's not always easy. It doesn't always lead to compliments and standing ovations. It can lead you to the strangest, wildest places. In the midst of war, for instance, you could find yourself fascinated by the mating rituals of a purple sunbird, or the secret life of captive goldfish, or an old aunt's descent into madness. And nobody can say that there isn't truth and art and beauty in that. Or, on the contrary, in the midst of putative peace, you could, like me, be unfortunate enough to stumble on a silent war. The trouble is that once you see it, you can't unsee it. And once you've seen it, keeping quiet, saying nothing, becomes as political an act as speaking out. There's no innocence. Either way, you're accountable.

Today, perhaps more so than in any other era in history, the writer's right to free speech is guarded and defended by the civil societies and state establishments of the most powerful countries in the world. Any overt attempt to silence or muffle a voice is met with furious opposition. The writer is embraced and protected. This is a wonderful thing. The writer, the actor, the musician, the film-maker—they have become radiant jewels in the crown of modern civilization. The artist, I imagine, is finally as free as he or she will ever be. Never before have so many writers had their books published. (And now, of course, we have the Internet.) Never before have we been more commercially viable. We live and prosper in the heart of the marketplace. True, for every so-called success there are hundreds who 'fail'. True, there are a myriad art forms, both folk and classical, myriad languages, myriad cultural and artistic traditions that are being crushed and cast aside in the stampede to the big bumper sale in Wonderland. Still, there have never been more writers, singers, actors, painters who have become influential, wealthy superstars. And they, the successful ones, spawn a million imitators, they become the torch-bearers, their work becomes the benchmark for what art is, or ought to be.

Nowadays in India the scene is almost farcical. Following the recent commercial success of some Indian authors, Western publishers are desperately prospecting for the next big Indo-Anglian work of fiction. They're doing everything short of interviewing English-speaking Indians for the post of 'writer'. Ambitious middle-class parents who, a few years ago, would only settle for a future in engineering, medicine or management for their children, now hopefully send them to creative writing schools. People like myself are constantly petitioned by computer companies, watch manufacturers, even media magnates, to endorse their products. A boutique owner in Bombay once asked me if he could 'display' my book (as though it was an accessory, a bracelet or a pair of earrings) while he filmed me shopping for clothes! Jhumpa Lahiri, the American writer of Indian origin who won the Pulitzer Prize, came to India recently to have a traditional Bengali wedding. The wedding was reported on the front page of national newspapers.

Now where does all this lead us? Is it just harmless nonsense, best ignored? How does all this ardent wooing affect our art? What kind of lenses does it put in our spectacles? How far does it remove us from the world around us?

There is very real danger that this neoteric seduction can shut us up far more effectively than violence and repression ever could. We have free speech. Maybe. But do we have Really Free Speech? If what we have to say doesn't 'sell', will we still say it? Can we? Or is everybody looking for Things That Sell to say? Could writers end up playing the role of palace entertainers? Or the subtle twenty-first-century version of court eunuchs attending to the pleasures of our incumbent CEOs? You know—naughty, but nice. Risqué perhaps, but not risky.

It has been some years now since my first, and so far only, novel, *The God of Small Things,* was published. In the early days, I used to be described—introduced—as the author of an almost freakishly 'successful' (if I may use so vulgar a term) first book. Nowadays I'm introduced as something of a freak myself. I am, apparently, what is known in twenty-first-century vernacular as a 'writer–activist'. (Like a sofa-bed.)

Why am I called a 'writer–activist' and why—even when it's used approvingly, admiringly—does that term make me flinch? I'm called a writer-activist because after writing *The God of Small Things* I wrote three political essays (the first three essays in this book): 'the end of imagination' about India's nuclear tests, 'the greater common good' about Big Dams and the 'development' debate, and 'power politics: the reincarnation of rumpelstiltskin' about the privatization and corporatization of essential infrastructure like water and electricity. Apart from the building of the temple in Ayodhya, these also currently happen to be the major preoccupations of the Indian government.

Now, I've been wondering why it should be that the person who wrote *The God of Small Things* is called a writer, and the person who wrote the political essays is called an activist? True, *The God of Small Things* is a work of fiction, but it's no less political than any of my essays. True, the essays are works of non-fiction, but since when did writers forgo the right to write non-fiction?

My thesis is that I've been saddled with this double-barrelled appellation, this awful professional label, not because my work is political, but because in my essays I take sides. I take a position. I have a point of view. What's worse, I make it clear that I think it's right and moral to take that position and what's even worse, use everything in my power to flagrantly solicit support for that position. For a writer of the twenty-first century, that's considered a pretty uncool, unsophisticated thing to do. It skates uncomfortably close to the territory occupied by political party ideologues—a breed of people that the world has learned (quite rightly) to mistrust. I'm aware of this. I'm all for being circumspect. I'm all for discretion, prudence, tentativeness, subtlety, ambiguity, complexity . . . I love the unanswered question, the unresolved story, the unclimbed mountain, the tender shard of an incomplete dream. Most of the time.

But is it mandatory for a writer to be ambiguous about everything? Isn't it true that there have been fearful episodes in human history when prudence and discretion would have just been euphemisms for pusillanimity? When caution was actually cowardice? When sophistication was disguised decadence? When circumspection was really a kind of espousal?

Isn't it true, or at least theoretically possible, that there are times in the life of a people or a nation when the political climate demands that we—even the most sophisticated of us—overtly take sides? I believe that such times are upon us. And I believe that in the coming years, intellectuals and artists will be called upon to take sides, and this time, unlike the struggle for Independence, we won't have the luxury of fighting a 'colonizing enemy'. We'll be fighting ourselves.

We will be forced to ask ourselves some very uncomfortable questions about our values and traditions, our vision for the future, our responsibilities as citizens, the legitimacy of our 'democratic institutions', the role of the state, the police, the army, the judiciary and the intellectual community.

Fifty years after Independence, India is still struggling with the legacy of colonialism, still flinching from the 'cultural insult'. As citizens, we're still caught up in the business of 'disproving' the white world's definition of us. Intellectually and emotionally, we have just begun to grapple with communal and caste politics that threaten to tear our society apart. But in the meanwhile something new looms on our horizon.

It's not war, it's not genocide, it's not ethnic cleansing, it's not a famine or an epidemic. On the face of it, it's just ordinary, day-to-day business. It lacks the drama, the large-format, epic magnificence of war or genocide. It's dull in comparison. It makes bad TV. It has to do with boring things like water supply, electricity, irrigation. But it also has to do with a process of barbaric dispossession on a scale that has few parallels in history. You may have guessed by now that I'm talking about the modern version of corporate globalization.

What is globalization? Who is it for? What is it going to do to a country like India in which social inequality has been institutionalized in the caste system for centuries? A country in which hundreds of millions of people live in rural areas.[4] In which eighty per cent of the landholdings are small farms. In which almost half the population cannot read or write.

Is the corporatization and globalization of agriculture, water supply, electricity and essential commodities going to pull India out of the stagnant morass of poverty, illiteracy and religious bigotry? Is the dismantling and auctioning off of elaborate public sector infrastructure, developed with public money over the last fifty years, really the way forward? Is corporate globalization going to close the gap between the privileged and the underprivileged, between the upper castes and the lower castes, between the educated and the illiterate? Or is it going to give those who already have a centuries-old head start a friendly helping hand?

Is corporate globalization about 'the eradication of world poverty' or is it a mutant variety of colonialism, remote controlled and digitally operated? These are huge, contentious questions. The answers vary depending on whether they come from the villages and fields of rural India, from the slums and shantytowns of urban India, from the living rooms of the burgeoning middle class or from the boardrooms of big business houses.

Today India produces more milk, more sugar, more food-grain than ever before. Government warehouses are over-flowing with forty-two million tonnes of foodgrain.[5] That's almost a quarter of the total annual foodgrain prod-uce. Farmers with too much grain on their hands were driven to despair. In regions that wielded enough political clout, the government went on a buying spree, pur-chasing more grain than it could possibly store or use. And yet, under the terms of its agreement with the World Trade Organization, the Indian government had to lift import restrictions on 1,400 commodities, including milk, grain, sugar, cotton, tea, coffee, rubber and palm oil.[6] This, despite the fact that there was a glut of these products in the market. While grain rots in government warehouses, hundreds of millions of Indian citizens live below the poverty line and do not have the means to eat a square meal a day. Starvation deaths (dressed up as measles and food-poisoning) are being reported from several parts of the country.

From 1 April 2001—April Fool's Day—once again ac-cording to the terms of its agreement with the WTO, the Indian government is contracted to drop its quantitative import restrictions. The Indian market is already flooded with cheaper imports. Though India is technically free to export its agricultural produce, in practice most of it can-not be exported because it doesn't meet the First World's 'environmental standards'. (Western consumers don't eat bruised mangoes, or bananas with mosquito bites, or rice with a few weevils in it. In India we don't mind the odd mosquito bite or the occasional weevil.)

Developed countries like the US, whose hugely sub-sidized farm industry engages only two to three per cent of its total population, are using the WTO to pressurize countries like India to drop agricultural subsidies in order to make the market 'competitive'. Huge, mechanized corporate enterprises working thousands of acres of farm-land want to compete with impoverished subsistence farmers who own only a couple of acres.

In effect, India's rural economy is being garrotted. Farmers who produce too much are in distress, farmers who produce too little are in distress, and landless agricul-tural labour is out of work as big estates and farms lay off their workers. They're all flocking to the cities in search of employment.

'Trade not Aid' is the rallying cry of the headmen of the new Global Village, headquartered in the shining offices of the WTO. Our British colonizers stepped onto our shores a few centuries ago disguised as traders. We all remember the East India Company. This time around, the colonizer doesn't even need a token white presence in the colonies. The CEOs and their men don't need to go to the trouble of tramping through the tropics risking malaria, diarrhoea, sunstroke and an early death. They don't have to maintain an army or a police force, or worry about insurrections and mutinies. They can have their colonies *and* an easy conscience. 'Creating a good investment climate' is the new euphemism for Third World repression. Besides, the responsibility for implementation rests with the local administration.

In India, in order to clear the way for 'development projects', the government is in the process of amending the present Land Acquisition Act (which, ironically, was drafted by the British in the nineteenth century) and making it more draconian than it already is.[7] State governments are preparing to ratify 'anti-terrorist' laws so that those who oppose development projects will be counted as terrorists. They can be held without trial for three years. They can have their lands and cattle seized.

Recently, corporate globalization has come in for some criticism. What happened in Seattle and Prague will go down in history. Each time the WTO or the World Economic Forum wants to have a meeting, they have to barricade themselves with thousands of heavily armed police. Still, all its admirers, from Bill Clinton, Kofi Annan and A.B. Vajpayee to the cheering brokers in the stalls, continue to say the same lofty things. If we have the right institutions of governance in place—effective courts, good laws, honest politicians, participatory democracy, a transparent administration that respects human rights and gives people a say in decisions that affect their lives—then the globalization project will work for the poor, as well. They call this 'globalization with a human face'.

The point is, if all this was in place, almost *anything* would succeed: socialism, capitalism, you name it. Everything works in Paradise, a Communist State as well as a Military Dictatorship! But in an imperfect world, is it corporate globalization that's going to bring us all this bounty? Is that what's happening in India now that it's on the fast track to the free market? Does any one thing on that lofty list apply to life in India today? Are state institutions transparent? Have people had a say? Have they even been informed—let alone consulted—about decisions that vitally affect their lives? And are Mr Clinton (or now Mr Bush) and Mr Vajpayee doing everything in their power to see that the 'right institutions of governance' are in place? Or are they involved in exactly the opposite enterprise? Do they mean something else altogether when they talk of the 'right institutions of governance'?

In November 2000, the World Commission on Dams report was released by Nelson Mandela. It is the first time ever that any serious attempt has been made to study the performance of Big Dams. For those of us who are opposed to Big Dams, the WCD report is a contested document with many unacceptable, wishy-washy clauses.

However, at least it *attempted* to address the serious social and ecological issues that have been raised and debated over the years. At least it *attempted* to set out guidelines for those governments and agencies engaged in building dams. At least it *attempted* to estimate how many people have been displaced by Big Dams.

India is the only country in the world that refused permission to the World Commission on Dams to hold a public hearing. The government of Gujarat, the state in which the Sardar Sarovar dam is being built, threatened members of the Commission with arrest.[8]

In February 2001, the Indian government formally rejected the World Commission on Dams report.[9] Does this sound like a transparent, accountable, participatory democracy?

Recently the Supreme Court ordered the closure of 77,000 'polluting and non-conforming' industrial units in Delhi.[10] The order will put 500,000 people out of work. What are these 'industrial units'? Who are these people? They're the millions who have migrated from their villages, some voluntarily, others involuntarily, in search of work. They're the people who aren't supposed to exist, the 'non-citizens' who survive in the folds and wrinkles, the cracks and fissures of the 'official' city. They exist just outside the net of the 'official' urban infrastructure.

Close to forty per cent of Delhi's population of twelve million—about five million people—live in slums and unauthorized colonies.[11] Most of them are not serviced by municipal facilities—no electricity, no water, no sewage systems. About 50,000 people are homeless and sleep on the streets. These 'non-citizens' are employed in what economists rather stuffily call the 'informal sector', the fragile but vibrant parallel economy that both shocks and delights the imagination. They work as hawkers, rickshaw pullers, garbage recyclers, car-battery rechargers, street tailors, transistor knob makers, buttonhole stitchers, paper bag makers, dyers, printers, barbers. These are the 'industrial units' that have been targeted by the Supreme Court. (Fortunately, I haven't had *that* knock on my door yet, though I'm as non-conforming a unit as the rest of them.)[12]

The trains that leave Delhi these days carry thousands of people who simply cannot survive in the city. They're returning to the villages they fled in the first place. Millions of others, because they're 'illegal', have become easy meat for the rapacious, bribe-seeking police and predatory government officials. They haven't yet been driven out of the city but now must live in perpetual fear and dread of that happening.

In India the times are full of talk of the 'free market', reforms, deregulation and the dismantling of the 'licence-raj'—all in the name of encouraging entrepreneurship and discouraging corruption. Yet when the state obliterates a flourishing market, when it breaks the backs of half a million imaginative, resourceful, small-scale entrepreneurs, and delivers millions of others as fodder to the doorstep of the corruption industry, few comment on the irony.

No doubt it's true that the informal sector is polluting and, according to a colonial understanding of urban land use, 'non-conforming'. But then we don't live in a clean, perfect world. What about the fact that sixty-seven per cent of Delhi's pollution comes from motor vehicles?[13] Is it conceivable that the Supreme Court will come up with an act that bans private cars, or limits the number of cars a household can own?

If pollution is indeed the main concern of our courts and government, why is it that they have shown no great enthusiasm for regulating big factories run by major industrialists that have polluted rivers, denuded forests, depleted and poisoned groundwater, and destroyed the livelihoods of thousands of people who depend on these resources for a living? The Grasim factory in Kerala, the Orient Paper Mill in Madhya Pradesh, the noxious 'sunrise belt' industries in Gujarat. The uranium mines in Jadugoda, the aluminum plants in Orissa. And hundreds of others.

This is our in-house version of First World bullying in the global warming debate, i.e., we pollute, you pay.

In circumstances like these, the term 'writer-activist' as a professional description of what I do makes me flinch doubly. First, because it is strategically positioned to diminish both writers and activists. It seeks to reduce the scope, the range, the sweep, of what a writer is and can be. It suggests, somehow, that writers by definition are too effete to come up with the clarity, the explicitness, the reasoning, the passion, the grit, the audacity and, if necessary, the vulgarity, to publicly take a political position. And conversely, it suggests that activists occupy the coarser, cruder end of the intellectual spectrum. That activists are by profession 'position-takers' and therefore lack complexity and intellectual sophistication, and are instead fuelled by a crude, simple-minded, one-sided understanding of things. But the more fundamental problem I have with the term is that this attempt to 'professionalize' protest has the effect of containing the problem and suggesting that it's up to the professionals—activists and writer-activists—to deal with it.

The fact is that what's happening today is not a 'problem', and the issues that some of us are raising are not 'causes'. They are huge political and social upheavals that are convulsing the world. One is not involved by virtue of being a writer or activist. One is involved because one is a human being. Writing about it just happens to be the most effective thing a writer can do. It is vital to de-professionalize the public debate on matters that vitally affect the lives of ordinary people. It's time to snatch our futures back from the 'experts'. Time to ask, in ordinary language, the public question and to demand in ordinary language, the public answer.

Frankly, however trenchantly, angrily, persuasively or poetically the case is made out, at the end of the day a writer is a citizen, only one of many, who is demanding public information, asking for a public explanation.

Speaking for myself, I have no personal or ideological axe to grind. I have no professional stakes to protect. I'm prepared to be persuaded. I'm prepared to change my mind. But instead of an argument, or an explanation, or a disputing of facts, one gets insults, invective and the Experts' Anthem: You don't understand and it's too complicated to explain. The subtext, of course, is: Don't worry your little head about it. Go and play with your toys. Leave the *real* world to us.

It's the old Brahminical instinct. Colonize knowledge, build four walls around it, and use it to your advantage. The *Manusmriti*, the Vedic Hindu code of conduct, says that if a Dalit overhears a *shloka* or any part of a sacred text, he must have molten lead poured into his ear. It isn't a coincidence that while India is poised to take her place at the forefront of the Information Revolution, millions of her citizens are illiterate. (It would be interesting, as an exercise, to find out how many 'experts'—scholars, professionals, consultants—in India are actually Brahmins or from the upper castes.)

If you're one of the lucky people with a berth booked on the small convoy, then Leaving it to the Experts is, or can be, a mutually beneficial proposition both for the expert and yourself. It's a convenient way of easing your conscience, shrugging off your own role in the circuitry. And it creates a huge professional market for all kinds of 'expertise'. There's a whole ugly universe waiting to be explored there. This is not at all to suggest that all consultants are racketeers or that expertise is unnecessary, but you've heard the saying—There's a lot of money in poverty. There are plenty of ethical questions to be asked of those who make a professional living off their expertise in poverty and despair.

For instance, at what point does a scholar stop being a scholar and become a parasite who feeds off despair and dispossession? Does the source of a scholar's funding compromise his or her scholarship? We know, after all, that World Bank studies are the most quoted studies in the world. Is the World Bank a dispassionate observer of the global situation? Are the studies it funds entirely devoid of self-interest?

Take, for example, the international dam industry. It's worth tens of billions of dollars a year.[14] It's bursting with experts and consultants. Given the number of studies, reports, books, PhDs, grants, loans, consultancies, EIAs—it's odd, wouldn't you say, that there is no really reliable estimate of how many people have been displaced by Big Dams in India? That there is no estimate for exactly what the contribution of Big Dams has been to overall food production? That there hasn't been an official audit, a comprehensive, honest, thoughtful, post-project evaluation of a single Big Dam to see whether or not it has achieved what it set out to achieve? Whether or not the costs were justified, or even what the costs actually were?

What *are* the experts up to?

On the whole, in India, the prognosis is—to put it mildly—Not Good. And yet, one cannot help but marvel at the fantastic range and depth and wisdom of the hundreds of people's resistance movements all over the county. They're being beaten down, but they simply refuse to lie down and die.

Their political ideologies and battle strategies span the range. We have the maverick Malayali professor who petitions the President every day against the communalization of history texts; Sunderlal Bahugana, who risks his life on indefinite hunger strikes protesting the Tehri dam;

the Adivasis in Jadugoda protesting uranium mining on their lands; the Koel Karo Sangathan resisting a mega-dam project in Jharkhand; the awe-inspiring Chattisgarh Mukti Morcha; the relentlessly dogged Mazdoor Kisan Shakti Sangathan; the Beej Bachao Andolan in Tehri-Garhwal fighting to save the biodiversity of seeds; and of course, the Narmada Bachao Andolan.

India's redemption lies in the inherent anarchy and fractiousness of its people and its political formations. Even our heel-clicking, boot-stamping Hindu fascists are undisciplined to the point of being chaotic. They can't bring themselves to agree with each other for more than five minutes at a time. Corporatizing India is like trying to impose an iron grid on a heaving ocean, forcing it to behave. My guess is that India will not behave. It cannot. It's too old and too clever to be made to jump through the hoops all over again. It's too diverse, too grand, too feral, and—eventually, I hope—too democratic to be lobotomized into believing in one single idea, which is, eventually, what corporate globalization really is: Life is Profit.

What is happening to the world lies, at the moment, just outside the realm of common human understanding. It is the writers, the poets, the artists, the singers, the filmmakers who can make the connections, who can find ways of bringing it into the realm of common understanding.

Who can translate cash-flow charts and scintillating board-room speeches into real stories about real people with real lives. Stories about what it's like to lose your home, your land, your job, your dignity, your past, and your future to an invisible force. To someone or something you can't see. You can't hate. You can't even imagine.

It's a new space that's been offered to us today. A new kind of challenge. It offers opportunities for a new kind of art. An art which can make the impalpable palpable, the intangible tangible, the invisible visible and the inevitable evitable. An art which can draw out the incorporeal adversary and make it real. Bring it to book.

Cynics say that real life is a choice between the failed revolution and the shabby deal. I don't know . . . maybe they're right. But even they should know that there's no limit to just how shabby that shabby deal can be. What we need to search for and find, what we need to hone and perfect into a magnificent, shining thing, is a new kind of politics. Not the politics of governance, but the politics of resistance. The politics of opposition. The politics of forcing accountability. The politics of joining hands across the world and preventing certain destruction. In the present circumstances, I'd say that the only thing worth globalizing is dissent. It's India's best export.

February 2001

the algebra of infinite justice

the algebra of infinite justice

In the aftermath of the unconscionable 11 September 2001 suicide attack on the Pentagon and the World Trade Center, an American newscaster said: 'Good and Evil rarely manifest themselves as clearly as they did last Tuesday. People who we don't know, massacred people who we do. And they did so with contemptuous glee.'[1] Then he broke down and wept.

Here's the rub: America is at war against people it doesn't know (because they don't appear much on TV). Before it has properly identified or even *begun* to comprehend the nature of its enemy, the US government has, in a rush of publicity and embarrassing rhetoric, cobbled together an 'International Coalition Against Terror', mobilized its army, its air force, its navy and its media, and committed them to battle.

The trouble is that once America goes off to war, it can't very well return without having fought one. If it doesn't find its enemy, for the sake of the enraged folks back home, it will have to manufacture one. Once war begins, it will develop a momentum, a logic and a justification of its own, and we'll lose sight of why it's being fought in the first place.

What we're witnessing here is the spectacle of the world's most powerful country, reaching reflexively, angrily, for an old instinct to fight a new kind of war. Suddenly, when it comes to defending itself, America's streamlined warships, its cruise missiles and F-16 jets look like obsolete, lumbering things. As deterrence, its arsenal of nuclear bombs is no longer worth its weight in scrap. Box-cutters, penknives and cold anger are the weapons with which the wars of the new century will be waged. Anger is the lock pick. It slips through customs unnoticed. Doesn't show up in baggage checks.

Who is America fighting? On 20 September, the FBI said that it had doubts about the identities of some of the hijackers. On the same day, President George Bush said, 'We know *exactly* who the terrorists were and which governments were supporting them.'[2] It sounds as though the President knows something that the FBI and the American public don't.

In his 20 September address to the US Congress, President George Bush called the enemies of America

'Enemies of Freedom'. 'Americans are asking why do they hate us?' he said. 'They hate our freedoms—our freedom of religion, our freedom of speech, our freedom to vote and assemble and disagree with each other.'[3] People are being asked to make two leaps of faith here. First, to assume that The Enemy is who the US government says it is, even though it has no substantial evidence to support that claim. And second, to assume that The Enemy's motives are what the US government says they are, and there's nothing to support that either.

For strategic, military and economic reasons, it is vital for the US government to persuade the American public that America's commitment to freedom and democracy and the American Way of Life is under attack. In the current atmosphere of grief, outrage and anger, it's an easy notion to peddle. However, if that were true, it's reasonable to wonder why the symbols of America's economic and military dominance—the World Trade Center and the Pentagon—were chosen as the targets of the attacks. Why not the Statue of Liberty? Could it be that the stygian anger that led to the attacks has its taproot not in American freedom and democracy, but in the US government's record of commitment and support to exactly the opposite things—to military and economic terrorism, insurgency, military dictatorship, religious bigotry and unimaginable genocide (*outside* America)?

It must be hard for ordinary Americans, so recently bereaved, to look up at the world with their eyes full of tears and encounter what might appear to them to be indifference. It isn't indifference. It's just augury. An absence of surprise. The tired wisdom of knowing that what goes around, eventually comes around. The American people ought to know that it is not them, but their government's policies that are so hated. All of us have been moved by the courage and grace shown by America's firefighters, rescue workers and ordinary office goers in the days that followed the attacks. The American people can't possibly doubt that they themselves, their extraordinary musicians, their writers, their actors, their spectacular sportsmen and their cinema, are universally welcomed.

America's grief at what happened has been immense and immensely public. It would be grotesque to expect it to calibrate or modulate its anguish. However, it will be a pity if, instead of using this as an opportunity to try and understand why 11 September happened, Americans use it as an opportunity to usurp the whole world's sorrow to mourn and avenge only their own. Because then it falls to the rest of us to ask the hard questions and say the harsh things. And for our pains, for our bad timing, we will be disliked, ignored and perhaps eventually silenced.

The world will probably never know what motivated those particular hijackers who flew planes into those particular American buildings. They were not glory boys. They left no suicide notes, no political messages, no organization has claimed credit for the attacks. All we know is that their belief in what they were doing out-stripped the natural human instinct for survival or any desire to be remembered. It's almost as though they could not scale down the enormity of their rage to anything smaller than their deeds. And what they did has blown a hole in the world as we knew it. In the absence of infor-mation, politicians, political commentators and writers (like myself) will invest the act with their own politics, with their own interpretations. This speculation, this analysis of the political climate in which the attacks took place, can only be a good thing.

But war is looming large. Whatever remains to be said, must be said quickly.

Before America places itself at the helm of the 'International Coalition Against Terror', before it invites (and coerces) countries to actively participate in its almost godlike mission— 'Operation Infinite Justice', until it was pointed out that this could be seen as an insult to Muslims, who believe that only Allah can mete out infinite justice, and was renamed 'Operation Enduring Freedom'—it would help if some small clarifications are made. For example, Infinite Justice/Enduring Freedom for whom? Is this America's War against Terror in America or against

Terror in general? What exactly is being avenged here? Is it the tragic loss of almost 7,000 lives, the gutting of fifteen million square feet of office space in Manhattan,[4] the destruction of a section of the Pentagon, the loss of several hundreds of thousands of jobs, the bankruptcy of some airline companies and the dip in the New York Stock Exchange? Or is it more than that?

In 1996, Madeleine Albright, then UN Ambassador to the United Nations, was asked on national television what she felt about the fact that 500,000 Iraqi children had died as a result of US economic sanctions. She replied that it was 'a very hard choice', but that all things considered, 'we think the price is worth it'.[5] Madeleine Albright never lost her job for saying this. She continued to travel the world representing the views and aspirations of the US government. More pertinently, the sanctions against Iraq remain in place. Children continue to die.

So here we have it. The equivocating distinction between civilization and savagery, between the 'massacre of inno-cent people' or, if you like, 'a clash of civilizations' and 'collateral damage'. The sophistry and fastidious algebra of Infinite Justice. How many dead Iraqis will it take to make the world a better place? How many dead Afghans for every dead American? How many dead children for every dead man? How many dead mujahedeen for each dead investment banker?

As we watch mesmerized, Operation Enduring Freedom unfolds on TV monitors across the world. A coalition of the world's superpowers is closing in on Afghanistan, one of the poorest, most ravaged, war-torn countries in the world, whose ruling Taliban government is sheltering Osama bin Laden, the man being held responsible for the 11 September attack. The only thing in Afghanistan that could possibly count as collateral value is its citizenry. (Among them, half a million maimed orphans. There are accounts of hobbling stampedes that occur when artificial limbs are airdropped into remote, inaccessible villages.)[6] Afghanistan's economy is in shambles. In fact, the problem for an invading army is that Afghanistan has no conventional co-ordinates or signposts to plot on a map—no military bases, no industrial complexes, no water treatment plants. Farms have been turned into mass graves. The countryside is littered with land mines—ten million is the most recent estimate.[7] The American army would first have to clear the mines and build roads in order to take its soldiers in. Fearing an attack from America, one million citizens have fled from their homes and arrived at the border between Pakistan and Afghanistan. The UN estimates that there are eight million Afghan citizens who will need emergency aid.[8] As supplies run out—Food and Aid agencies have been evacuated—the BBC reports that one of the worst humanitarian disasters of recent times has begun to unfold.[9] Witness the Infinite Justice of the new century.

Civilians starving to death, while they're waiting to be killed.

In America there has been rough talk of 'bombing Afghanistan back to the Stone Age'. Someone please break the news that Afghanistan is already there.[10] And if it's any consolation, America played no small part in helping it on its way. The American people may be a little fuzzy about where exactly Afghanistan is (we hear reports that there's a run on maps of the country),[11] but the US government and Afghanistan are old friends. In 1979, after the Soviet invasion of Afghanistan, the CIA and Pakistan's ISI (Inter Services Intelligence) launched the CIA's largest covert operation since the Vietnam War.[12] Their purpose was to harness the energy of Afghan resistance to the Soviets and expand it into a holy war, an Islamic jihad, which would turn Muslim countries within the Soviet Union against the communist regime and eventually destabilize it. When it began, it was meant to be the Soviet Union's Vietnam. It turned out to be much more than that. Over the years, through the ISI, the CIA funded and recruited tens of thousands of radical mujahedeen from forty Islamic countries as soldiers for America's proxy war.[13] The rank and file of the mujahedeen were unaware that their jihad was actually being fought on behalf of Uncle Sam. (The irony is that America was equally unaware that it was financing a future war against itself.)

The CIA poured in money and military equipment, but the overheads had become immense, and more money was needed. The mujahedeen ordered farmers to plant opium as 'revolutionary tax'.[14] Under the protection of the ISI, hundreds of heroin processing laboratories were set up across Afghanistan. Within two years of the CIA's arrival, the Pakistan–Afghanistan borderland had become the biggest producer of heroin in the world, and the single biggest source on American streets. The annual profits, said to be between $100 and $200 billion, were ploughed back into training and arming militants.[15] By 1989, after being bloodied by ten years of relentless conflict, the Russians withdrew, leaving behind a civilization reduced to rubble. Civil war in Afghanistan raged on. The jihad spread to Chechnya, Kosovo and eventually to Kashmir.

In 1996, the Taliban—then a marginal sect of dangerous, hard-line fundamentalists—fought its way to power in Afghanistan. It was funded by the ISI, that old cohort of the CIA, and supported by many political parties in Pakistan.[16] The Taliban unleashed a regime of terror. Its first victims were its own people, particularly women. It closed down girls' schools, dismissed women from government jobs, and enforced Sharia laws under which women deemed to be 'immoral' are stoned to death and widows guilty of being adulterous are buried alive.[17] Given the Taliban government's human rights track record, it seems unlikely that it will in any way be intimidated or swerved from its purpose by the prospect of war, or the threat to the lives of its civilians.

After all that has happened, can there be anything more ironic than Russia and America joining hands to re-destroy Afghanistan? The question is, can you destroy destruction? Dropping more bombs on Afghanistan will only shuffle the rubble, scramble some old graves and disturb the dead. The desolate landscape of Afghanistan was the burial ground of Soviet communism and the springboard of a uni-polar world dominated by America. It made the space for neo-capitalism and corporate globalization, again dominated by America. And now Afghanistan is poised to be the graveyard for the unlikely soldiers who fought and won this war for America.

And what of America's trusted ally? Pakistan too has suffered enormously. The US government has not been shy of supporting military dictators who have blocked the idea of democracy from taking root in the country. Before the CIA arrived, there was a small rural market for opium in Pakistan. Between 1979 and 1985, the number of heroin addicts grew from next to nothing to a massive number.[18] Even before 11 September, there were millions of Afghan refugees living in tented camps along the border. Pakistan's economy is crumbling. Sectarian violence, globalization's Structural Adjustment Programmes and drug lords are tearing the country to pieces.[19] Set up to fight the

Soviets, the terrorist training centres and madrassas, sown like dragon's teeth across the country, produced fundamentalists with tremendous popular appeal *within* Pakistan itself. The Taliban, which the Pakistan government has supported, funded and propped up for years, has material and strategic alliances with Pakistan's own political parties.[20] Now the US government is asking (*asking?*) Pakistan to garrot the pet it has hand-reared in its backyard for so many years. President Musharraf, having pledged his support to the US, could well find he has something resembling civil war on his hands.[21]

India, thanks in part to its geography, and in part to the vision of its former leaders, has so far been fortunate enough to be left out of this Great Game. Had it been drawn in, it's more than likely that our democracy, such as it is, would not have survived. Today, as some of us watch in horror, the Indian government is furiously gyrating its hips, begging the US to set up its base in India rather than Pakistan.[22] Having had this ringside view of Pakistan's sordid fate, it isn't just odd, it's *unthinkable*, that India should want to do this. Any Third World country with a fragile economy and a complex social base should know by now that to invite a Superpower like America in (whether it says it's staying or just passing through) would be like inviting a brick to drop through your windscreen.

In the media blitz that followed 11 September, mainstream TV stations largely ignored the story of America's involvement with Afghanistan. So, to those unfamiliar with the story, the coverage of the attacks could have been moving, disturbing and perhaps, to cynics, self-indulgent. However, to those of us who *are* familiar with Afghanistan's recent history, American television coverage and the rhetoric of the 'International Coalition Against Terror' is just plain insulting. America's 'free press' like its 'free market' has a lot to account for.

Operation Enduring Freedom is ostensibly being fought to uphold the American Way of Life. It'll probably end up undermining it completely. It will spawn more anger and more terror across the world. For ordinary people in America, it will mean lives lived in a climate of sickening uncertainty: Will my child be safe in school? Will there be nerve gas in the subway? A bomb in the cinema hall? Will my love come home tonight? There have been warnings about the possibility of biological warfare—smallpox, bubonic plague, anthrax—the deadly payload of innocuous crop duster aircraft.[23] Being picked off a few at a time may end up being worse than being annihilated all at once by a nuclear bomb.

The US government, and no doubt governments all over the world, will use the climate of war as an excuse to curtail civil liberties, deny free speech, lay off workers, harass ethnic and religious minorities, cut back on public spending and divert huge amounts of money to the defence industry. To what purpose? President George Bush can no more 'rid the world of evil-doers' than he can stock it with saints.[24] It's absurd for the US government to even toy with the notion that it can stamp out terrorism with more violence and oppression. Terrorism is the symptom, not the disease. Terrorism has no country. It's transnational, as global an enterprise as Coke or Pepsi or Nike. At the first sign of trouble, terrorists can pull up stakes and move their 'factories' from country to country in search of a better deal. Just like the multinationals.

Terrorism as a phenomenon may never go away. But if it is to be contained, the first step is for America to at least *acknowledge* that it shares the planet with other nations, with other human beings, who, even if they are not on TV, have loves and griefs and stories and songs and sorrows and, for heaven's sake, *rights*. Instead, when Donald Rumsfeld, the US Defense Secretary, was asked what he would call a victory in America's New War, he said that if he could convince the world that Americans must be allowed to continue with their way of life, he would consider it a victory.[25]

The 11 September attack was a monstrous calling card from a world gone horribly wrong. The message may have been written by bin Laden (who knows?) and delivered by his couriers, but it could well have been signed by the ghosts of the victims of America's old wars.

The millions killed in Korea, Vietnam and Cambodia, the 17,500 killed when Israel—backed by the US—invaded Lebanon in 1982, the tens of thousands of Iraqis killed in Operation Desert Storm, the thousands of Palestinians who have died fighting Israel's occupation of the West Bank.[26] And the millions who died in Yugoslavia, Somalia, Haiti, Chile, Nicaragua, El Salvador, the Dominican Republic and Panama, at the hands of all the terrorists, dictators and genocidists who the American government supported, trained, bankrolled and supplied with arms. And this is far from being a comprehensive list.

For a country involved in so much warfare and conflict, the American people have been extremely fortunate. The strikes on 11 September were only the second on American soil in over a century. The first was Pearl Harbor. The reprisal for this took a long route, but ended with Hiroshima and Nagasaki. This time the world waits with bated breath for the horrors to come.

Someone recently said that if Osama bin Laden didn't exist, America would have had to invent him.[27] But in a way, America *did* invent him. He was among the jihadis who moved to Afghanistan after 1979 when the CIA commenced operations there. He has the distinction of being created by the CIA and wanted by the FBI. In the course of a fortnight he has been promoted from Suspect to Prime Suspect and then, despite the lack of any real evidence, straight up the charts to being 'wanted dead or alive'.

From all accounts, it will be impossible to produce evidence (of the sort that would stand scrutiny in a court of law) to link bin Laden to the 11 September attack.[28] So far, it appears that the most incriminating piece of evidence against him is the fact that he has not condemned them. From what is known about the location of bin Laden and the living conditions from which he operates, it's entirely possible that he did not personally plan and carry out the attack—that he is the inspirational figure, 'the CEO of the Holding Company'.[29] The Taliban's response to US demands for the extradition of bin Laden has been uncharacteristically reasonable: produce the evidence, we'll hand him over. President Bush's response is that the demand is 'non-negotiable'.[30]

(While talks are on for the extradition of CEOs—can India put in a side-request for the extradition of Warren Anderson of the USA? He was Chairman of Union Carbide, responsible for the 1984 Bhopal gas leak that killed 16,000 people. We *have* collated the necessary evidence. It's all in the files. Could we have him, please?)[31]

But who is Osama bin Laden *really*?

Let me rephrase that. *What* is Osama bin Laden?

He is America's family secret. He is the American President's dark doppelganger. The savage twin of all that purports to be beautiful and civilized. He has been sculpted from the spare rib of a world laid to waste by America's foreign policy: its gunboat diplomacy, its nuclear arsenal, its vulgarly stated policy of 'full spectrum dominance', its chilling disregard for non-American lives, its barbarous military interventions, its support for despotic and dictatorial regimes, its merciless economic agenda that has munched through the economies of poor countries like a cloud of locusts.[32] Its marauding multinationals who are taking over the air we breathe, the ground we stand on, the water we drink, the thoughts we think.

Now that the family secret has been spilled, the twins are blurring into one another and gradually becoming interchangeable. Their guns, bombs, money and drugs have been going around in the loop for a while. (The Stinger missiles that will greet US helicopters were supplied by the CIA. The heroin used by America's drug-addicts comes from Afghanistan. The Bush administration recently gave Afghanistan a $43 million subsidy for a 'war on drugs'. . .)[33] Now they've even begun to borrow each other's rhetoric. Each refers to the other as 'the head of the snake'. Both invoke God and use the loose millenarian currency of Good and Evil as their terms of reference. Both are engaged in unequivocal political crimes. Both are dangerously armed—one with the nuclear arsenal of the obscenely powerful, the other with the incandescent, destructive power of the utterly hopeless. The fireball and the ice pick. The bludgeon and the axe. The important thing to keep in mind is that neither is an acceptable alternative to the other.

President Bush's ultimatum to the people of the world— 'Either you are with us or you are with the terrorists'—is a piece of presumptuous arrogance.[34]

It's not a choice that people want to, need to, or should have to make.

October 2001

war is peace

As darkness deepened over Afghanistan on Sunday, 7 October 2001, the US government, backed by the International Coalition Against Terror (the new, amenable surrogate for the United Nations), launched air strikes against Afghanistan. TV channels lingered on computer-animated images of cruise missiles, stealth bombers, tomahawks, 'bunker-busting' missiles and Mark 82 high drag bombs.[1] All over the world, little boys watched goggle-eyed and stopped clamouring for new video games.

The UN, reduced now to an ineffective acronym, wasn't even asked to mandate the air strikes. (As Madeleine Albright once said, 'We will behave multilaterally when we can, and unilaterally when we must.')[2]

The 'evidence' against the terrorists was shared amongst friends in the 'Coalition'. After conferring, they announced that it didn't matter whether or not the 'evidence' would stand up in a court of law.[3] Thus, in an instant, were centuries of jurisprudence carelessly trashed.

Nothing can excuse or justify an act of terrorism, whether it is committed by religious fundamentalists, private militia, people's resistance movements—or whether it's dressed up as a war of retribution by a recognized government. The bombing of Afghanistan is not revenge for New York and Washington. It is yet another act of terror against the people of the world. Each innocent person that is killed must be *added to*, not set off against, the grisly toll of civilians who died in New York and Washington.

People rarely win wars, governments rarely lose them. People get killed. Governments moult and regroup, hydra-headed. They first use flags to shrink-wrap people's minds and smother real thought, and then as ceremonial shrouds to bury their willing dead. On both sides, in Afghanistan as well as America, civilians are now hostage to the actions of their own governments. Unknowingly, ordinary people in both countries share a common bond —they have to live with the phenomenon of blind, unpredictable terror. Each batch of bombs that is dropped on Afghanistan is matched by a corresponding escalation of mass hysteria in America about anthrax, more hijackings and other terrorist acts.

There is no easy way out of the spiralling morass of terror and brutality that confronts the world today. It is time now for the human race to hold still, to delve into its wells of collective wisdom, both ancient and modern. What happened on 11 September changed the world forever. Freedom, progress, wealth, technology, war—these words have taken on new meaning. Governments have to acknowledge this transformation, and approach their new tasks with a modicum of honesty and humility. Unfortunately, up to now, there has been no sign of any introspection from the leaders of the International Coalition. Or the Taliban.

When he announced the air strikes, President George Bush said, 'We're a peaceful nation.' America's favourite Ambassador, Tony Blair (who also holds the portfolio of Prime Minister of the UK), echoed him: 'We're a peaceful people.'[4]

So now we know. Pigs are horses. Girls are boys. War is Peace.

Speaking at the FBI headquarters a few days later, President Bush said, 'This is the calling of the United States of America. The most free nation in the world. A nation built on fundamental values; that rejects hate, rejects violence, rejects murderers and rejects evil. And we will not tire.'[5]

Here is a list of the countries that America has been at war with—and bombed—since World War II: China (1945–46, 1950–53), Korea (1950–53), Guatemala (1954, 1967–69), Indonesia (1958), Cuba (1959–60), the Belgian Congo (1964), Peru (1965), Laos (1964–73), Vietnam (1961–73), Cambodia (1969–70), Grenada (1983), Libya (1986), El Salvador (1980s), Nicaragua (1980s), Panama (1989), Iraq (1991–99), Bosnia (1995), Sudan (1998), Yugoslavia (1999). And now Afghanistan.

Certainly it does not tire—this, the Most Free nation in the world. What freedoms does it uphold? *Within* its borders, the freedoms of speech, religion, thought; of artistic expression, food habits, sexual preferences (well, to some extent) and many other exemplary, wonderful things. *Outside* its borders, the freedom to dominate, humiliate and subjugate—usually in the service of America's real religion, the 'free market'. So when the US government christens a war 'Operation Infinite Justice', or 'Operation Enduring Freedom', we in the Third World feel more than a tremor of fear. Because we know that Infinite Justice for some means Infinite Injustice for others. And Enduring Freedom for some means Enduring Subjugation for others.

The International Coalition Against Terror is largely a cabal of the richest countries in the world. Between them, they manufacture and sell almost all of the world's weapons, they possess the largest stockpile of weapons of mass destruction—chemical, biological and nuclear. They have fought the most wars, account for most of the genocide, subjection, ethnic cleansing and human rights violations in modern history, and have sponsored, armed and financed untold numbers of dictators and despots. Between them, they have worshipped, almost deified, the cult of violence and war. For all its appalling sins, the Taliban just isn't in the same league.

The Taliban was compounded in the crumbling crucible of rubble, heroin and landmines in the backwash of the Cold War. Its oldest leaders are in their early forties. Many of them are disfigured and handicapped, missing an eye, an arm or a leg. They grew up in a society scarred and devastated by war. Between the Soviet Union and America, over twenty years, about $45 billion worth of arms and ammunition was poured into Afghanistan.[6]

The latest weaponry was the only shard of modernity to intrude upon a thoroughly medieval society. Young boys—many of them orphans—who grew up in those times, had guns for toys, never knew the security and comfort of family life, never experienced the company of women. Now, as adults and rulers, the Taliban beat, stone, rape and brutalize women, they don't seem to know what else to do with them. Years of war has stripped them of gentleness, inured them to kindness and human compassion. They dance to the percussive rhythms of bombs raining down around them. Now they've turned their monstrosity on their own people.

With all due respect to President Bush, the people of the world do *not* have to choose between the Taliban and the US government. All the beauty of human civilization—our art, our music, our literature—lies beyond these two fundamentalist, ideological poles. There is as little chance that the people of the world can all become middle-class consumers as there is that they will all embrace any one particular religion. The issue is not about Good vs Evil or Islam vs Christianity as much as it is about *space*. About how to accommodate diversity, how to contain the impulse towards hegemony—every kind of hegemony, economic, military, linguistic, religious and cultural. Any ecologist will tell you how dangerous and fragile a mono-culture is. A hegemonic world is like having a government without a healthy opposition. It becomes a kind of dictatorship. It's like putting a plastic bag over the world, and preventing it from breathing. Eventually, it will be torn open.

One and a half million Afghan people lost their lives in the twenty years of conflict that preceded this new war.[7]

Afghanistan was reduced to rubble, and now, the rubble is being pounded into finer dust. By the second day of the air strikes, US pilots were returning to their bases without dropping their assigned payload of bombs.[8] As one pilot put it, Afghanistan is 'not a target-rich environment'.[9] At a press briefing at the Pentagon, Donald Rumsfeld, US Defense Secretary, was asked if America had run out of targets. 'First we're going to re-hit targets,' he said, 'and second, *we're* not running out of targets, Afghanistan is . . .' This was greeted with gales of laughter in the Briefing Room.[10]

By the third day of the strikes, the US Defense Department boasted that it had 'achieved air supremacy over Afghanistan'.[11] (Did they mean that they had destroyed *both*, or maybe all sixteen, of Afghanistan's planes?)

On the ground in Afghanistan, the Northern Alliance—the Taliban's old enemy, and therefore the International Coalition's newest friend—is making headway in its push to capture Kabul. (For the archives, let it be said that the Northern Alliance's track record is not very different from the Taliban's. But for now, because it's inconvenient, that little detail is being glossed over.)[12]

The visible, moderate, 'acceptable' leader of the Alliance, Ahmed Shah Masud, was killed in a suicide-bomb attack early in September.[13] The rest of the Nothern Alliance is a brittle confederation of brutal warlords, ex-communists and unbending clerics. It is a disparate group divided along ethnic lines, some of whom have tasted power in Afghanistan in the past.

Until the US air strikes, the Northern Alliance controlled about five per cent of the geographical area of Afghanistan. Now, with the Coalition's help and 'air cover', it is poised to topple the Taliban.[14] Meanwhile, Taliban soldiers, sensing imminent defeat, have begun to defect to the Alliance. So the fighting forces are busy switching sides and changing uniforms. But in an enterprise as cynical as this one, it hardly seems to matter at all. Love is hate, north is south, peace is war.

Among the global powers, there is talk of 'putting in a representative government'. Or, on the other hand, of 'restoring' the Kingdom to Afghanistan's eighty-nine-year-old former King Zahir Shah, who has lived in exile in Rome since 1973.[15] That's the way the game goes— support Saddam Hussein, then 'take him out'; finance the mujahedeen, then bomb them to smithereens; put in Zahir Shah and see if he's going to be a good boy. (Is it possible to 'put in' a representative government? Can you place an order for Democracy—with extra cheese and jalapeño peppers?)

Reports have begun to trickle in about civilian casualties, about cities emptying out as Afghan civilians flock to the borders which have been closed.[16] Main arterial roads have been blown up or sealed off. Those who have experience of working in Afghanistan say that by early November, food convoys will not be able to reach the millions of Afghans (7.5 million according to the UN) who run the very real risk of starving to death during the course of this winter.[17] They say that in the days that are left before winter sets in, there can *either* be a war, *or* an attempt to reach food to the hungry. Not both.

As a gesture of humanitarian support, the US government air-dropped 37,000 packets of emergency rations into Afghanistan. It says it plans to drop more than 500,000 packets. That will still only add up to a single meal for half a million people out of the several million in dire need of food. Aid workers have condemned it as a cynical, dangerous, public-relations exercise. They say that air-dropping food packets is worse than futile. First, because the food will never get to those who really need it. More dangerously, those who run out to retrieve the packets risk being blown up by land mines.[18] A tragic alms race.

Nevertheless, the food packets had a photo-op all to themselves. Their contents were listed in major newspapers. They were vegetarian, we're told, as per Muslim Dietary Law (!). Each yellow packet, decorated with the American flag, contained: rice, peanut butter, bean salad, strawberry jam, crackers, raisins, flat bread, an apple fruit bar, seasoning, matches, a set of plastic cutlery, a serviette and illustrated user instructions.[19]

After three years of unremitting drought, an air-dropped airline meal in Jalalabad! The level of cultural ineptitude, the failure to understand what months of relentless hunger and grinding poverty *really* mean, the US government's attempt to use even this abject misery to boost its self-image, beggars description.

Reverse the scenario for a moment. Imagine if the Taliban government was to bomb New York City, saying all the while that its *real* target was the US government and its policies. And suppose, during breaks between the bombing, the Taliban dropped a few thousand packets containing *nan* and *kababs* impaled on an Afghan flag. Would the good people of New York ever find it in themselves to forgive the Afghan government? Even if they were hungry, even if they needed the food, even if they *ate* it, how would they ever forget the insult, the condescension? Rudi Guiliani, Mayor of New York City, returned a gift of $10 million from a Saudi prince because it came with a few words of friendly advice about American policy in the Middle East.[20] Is pride a luxury that only the rich are entitled to?

Far from stamping it out, igniting this kind of rage is what *creates* terrorism. Hate and retribution don't go back into the box once you've let them out. For every 'terrorist' or his 'supporter' that is killed, hundreds of innocent people are being killed too. And for every hundred innocent people killed, there is a good chance that several future terrorists will be created.

Where will it all lead?

Setting aside the rhetoric for a moment, consider the fact that the world has not yet found an acceptable definition of what 'terrorism' is. One country's terrorist is too often another's freedom fighter. At the heart of the matter lies the world's deep-seated ambivalence towards violence. Once violence is accepted as a legitimate political instrument, then the morality and political acceptability of terrorists (insurgents or freedom fighters) becomes contentious, bumpy terrain. The US government itself has funded, armed and sheltered plenty of rebels and insurgents around the world. While President Reagan praised them as freedom fighters, the CIA and Pakistan's ISI trained and armed the mujahedeen who, in the eighties, were seen as terrorists by the government in Soviet-occupied Afghanistan.[21]

Today, Pakistan—America's ally in this new war—sponsors insurgents who cross the border into Kashmir in India. Pakistan lauds them as 'freedom fighters', India calls them 'terrorists'. India, for its part, denounces countries who sponsor and abet terrorism, but the Indian army has, in the past, trained separatist Tamil rebels asking for a homeland in Sri Lanka—the LTTE, responsible for countless acts of bloody terrorism. (Just as the CIA abandoned the mujahedeen after they had served its purpose, India abruptly turned its back on the LTTE for a host of political reasons. It was an enraged LTTE suicide bomber who assassinated former Indian Prime Minister Rajiv Gandhi in 1991.)

It is important for governments and politicians to understand that manipulating these huge, raging human feelings for their own narrow purposes may yield instant results, but, eventually and inexorably, they have disastrous consequences. Igniting and exploiting religious sentiments for reasons of political expediency is the most dangerous legacy that governments or politicians can bequeath to *any* people—including their own. People who live in societies ravaged by religious or communal bigotry know that every religious text—from the Bible to the Bhagwad Gita—can be mined and misinterpreted to justify anything, from nuclear war to genocide to corporate globalization.

This is not to suggest that the terrorists who perpetrated the outrage on 11 September should not be hunted down and brought to book. They must be. But is war the best way to track them down? Will burning the haystack find you the needle? Or will it escalate the anger and make the world a living hell for all of us?

At the end of the day, how many people can you spy on, how many bank accounts can you freeze, how many conversations can you eavesdrop on, how many e-mails can you intercept, how many letters can you open, how many phones can you tap? Even before 11 September, the CIA had accumulated more information than is humanly possible to process. (Sometimes, too much data can actually hinder intelligence—small wonder the US spy satellites completely missed the preparation that preceded India's nuclear tests in 1998.)

The sheer scale of the surveillance will become a logistical, ethical and civil rights nightmare. It will drive everybody clean crazy. And freedom—that precious, precious thing —will be the first casualty. It's already hurt and haemorrhaging dangerously.

Governments across the world are cynically using the prevailing paranoia to promote their own interests. All kinds of unpredictable political forces are being unleashed. In India, for instance, members of the All India People's Resistance Forum, who were distributing anti-war and anti-US pamphlets in Delhi, have been jailed. Even the printer of the leaflets was arrested.[22] The right-wing government (while it shelters Hindu extremist groups like the Vishwa Hindu Parishad and the Bajrang Dal) has banned the Students Islamic Movement of India and is trying to revive an anti-terrorist Act which had been withdrawn after the Human Rights Commission reported that it had been more abused than used.[23] Millions of Indian citizens are Muslim. Can *anything* be gained by alienating them?

Every day that the war goes on, raging emotions are being let loose into the world. The international press has little or no independent access to the war zone. In any case, the mainstream media, particularly in the US, has more or less rolled over, allowing itself to be tickled on the stomach with press hand-outs from military men and government officials. Afghan radio stations have been destroyed by the bombing. The Taliban has always been deeply suspicious of the Press. In the propaganda war, there is no accurate estimate of how many people have been killed, or how much destruction has taken place. In the absence of reliable information, wild rumours spread.

Put your ear to the ground in this part of the world, and you can hear the thrumming, the deadly drumbeat of burgeoning anger. Please. *Please*, stop the war now. Enough people have died. The smart missiles are just not smart enough. They're blowing up whole warehouses of suppressed fury.

President George Bush recently boasted, 'When I take action, I'm not going to fire a $2 million missile at a ten-dollar empty tent and hit a camel in the butt. It's going to be decisive.'[24] President Bush should know that there are no targets in Afghanistan that will give his missiles their money's worth. Perhaps, if only to balance his books, he should develop some cheaper missiles to use on cheaper targets and cheaper lives in the poor countries of the world. But then, that may not make good business sense to the Coalition's weapons manufacturers. It wouldn't make any sense at all, for example, to the Carlyle Group —described by the Industry Standard as 'one of the world's largest private investment funds,' with $13 billion under management.[25] Carlyle invests in the defence sector and makes its money from military conflicts and weapons spending.

Carlyle is run by men with impeccable credentials. Former US Defense Secretary Frank Carlucci is Carlyle's Chairman and Managing Director. He was a college roommate of Donald Rumsfeld's. Carlyle's other partners include former US Secretary of State James A. Baker III, George Soros and Fred Malek (George Bush Sr's campaign manager). An American paper—the *Baltimore Chronicle and Sentinel*—says that former President George Bush Sr is reported to be seeking investments for the Carlyle Group from Asian markets. He is reportedly paid not inconsiderable sums of money to make 'presentations' to potential government-clients.[26]

Ho hum. As the tired saying goes, it's all in the family.

Then there's that other branch of traditional family business—oil. Remember, President George Bush Jr and Vice-President Dick Cheney both made their fortunes working in the US oil industry.

Turkmenistan, which borders the north-west of Afghanistan, holds the world's third largest gas reserves and an estimated six billion barrels of oil reserves. Enough, experts say, to meet American energy needs for the next thirty years (or a developing country's energy requirements for a couple of centuries).[27]

America has always viewed oil as a security consideration, and protected it by any means it deems necessary. Few of us doubt that its military presence in the Gulf has little to do with its concern for human rights and almost entirely to do with its strategic interest in oil.

Oil and gas from the Caspian region currently moves northward to European markets. Geographically and politically, Iran and Russia are major impediments to American interests. In 1998, Dick Cheney—then CEO of Halliburton, a major player in the oil industry—said, 'I can't think of a time when we've had a region emerge as suddenly to become as strategically significant as the Caspian. It's almost as if the opportunities have arisen overnight.'[28] True enough.

For some years now, an American oil giant called Unocal has been negotiating with the Taliban for permission to construct an oil pipeline through Afghanistan to Pakistan and out to the Arabian Sea. From here, Unocal hopes to access the lucrative 'emerging markets' in South and South-east Asia. In December 1997, a delegation of Taliban mullahs travelled to America and even met US State Department officials and Unocal executives in Houston.[29] At that time the Taliban's taste for public executions and its treatment of Afghan women were not made out to be the crimes against humanity that they are now. Over the next six months, pressure from hundreds of outraged American feminist groups was brought to bear on the Clinton administration. Fortunately, they managed to scuttle the deal. And now comes the US oil industry's big chance.

In America, the arms industry, the oil industry, the major media networks and, indeed, US foreign policy, are all controlled by the same business combines. Therefore it would be foolish to expect this talk of guns and oil and defence deals to get any real play in the media. In any case, to a distraught, confused people whose pride has just been wounded, whose loved ones have been tragically killed, whose anger is fresh and sharp, the inanities about the 'Clash of Civilizations' and the 'Good vs Evil' discourse home in unerringly. They are cynically doled out by government spokesmen like a daily dose of vitamins or anti-depressants. Regular medication ensures that mainland America continues to remain the enigma it has always been—a curiously insular people, administered by a pathologically meddlesome, promiscuous government.

And what of the rest of us, the numb recipients of this onslaught of what we know to be preposterous propaganda? The daily consumers of the lies and brutality smeared in peanut butter and strawberry jam being air-dropped into our minds just like those yellow food packets. Shall we look away and eat because we're hungry, or shall we stare unblinking at the grim theatre unfolding in Afghanistan until we retch collectively and say, in one voice, that we have had enough?

As the first year of the new millennium rushes to a close, one wonders—have we forfeited our right to dream? Will we ever be able to re-imagine beauty? Will it be possible ever again to watch the slow, amazed blink of a new-born gecko in the sun, or whisper back to the marmot who has just whispered in your ear—without thinking of the World Trade Center and Afghanistan?

October 2001

democracy

Who's She When She's at Home?

Last night a friend from Baroda called. Weeping. It took her fifteen minutes to tell me what the matter was. It wasn't very complicated. Only that a friend of hers, Sayeeda,[1] had been caught by a mob. Only that her stomach had been ripped open and stuffed with burning rags. Only that after she died someone carved 'Om' on her forehead. [2]

Precisely which Hindu scripture preaches this?

Our Prime Minister, Mr A.B. Vajpayee, justified this as part of the retaliation by outraged Hindus against Muslim 'terrorists' who burned alive fifty-eight Hindu passengers on the Sabarmati Express in Godhra.[3] Each of those who died that hideous death was someone's brother, someone's mother, someone's child. Of course they were.

Which particular verse in the Koran required that they be roasted alive?

The more the two sides try and call attention to their religious differences by slaughtering each other, the less there is to distinguish them from one another. They worship at the same altar. They're both apostles of the same murderous god, whoever he is. In an atmosphere so vitiated, for anybody, and in particular the Prime Minister, to arbitrarily decree exactly where the cycle started is malevolent and irresponsible.

Right now we're sipping from a poisoned chalice—a flawed democracy laced with religious fascism. Pure arsenic.

What shall we do? What *can* we do?

We have a ruling party that's haemorrhaging. Its rhetoric against Terrorism, the passing of the Prevention of Terrorism Act (POTA), the sabre-rattling against Pakistan (with the underlying nuclear threat), the massing of almost a million soldiers on the border on hair-trigger alert and, most dangerous of all, the attempt to communalize and falsify school history textbooks—none of this has prevented it from being humiliated in election after election.[4] Even its old party trick—the revival of the Ram Mandir plans in Ayodhya—didn't quite work out.[5] Desperate now, it has turned for succour to the state of Gujarat.

Gujarat, the only major state in India to have a Baratya Janata Party (BJP) government, has, for some years, been the petri dish in which Hindu fascism has been fomenting an elaborate political experiment. In March 2002, the initial results were put on public display.

Within hours of the Godhra outrage, a meticulously planned pogrom was unleashed against the Muslim community. It was led from the front by the Hindu nationalist Vishwa Hindu Parishad (VHP) and the Bajrang Dal. Officially the number of dead is 800. Independent reports put the figure as high as 2,000.[6] More than 150,000 people, driven from their homes, now live in refugee camps.[7] Women were stripped, gang-raped; parents were bludgeoned to death in front of their children.[8] Two hundred and forty dargahs and 180 masjids were destroyed. In Ahmedabad the tomb of Wali Gujarati, the founder of the modern Urdu poem, was demolished and paved over in the course of a night.[9] The tomb of the musician Ustad Faiyaz Ali Khan was desecrated and wreathed in burning tyres.[10] Arsonists burned and looted shops, homes, hotels, textiles mills, buses and private cars. Tens of thousands have lost their jobs.[11]

A mob surrounded the house of former Congress MP Ehsan Jaffri. His phone calls to the Director General of Police, the Police Commissioner, the Chief Secretary, the Additional Chief Secretary (Home) were ignored. The mobile police vans around his house did not intervene. The mob dragged Ehsan Jaffri out of his house, and dismembered him.[12] Of course it's only a coincidence that Jaffri was a trenchant critic of Gujarat's Chief Minister, Narendra Modi, during his campaign for the Rajkot Assembly by-election in February.

Across Gujarat, thousands of people made up the mobs. They were armed with petrol bombs, guns, knives, swords and tridents.[13] Apart from the VHP and Bajrang Dal's usual lumpen constituency, there were Dalits and Adivasis who were brought in buses and trucks. Middle-class people participated in the looting. (On one memorable occasion a family arrived in a Mitsubishi Lancer.[14]) There was a deliberate, systematic attempt to destroy the economic base of the Muslim community. The leaders of the mob had computer-generated cadastral lists marking out Muslim homes, shops, businesses and even partnerships. They had mobile phones to coordinate the action. They had trucks loaded with thousands of gas cylinders, hoarded weeks in advance, which they used to blow up Muslim commercial establishments. They had not just police protection and police connivance but also covering fire.[15]

While Gujarat burned, our Prime Minister was on MTV promoting his new poems.[16] (Reports say cassettes have sold a hundred thousand copies.) It took him more than a month—and two vacations in the hills—to make it to Gujarat.[17] When he did, shadowed by the chilling Mr Modi, he gave a speech at the Shah Alam refugee camp.[18] His mouth moved, he tried to express concern, but no real sound emerged except the mocking of the wind whistling through a burned, bloodied, broken world. Next we knew, he was bobbing around in a golf cart, striking business deals in Singapore.[19]

It is important to remember that the violence that convulsed Gujarat did not spill across the borders into other states. Rajasthan, Maharashtra, Madhya Pradesh—all communally sensitive states—remained calm. So did Bihar and Uttar Pradesh. It is not a coincidence that none of these states had a BJP government.

The killers still stalk Gujarat's streets. For weeks the lynch mob was the arbiter of the routine affairs of daily life: who can live where, who can say what, who can meet whom, and where and when. Its mandate expanded from religious affairs, to property disputes, family altercations, the planning and allocation of water resources . . . (which is why Medha Patkar of the NBA was assaulted).[20] Muslim businesses have been shut down. Muslim people are not served in restaurants. Muslim children are not welcome in schools. Muslim students are too terrified to sit for their exams.[21] Muslim parents live in dread that their infants might forget what they've been told and give themselves away by saying 'Ammi!' or 'Abba!' in public and invite sudden and violent death.

Notice has been given: *this is just the beginning.*

Is this the Hindu Rashtra (Nation) that we've all been asked to look forward to? Once the Muslims have been 'shown their place', will milk and Coca-Cola flow across the land? Once the Ram Mandir (Temple) is built, will there be a shirt on every back and a roti in every belly?[22] Will every tear be wiped from every eye? Can we expect an anniversary celebration next year? Or will there be someone else to hate by then? Alphabetically: Adivasis, Buddhists, Christians, Dalits, Parsis, Sikhs? Those who wear jeans or speak English or those who have thick lips or curly hair? We won't have to wait long. It's started already. Will the established rituals continue? Will people be beheaded, dismembered and urinated upon? Will foetuses be ripped from their mothers' wombs and slaugh-tered? (What kind of depraved vision can even *imagine* India without the range and beauty and spectacular anar-chy of all these cultures? India would become a tomb and smell like a crematorium.)

No matter who they were, or how they were killed, each person who died in Gujarat in the weeks gone by deserves to be mourned. There have been hundreds of outraged letters to journals and newspapers asking why the 'pseudo-secularists' do not condemn the burning of the Sabarmati Express in Godhra with the same degree of outrage with which they condemn the killings in the rest of Gujarat. What they don't seem to understand is that there *is* a fundamental difference between a pogrom such as the one taking place in Gujarat now and the burning of the Sabarmati Express in Godhra. We still don't know who exactly was responsible for the carnage in Godhra.[23] Whoever did it, whatever their political or religious persuasion, committed a terrible crime. But every independent report says the pogrom against the Muslim community in Gujarat—billed by the Government as spontaneous 'reaction'—has at best been conducted under the benign gaze of the State and, at worst, with active State collusion.[24] Either way, the State is criminally culpable. And the State acts in the name of its citizens. So as a citizen, I am forced to acknowledge that I am somehow made complicit in the Gujarat pogrom. It is this that outrages me. And it is this that puts a completely different complexion on the two massacres.

After the Gujarat massacres, at its convention in Bangalore, the Rashtriya Swayamsewak Sangh (RSS), the moral and cultural guild of the BJP, of which the Prime

Minister, the Home Minister and Chief Minister Modi himself are all members, called upon Muslims to earn the 'goodwill' of the majority community.[25] At the meeting of the national executive of the BJP in Goa, Narendra Modi was greeted as a hero. His smirking offer to resign from the Chief Minister's post was unanimously turned down.[26] In a recent public speech he compared the events of the last few weeks in Gujarat to Gandhi's Dandi March—both, according to him, significant moments in the Struggle for Freedom.[27]

While the parallels between contemporary India and pre-war Germany are chilling, they're not surprising. (The founders of the RSS have, in their writings, been frank in their admiration for Hitler and his methods.[28]) One difference is that here in India we don't have a Hitler. We have, instead, a travelling extravaganza, a mobile symphonic orchestra. The hydra-headed, many-armed Sangh Parivar —the 'joint family' of Hindu political and cultural organizations—with the BJP, the RSS, the VHP and the Bajrang Dal each playing a different instrument. Its utter genius lies in its apparent ability to be all things to all people at all times.

The Parivar has an appropriate head for every occasion. An old versifier with rhetoric for every season. A rabble-rousing hardliner, Lal Krishna Advani, for Home Affairs; a suave one, Jaswant Singh, for Foreign Affairs; a smooth,

English-speaking lawyer, Arun Jaitley, to handle TV
debates; a cold-blooded creature, Narendra Modi, for a
Chief Minister; and the Bajrang Dal and the VHP, grass-
roots workers in charge of the physical labour that goes
into the business of genocide. Finally, this many-headed
extravaganza has a lizard's tail which drops off when it's in
trouble and grows back again: a specious socialist dressed
up as Defence Minister, whom it sends on its damage-
limitation missions—wars, cyclones, genocides. They trust
him to press the right buttons, hit the right note.

The Sangh Parivar speaks in as many tongues as a whole
corsage of tridents. It can say several contradictory things
simultaneously. While one of its heads (the VHP) exhorts
millions of its cadres to prepare for the Final Solution, its
titular head (the Prime Minister) assures the nation that
all citizens, regardless of their religion, will be treated
equally. It can ban books and films and burn paintings for
'insulting Indian culture'. Simultaneously, it can mortgage
the equivalent of sixty per cent of the entire country's
rural development budget as profit to Enron.[29] It contains
within itself the full spectrum of political opinion, so what
would normally be a public fight between two adversarial
political parties is now just a Family Matter. However acrimonious the quarrel, it's *always* conducted in
public, always resolved amicably, and the audience always
goes away satisfied it's got value for money—anger,
action, revenge, intrigue, remorse, poetry and plenty of

gore. It's our own vernacular version of Full Spectrum Dominance.[30]

But when the chips are down, *really* down, the squabbling heads quieten, and it becomes chillingly apparent that underneath all the clamour and the noise a single heart beats. And an unforgiving mind with saffron-saturated tunnel vision works overtime.

There have been pogroms in India before, every kind of pogrom—directed at particular castes, tribes, religious faiths. In 1984, following the assassination of Indira Gandhi, the Congress Party presided over the massacre of 3,000 Sikhs in Delhi, every bit as macabre as the one in Gujarat.[31] At the time, Rajiv Gandhi, never known for an elegant turn of phrase, said, 'When a large tree falls, the earth shakes.'[32] In 1985 the Congress swept the polls. On a *sympathy* wave! Eighteen years have gone by, and almost no one has been punished.

Take any politically volatile issue—the nuclear tests, the Babri Masjid, the Tehelka scam, the stirring of the communal cauldron for electoral advantage—and you'll see the Congress Party has been there before. In every case, the Congress sowed the seed and the BJP has swept in to reap the hideous harvest. So in the event that we're called upon to vote, *is* there a difference between the two? The answer is a faltering but distinct 'yes'. Here's why: It's true that the Congress Party has sinned, and grievously, and for decades together. But it has done by night what the BJP does by day. It has done covertly, stealthily, hypocritically, shamefacedly what the BJP does with pride. And this is an important difference.

Whipping up communal hatred is part of the mandate of the Sangh Parivar. It has been planned for *years*. It has been injecting a slow-release poison directly into civil society's bloodstream. Hundreds of RSS shakhas ('educational cells') and Saraswati shishu mandirs across the country have been indoctrinating thousands of children and young people, stunting their minds with religious hatred and falsified history, inluding unfactual or wildly exaggerated accounts of the rape and pillaging of Hindu women and Hindu temples by Muslim rulers in the pre-colonial period. They're no different from, and no less dangerous than, the madrassas all over Pakistan and Afghanistan which spawned the Taliban. In states like Gujarat, the police, the administration and the political cadres at every level have been systematically penetrated.[33] It has huge popular appeal, which it would be foolish to underestimate or misunderstand. The whole enterprise has a formidable religious, ideological, political and administrative underpinning. This kind of power, this kind of reach, can only be achieved with State backing.

Some madrassas, the Muslim equivalent of hothouses cultivating religious hatred, try and make up in frenzy and foreign funding what they lack in State support. They provide the perfect foil for Hindu communalists to dance their dance of mass paranoia and hatred. (In fact they serve that purpose so perfectly they might just as well be working as a team.)

Under this relentless pressure, what will most likely happen is that the majority of the Muslim community will resign itself to living in ghettos as second-class citizens, in constant fear, with no civil rights and no recourse to justice. What will daily life be like for them? Any little thing, an altercation in a cinema queue or a fracas at a traffic light, could turn lethal. So they will learn to keep very quiet, to accept their lot, to creep around the edges of the society in which they live. Their fear will transmit itself to other minorities. Many, particularly the young, will probably turn to militancy. They will do terrible things. Civil society will be called upon to condemn them. Then President Bush's canon will come back to us: 'Either you are with us or you are with the terrorists.'[34]

Those words hang frozen in time like icicles. For years to come, butchers and genocidists will fit their grisly mouths around them ('lip-synch', film-makers call it) in order to justify their butchery.

Mr Bal Thackeray of the Shiv Sena, who has lately been feeling a little upstaged by Mr Modi, has the lasting solution. He's called for civil war. Isn't that just perfect? Then Pakistan won't need to bomb us, we can bomb ourselves. Let's turn all of India into Kashmir. Or Bosnia. Or Palestine. Or Rwanda. Let's all suffer forever. Let's buy expensive guns and explosives to kill each other with. Let the British arms dealers and the American weapons manufacturers grow fat on our spilled blood.[35] We could ask the Carlyle group—of which the Bush and bin Laden families were both shareholders—for a bulk discount.[36] Maybe if things go really well, we'll become like Afghanistan. (And look at the publicity they've gone and got themselves.) When all our farmlands are mined, our buildings destroyed, our infrastructure reduced to rubble, our children physically maimed and mentally wrecked, when we've nearly wiped ourselves out with self-manufactured hatred, maybe we can appeal to the Americans to help us out. Airdropped airline meals, anyone?

How close we have come to self-destruction! Another step and we'll be in free-fall. And yet the Government presses on. At the Goa meeting of the BJP's national executive, the Prime Minister of Secular, Democratic India, Mr A.B. Vajpayee, made history. He became the first Indian Prime Minister to cross the threshold and publicly unveil an unconscionable bigotry against Muslims, which even George Bush and Donald Rumsfeld would be embarrassed to own up to. 'Wherever Muslims are living,' he said, 'they don't want to live in harmony. They don't mix with the society. They are not interested in living in peace.'[37]

Shame on him. But if only it were just him: in the immediate aftermath of the Gujarat holocaust, confident of the success of its 'experiment', the BJP wants a snap poll. 'The *gentlest* of people,' my friend from Baroda said to me, 'the *gentlest* of people, in the gentlest of voices, says "Modi is our hero".'

Some of us nurtured the naive hope that the magnitude of the horror of the last few weeks would make the secular parties, however self-serving, unite in sheer outrage. On its own, the BJP does not have the mandate of the people of India. It does not have the mandate to push through the Hindutva project. We hoped that the twenty-two allies that make up the BJP-led coalition at the Centre would withdraw their support. We thought, quite stupidly, that they would see that there could be no bigger test of their moral fibre, of their commitment to their avowed principles of secularism.

It's a sign of the times that not a single one of the BJP's allies has withdrawn support. In every shifty eye you see that faraway look of someone doing mental maths to calculate which constituencies and portfolios they'll retain and which ones they'll lose if they pull out. Deepak Parekh of HDFC is one of the only CEOs of India's corporate community to condemn what happened.[38] Farooq Abdullah, Chief Minister of Jammu and Kashmir and the only prominent Muslim politician left in India, is currying favour with the Government by supporting Modi because he nurses the dim hope that he might become Vice-President of India very soon.[39] And worst of all, Mayawati, leader of the Bahujan Samaj Party (BSP), the People's Socialist Party, the great hope of the lower castes, has forged an alliance with the BJP in Uttar Pradesh.[40]

The Congress and the Left parties have launched a public agitation asking for Modi's resignation. *Resignation?*[41] Have we lost all sense of proportion? Criminals are not meant to *resign*. They're meant to be charged, tried and convicted. As those who burned the train in Godhra should be. As the mobs and those members of the police force and the administration who planned and partici-pated in the pogrom in the rest of Gujarat should be. As those responsible for raising the pitch of the frenzy to boiling point must be. The Supreme Court has the option of acting against Modi and the Bajrang Dal and the VHP suo motu (when the Court itself files charges). There are hundreds of testimonies. There are masses of evidence.

But in India if you are a butcher or a genocidist who happens to be a politician, you have every reason to be optimistic. No one even *expects* politicians to be prosecuted. To demand that Modi and his henchmen be arraigned and put away would make other politicians vulnerable to their own unsavoury pasts. So instead they disrupt Parliament, shout a lot, eventually those in power set up commissions of inquiry, ignore the findings and between themselves makes sure the juggernaut chugs on.

Already the issue has begun to morph. Should elections be allowed or not? Should the Election Commission decide that? Or the Supreme Court? Either way, whether elections are held or deferred, by allowing Modi to walk free, by allowing him to continue with his career as a politician, the fundamental, governing principles of democracy are not just being subverted but deliberately sabotaged. This kind of democracy is the *problem*, not the solution. Our society's greatest strength is being turned into her deadliest enemy. What's the point of us all going on about 'deepening democracy', when it's being bent and twisted into something unrecognizable?

What if the BJP *does* win the elections? After all George Bush had a sixty per cent rating in his War Against Terror, and Ariel Sharon has an even stronger mandate for his bestial invasion of Palestine.[42] Does that make everything all right? Why not dispense with the legal system, the constitution, the press—the whole shebang— morality *itself*, why not chuck it and put everything up for a vote? Genocides can become the subject of opinion polls and massacres can have marketing campaigns.

Fascism's firm footprint has appeared in India. Let's mark the date: Spring, 2002. While we can thank the American President and the Coalition Against Terror for creating a congenial international atmosphere for its ghastly debut, we cannot credit them for the years it has been brewing in our public and private lives.

It breezed in in the wake of the Pokhran nuclear tests in 1998.[43] From then onwards, the massed energy of blood-thirsty patriotism became openly acceptable political currency. The 'weapons of peace' trapped India and Pakistan in a spiral of brinkmanship—threat and counter-threat, taunt and counter-taunt.[44] And now, one war and hundreds of dead later,[45] more than a million soldiers from both armies are massed at the border, eyeball to eyeball, locked in a pointless nuclear standoff. The escalating belligerence against Pakistan has ricocheted off the border and entered our own body politic, like a sharp blade slicing through the vestiges of communal harmony and tolerance between the Hindu and Muslim communities. In no time at all, the godsquadders from hell have colonized the public imagination. And we allowed them in. Each time the hostility between India and Pakistan is cranked up, within India there's a corresponding increase in the hostility towards the Muslims. With each battle cry against Pakistan, we inflict a wound on ourselves, on our way of life, on our spectacularly diverse and ancient civilization, on everything that makes India different from Pakistan. Increasingly, Indian Nationalism has come to mean Hindu Nationalism, which defines itself not through a respect or regard for itself, but through a hatred of the Other. And the Other, for the moment, is not just Pakistan, it's Muslim. It's disturbing to see how neatly nationalism dovetails into fascism. While we must not allow the fascists to define what the nation is, or who it belongs to, it's worth keeping in mind that nationalism —in all its many avatars: socialist, capitalist and fascist— has been at the root of almost all the genocide of the twentieth century. On the issue of nationalism, it's wise to proceed with caution.

Can we not find it in ourselves to belong to an ancient civilization instead of to just a recent nation? To love a *land* instead of just patrolling a territory? The Sangh Parivar understands nothing of what civilization means. It seeks to limit, reduce, define, dismember and desecrate the memory of what we were, our understanding of what we are, and our dreams of who we want to be. What kind of India do they want? A limbless, headless, soulless torso, left bleeding under the butchers' cleaver with a flag driven deep into her mutilated heart? Can we let that happen? Have we let it happen?

The incipient, creeping fascism of the past few years has been groomed by many of our 'democratic' institutions. Everyone has flirted with it—Parliament, the press, the police, the administration, the public. Even 'secularists' have been guilty of helping to create the right climate. Each time you defend the right of an institution, *any* institution (including the Supreme Court), to exercise unfettered, unaccountable powers that must never be challenged, you move towards fascism. To be fair, perhaps not everyone recognized the early signs for what they were.

The national press has been startlingly courageous in its denunciation of the events of the last few weeks. Many of the BJP's fellow travellers who have journeyed with it to the brink are now looking down the abyss into the hell that was once Gujarat and turning away in genuine dismay. But how hard and for how long will they fight? This is not going to be like a publicity campaign for an upcoming cricket season. And there will not always be spectacular carnage to report on. Fascism is also about the slow, steady infiltration of all the instruments of State power. It's about the slow erosion of civil liberties, about unspectacular day-to-day injustices. Fighting it means fighting to win back the minds and hearts of people. Fighting it does not mean asking for RSS shakhas and the madrassas that are overtly communal to be banned, it means working towards the day when they're voluntarily abandoned as bad ideas. It means keeping an eagle eye on public institutions and demanding accountability. It means putting your ear to the ground and listening to the whispering of the truly powerless. It means giving a forum to the myriad voices from the hundreds of resistance movements across the country who are speaking about *real* things—about bonded labour, marital rape, sexual preferences, women's wages, uranium dumping, unsustainable mining, weavers' woes, farmers' worries. It means fighting displacement and dispossession and the relentless, everyday violence of abject poverty. Fighting it also means not allowing your newspaper columns and prime-time TV spots to be hijacked by their spurious passions and their staged theatrics, which are designed to divert attention from everything else.

While most people in India have been horrified by what happened in Gujarat, many thousands of the indoctrinated are preparing to journey deeper into the heart of the horror. Look around you and you'll see in little parks, in big maidans, in empty lots, in village commons, the RSS is marching, hoisting its saffron flag. Suddenly they're everywhere, grown men in khaki shorts marching, marching, marching. To *where*? For *what*? Their disregard for history shields them from the knowledge that fascism will thrive for a short while and then self-annihilate because of its inherent stupidity. But unfortunately, like the radioactive fallout of a nuclear strike, it has a half-life that will cripple generations to come.

These levels of rage and hatred cannot be contained, cannot be expected to subside, with public censure and denunciation. Hymns of brotherhood and love are great, but not enough.

Historically, fascist movements have been fuelled by feelings of national disillusionment. Fascism has come to India after the dreams that fuelled the Freedom Struggle have been frittered away like so much loose change.

Independence itself came to us as what Gandhi famously called a 'wooden loaf'—a notional freedom tainted by the blood of the thousands who died during Partition.[46] For more than half a century now, the hatred and mutual distrust have been exacerbated, toyed with and never allowed to heal by politicians, led from the front by Mrs Indira Gandhi. Every political party has tilled the marrow of our secular parliamentary democracy, mining it for electoral advantage. Like termites excavating a mound, they've made tunnels and underground passages, undermining the meaning of 'secular', until it has just become an empty shell that's about to implode. Their tilling has weakened the foundations of the structure that connects the Constitution, Parliament and the courts of law— the configuration of checks and balances that forms the backbone of a parliamentary democracy. Under the circumstances, it's futile to go on blaming politicians and demanding from them a morality they're incapable of.

There's something pitiable about a people that constantly bemoans its leaders. If they've let us down, it's only because we've allowed them to. It could be argued that civil society has failed its leaders as much as leaders have failed civil society. We have to accept that there is a dangerous, systemic flaw in our parliamentary democracy that politicians *will* exploit. And that's what results in the kind of conflagration that we have witnessed in Gujarat. There's fire in the ducts. We have to address this issue and come up with a *systemic* solution.

But politicians' exploitation of communal divides is by no means the only reason that fascism has arrived on our shores.

Over the past fifty years, ordinary citizens' modest hopes for lives of dignity, security and relief from abject poverty have been systematically snuffed out. Every 'democratic' institution in this country has shown itself to be unaccountable, inaccessible to the ordinary citizen, and either unwilling or incapable of acting in the interests of genuine social justice. *Every* strategy for real social change —land reform, education, public health, the equitable distribution of natural resources, the implementation of positive discrimination—has been cleverly, cunningly and consistently scuttled and rendered ineffectual by those castes and that class of people who have a stranglehold on the political process. And now corporate globalization is being relentlessly and arbitrarily imposed on an essentially feudal society, tearing through its complex, tiered, social fabric, ripping it apart culturally and economically.

There is very real grievance here. And the fascists didn't create it. But they have seized upon it, upturned it and forged from it a hideous, bogus sense of pride. They have mobilized human beings using the lowest common denominator—religion. People who have lost control over their lives, people who have been uprooted from their homes and communities, who have lost their culture and their language, are being made to feel proud of *something*. Not something they have striven for and achieved, not something they can count as a personal accomplishment, but something they just happen to be. Or, more accurately, something they happen *not* to be. And the falseness, the emptiness of that pride, is fuelling a gladiatorial anger that is then directed towards a simulated target that has been wheeled into the amphitheatre.

How else can you explain the project of trying to disenfranchise, drive out or exterminate the second poorest community in this country, using as your foot soldiers the very poorest (Dalits and Adivasis)? How else can you explain why Dalits in Gujarat, who have been despised, oppressed and treated worse than refuse by the upper castes for thousands of years, have joined hands with their oppressors to turn on those who are only marginally less unfortunate than they themselves? Are they just wage slaves, mercenaries for hire? Is it all right to patronize them and absolve them of responsibility for their own actions? Or am I being obtuse? Perhaps it's common practice for the unfortunate to vent their rage and hatred on the *next* most unfortunate, because their *real* adversaries are inaccessible, seemingly invincible and completely out of range? Because their own leaders have cut loose and are feasting at the high table, leaving them to wander rudderless in the wilderness, spouting nonsense about returning to the Hindu fold. (The first step, presumably, towards founding a Global Hindu Empire, as realistic a goal as Fascism's previously failed projects—the restoration of Roman Glory, the purification of the German race or the establishment of an Islamic Sultanate.)

One hundred and thirty million Muslims live in India.[47] Hindu fascists regard them as legitimate prey. Do people like Modi and Bal Thackeray think that the world will stand by and watch while they're liquidated in a 'civil war'? Press reports say that the European Union and several other countries have condemned what happened in Gujarat and likened it to Nazi rule.[48] The Indian government's portentous response is that foreigners should not use the Indian media to comment on what is an 'internal matter' (like the chilling goings on in Kashmir?).[49] What next? Censorship? Closing down the Internet? Blocking international calls? Killing the wrong 'terrorists' and fudging the DNA samples? There is no terrorism like State terrorism.

But who will take them on? Their fascist cant can perhaps be dented by some blood and thunder from the Opposition. So far only Laloo Yadav, head of the Rashtriya Janata Dal (RJD), the National People's Party, in Bihar, has shown himself to be truly passionate: '*Kaun mai ka lal kehtha hai ki yeh Hindu Rashtra hai? Usko yahan bhej do, chhaahti phad doonga!*'[17] ('Which mother's son says this is a Hindu Nation? Send him here, I'll tear his chest open.')[50]

Unfortunately there's no quick fix. Fascism itself can only be turned away if all those who are outraged by it show a commitment to social justice that equals the intensity of their indignation.

Are we ready to get off our starting blocks? Are we ready, many millions of us, to rally not just on the streets, but at work and in schools and in our homes, in every decision we take, and every choice we make?

Or not just yet . . .

If not, then years from now, when the rest of the world has shunned us (as it should), like the ordinary citizens of Hitler's Germany, we too will learn to recognize revulsion in the gaze of our fellow human beings. We too will find ourselves unable to look our own children in the eye, for the shame of what we did and didn't do. For the shame of what we allowed to happen.

This is *us*. In *India*. Heaven help us make it through the night.

April 2002

war talk

Summer Games with Nuclear Bombs

When India and Pakistan conducted their nuclear tests in 1998, even those of us who condemned them balked at the hypocrisy of Western nuclear powers. Implicit in their denunciation of the tests was the notion that Blacks cannot be trusted with the Bomb. Now we are presented with the spectacle of our governments competing to confirm that belief.

As diplomats' families and tourists disappear from the subcontinent, Western journalists arrive in Delhi in droves. Many call me. 'Why haven't you left the city?' they ask. 'Isn't nuclear war a real possibility? Isn't Delhi a prime target?'

If nuclear weapons exist, then nuclear war is a real possibility. And Delhi is a prime target. It is.

But where shall we go? Is it possible to go out and buy another life because this one's not panning out?

If I go away, and everything and everyone—every friend, every tree, every home, every dog, squirrel and bird that I have known and loved—is incinerated, how shall I live on? Whom shall I love? And who will love me back? Which society will welcome me and allow me to be the hooligan that I am here, at home?

So we're all staying. We huddle together. We realize how much we love each other. And we think, what a shame it would be to die now. Life's normal only because the macabre has become normal. While we wait for rain, for football, for justice, the old generals and eager boy-anchors on TV talk of first-strike and second-strike capabilities as though they're discussing a family board game.

My friends and I discuss *Prophecy*, the documentary about the bombing of Hiroshima and Nagasaki.[1] The fireball. The dead bodies choking the river. The living stripped of skin and hair. The singed, bald children, still alive, their clothes burned into their bodies. The thick, black, toxic water. The scorched, burning air. The cancers, implanted genetically, a malignant letter to the unborn. We remember especially the man who just melted into the steps of a building. We imagine ourselves like that. As stains on staircases. I imagine future generations of hushed schoolchildren pointing at my stain . . . that was a writer. Not She or He. *That.*

I'm sorry if my thoughts are stray and disconnected, not always worthy. Often ridiculous.

I think of a little mixed-breed dog I know. Each of his toes is a different colour. Will he become a radioactive stain on a staircase too? My husband's writing a book on trees. He has a section on how figs are pollinated. Each fig only by its own specialized fig wasp. There are nearly a thousand different species of fig wasps, each a precise, exquisite synchrony, the product of millions of years of evolution.

All the fig wasps will be nuked. Zzzz. Ash. And my husband. And his book.

A dear friend, who's an activist in the anti-dam movement in the Narmada valley, is on indefinite hunger strike. Today is the fourteenth day of her fast. She and the others fasting with her are weakening quickly. They're protesting because the Madhya Pradesh government is bulldozing schools, clear-felling forests, uprooting hand pumps, forcing people from their villages to make way for the Maan dam. The people have nowhere to go. And so, the hunger strike.[2]

What an act of faith and hope! How brave it is to believe that in today's world, reasoned, closely argued, non-violent protest will register, will matter. But will it? To governments that are comfortable with the notion of a wasted world, what's a wasted valley?

The threshold of horror has been ratcheted up so high that nothing short of genocide or the prospect of nuclear war merits mention. Peaceful resistance is treated with contempt. Terrorism's the real thing. The underlying principle of the War Against Terror, the very notion that war is an acceptable solution to terrorism, has ensured that terrorists in the subcontinent now have the power to trigger a nuclear war.

Displacement, dispossession, starvation, poverty, disease— these are now just the funnies, the comic-strip items. Our Home Minister says that Amartya Sen has it all wrong —the key to India's development is not education and health but Defence[3] (and don't forget the kickbacks, O Best Beloved).

Perhaps what he really meant was that war is the key to distracting the world's attention from fascism and genocide. To avoid dealing with any single issue of real governance that urgently needs to be addressed.

For the governments of India and Pakistan, Kashmir is not a *problem*, it's their perennial and spectacularly successful *solution*. Kashmir is the rabbit they pull out of their hats every time they need a rabbit. Unfortunately, it's a radio-active rabbit now, and it's careening out of control.

No doubt there is Pakistan-sponsored cross-border terror-ism in Kashmir. But there are other kinds of terror in the valley. There's the inchoate nexus between jihadi mili-tants, ex-militants, foreign mercenaries, local mercenaries, underworld Mafiosi, security forces, arms dealers and criminalized politicians and officials on both sides of the border. There's also rigged elections, daily humiliation, 'disappearances' and staged 'encounters'.[4]

And now the cry has gone up in the heartland: India is a Hindu country. Muslims can be murdered under the benign gaze of the State. Mass murderers will not be brought to justice. Indeed, they will stand for elections. Is India to be a Hindu nation in the heartland and a secular one around the edges?

Meanwhile the International Coalition Against Terror makes war and preaches restraint. While India and Paki-stan bay for each other's blood the Coalition is quietly laying gas pipelines, selling us weapons and pushing through their business deals. (Buy now pay later.) Britain, for example, is busy arming both sides.[5] Tony Blair's 'peace' mission in January 2002 was actually a business trip to discuss a one-billion-pound deal (and don't forget the kickbacks, O Best Beloved) to sell Hawk fighter-bombers to India.[6] Roughly, for the price of a *single* Hawk bomber, the government could provide one and a half million people with clean drinking water for life.[7]

'Why isn't there a peace movement?' Western journalists ask me ingenuously. How can there be a peace movement when, for most people in India, peace means a daily battle: for food, for water, for shelter, for dignity? War, on the other hand, is something professional soldiers fight far away on the border. And nuclear war—well, that's completely outside the realm of most people's comprehension. No one knows what a nuclear bomb is. No one cares to explain. As the Home Minister said, education is not a pressing priority.

The last question every visiting journalist always asks me is: Are you writing another book? That question mocks me. Another book? Right *now*? This talk of nuclear war displays such contempt for music, art, literature and everything else that defines civilization. So what kind of book should I write?

It's not just the one million soldiers on the border who are living on hair-trigger alert. It's all of us. That's what nuclear bombs do. Whether they're used or not, they vio-

late everything that is humane. They alter the meaning of
life itself.

Why do we tolerate them? Why do we tolerate the men
who use nuclear weapons to blackmail the entire human
race?

June 2002

come september

come september

Quite often these days, I find myself being described as a 'social activist'. Those who agree with my views, call me 'courageous'. Those who don't, call me all kinds of rude names which I won't repeat. I am not a social activist, neither am I particularly courageous. . . . So please do not underestimate the trepidation with which I stand here to say what I must say.

Writers imagine that they cull stories from the world. I'm beginning to believe that vanity makes them think so. That it's actually the other way around. Stories cull writers from the world. Stories reveal themselves to us. The public narrative, the private narrative—they colonize us. They commission us. They insist on being told. Fiction and non-fiction are only different techniques of story telling. For reasons I do not fully understand, fiction dances out of me. Non-fiction is wrenched out by the aching, broken world I wake up to every morning.

The theme of much of what I write, fiction as well as non-fiction, is the relationship between power and power-lessness and the endless, circular conflict they're engaged in. John Berger, that most wonderful writer, once wrote: *Never again will a single story be told as though it's the only one.* There can never be a single story. There are only ways of seeing. So when I tell a story, I tell it not as an ideologue who wants to pit one absolutist ideology against another, but as a story-teller who wants to share her way of seeing. Though it might appear otherwise, my writing is not really about nations and histories, it's about power. About the paranoia and ruthlessness of power. About the physics of power. I believe that the accumulation of vast unfettered power by a State or a country, a corporation or an institution—or even an individual, a spouse, friend or sibling—regardless of ideology, results in excesses such as the ones I will recount here.

Living as I do, as millions of us do, in the shadow of the nuclear holocaust that the governments of India and Pakistan keep promising their brain-washed citizenry, and in the global neighbourhood of the War against Terror (what President Bush rather biblically calls 'The Task That Never Ends'), I find myself thinking a great deal about the relationship between Citizens and the State.

In India, those of us who have expressed views on Nuclear Bombs, Big Dams, Corporate Globalization and the rising threat of communal Hindu fascism—views that are at variance with the Indian Government's—are branded 'anti-national'. While this accusation does not fill me with indignation, it's not an accurate description of what I do or how I think. An 'anti-national' is a person who is against his/her own nation and, by inference, is pro some other one. But it isn't necessary to be 'anti-national' to be deeply suspicious of all nationalism, to be anti-national*ism*. Nationalism of one kind or another was the cause of most of the genocide of the twentieth century. Flags are bits of coloured cloth that governments use first to shrink-wrap peoples' minds and then as ceremonial shrouds to bury the dead. When independent, thinking people (and here I do not include the corporate media) begin to rally under flags, when writers, painters, musicians, film makers suspend their judgment and blindly yoke their art to the service of the 'Nation', it's time for all of us to sit up and worry. In India we saw it happen soon after the nuclear tests in 1998 and during the Kargil War against Pakistan in 1999. In the US we saw it during the Gulf War and we see it now, during the 'War against Terror'. That blizzard of Made-in-China American flags.

Recently, those who have criticized the actions of the US Government (myself included) have been called 'anti-American'. Anti-Americanism is in the process of being consecrated into an ideology.

The term 'anti-American' is usually used by the American establishment to discredit and, not falsely—but, shall we say, inaccurately—define its critics. Once someone is branded anti-American, the chances are that he or she will be judged before they're heard and the argument will be lost in the welter of bruised national pride.

What does the term 'anti-American' *mean*? Does it mean you're anti-jazz? Or that you're opposed to free speech? That you don't delight in Toni Morrison or John Updike? That you have a quarrel with giant Sequoias? Does it mean you don't admire the hundreds of thousands of American citizens who marched against nuclear weapons, or the thousands of war resisters who forced their government to withdraw from Vietnam? Does it mean that you hate all Americans?

This sly conflation of America's culture, music, literature, the breathtaking physical beauty of the land, the ordinary pleasures of ordinary people with criticism of the US government's foreign policy (about which, thanks to America's 'free press,' sadly most Americans know very little) is a deliberate and extremely effective strategy. It's like a retreating army taking cover in a heavily populated city, hoping that the prospect of hitting civilian targets will deter enemy fire.

There are many Americans who would be mortified to be associated with their government's policies. The most scholarly, scathing, incisive, hilarious critiques of the hypocrisy and the contradictions in US government policy come from American citizens. When the rest of the world wants to know what the US government is up to, we turn to Noam Chomsky, Edward Said, Howard Zinn, Ed Herman, Amy Goodman, Michael Albert, Chalmers Johnson, William Blum and Anthony Arnove to tell us what's really going on.

Similarly, in India, not hundreds, but millions of us would be ashamed and offended if we were in any way implicated with the present Indian government's fascist policies which, apart from the perpetration of State terrorism in the valley of Kashmir (in the name of fighting terrorism), have also turned a blind eye to the recent state-supervised pogrom against Muslims in Gujarat. It would be absurd to think that those who criticize the Indian government are 'anti-Indian'—although the government itself never hesitates to take that line. It is dangerous to cede to the Indian Government or the American Government or *anyone* for that matter, the right to define what 'India' or 'America' are, or ought to be.

To call someone 'anti-American', indeed, to *be* anti-American, (or for that matter anti-Indian, or anti-Timbuktuan) is not just racist, it's a failure of the imagination. An inability to see the world in terms other than those that the establishment has set out for you: If you're not a Bushie, you're a Taliban. If you don't love us, you hate us. If you're not Good, you're Evil. If you're not with us, you're with the terrorists.

Last year, like many others, I too made the mistake of scoffing at this post–September–11th rhetoric, dismissing it as foolish and arrogant. I've realized that it's not foolish at all. It's actually a canny recruitment drive for a misconceived, dangerous war. Every day I'm taken aback at how many people believe that opposing the war in Afghanistan amounts to supporting terrorism, or voting for the Taliban. Now that the initial aim of the war—capturing Osama Bin Laden (dead or alive)—seems to have run into bad weather, the goal posts have been moved. It's being made out that the whole point of the war was to topple the Taliban regime and liberate Afghan women from their burqas. We're being asked to believe that the US marines are actually on a feminist mission. (If so, will their next stop be America's military ally Saudi Arabia?) Think of it this way: In India there are some pretty reprehensible social practices, against 'untouchables', against Christians and Muslims, against women. Pakistan and Bangladesh have even worse ways of dealing with minority communities and women. Should they be bombed? Should Delhi, Islamabad, and Dhaka be destroyed? Is it possible to bomb bigotry out of India? Can we bomb our way to a feminist paradise? Is that how women won the vote in the US? Or how slavery was abolished? Can we win redress for the genocide of the millions of Native Americans upon whose corpses the United States was founded—by bombing Santa Fe?

None of us need anniversaries to remind us of what we cannot forget. So it is no more than coincidence that I happen to be here, on American soil, in September—this month of dreadful anniversaries. Uppermost on everybody's mind of course, particularly here in America, is the horror of what has come to be known as Nine Eleven. Nearly three thousand civilians lost their lives in that lethal terrorist strike. The grief is still deep. The rage still sharp. The tears have not dried. And a strange, deadly war is raging around the world. Yet, each person who has lost a loved one surely knows secretly, deeply, that no war, no act of revenge, no daisy-cutters dropped on someone else's loved ones or someone else's children will blunt the edges of their pain or bring their own loved ones back. War cannot avenge those who have died. War is only a brutal desecration of their memory.

To fuel yet another war—this time against Iraq—by cynically manipulating people's grief, by packaging it for TV specials sponsored by corporations selling detergent or running shoes, is to cheapen and devalue grief, to drain it of meaning. What we are seeing now is a vulgar display of the *business* of grief, the commerce of grief, the pillaging of even the most private human feelings for political purpose. It is a terrible, violent thing for a State to do to its people.

It's not a clever enough subject to speak of from a public platform, but what I would really love to talk to you about is Loss. Loss and losing. Grief, failure, brokenness, numbness, uncertainty, fear, the death of feeling, the death of dreaming. The absolute, relentless, endless, habitual unfairness of the world. What does loss mean to individuals? What does it mean to whole cultures, whole peoples who have learned to live with it as a constant companion?

Since it is September 11th that we're talking about, perhaps it's in the fitness of the things that we remember what that date means, not only to those who lost their loved ones in America last year, but to those in other parts of the world to whom that date has long held significance. This historical dredging is not offered as an accusation or a provocation. But just to share the grief of history. To thin the mist a little. To say to the citizens of America, in the gentlest, most human way: Welcome to the World.

Twenty-nine years ago, in Chile, on the 11th of September 1973, General Pinochet overthrew the democratically elected government of Salvador Allende in a CIA-backed coup. '*Chile shouldn't be allowed to go Marxist just because its people are irresponsible,'* said Henry Kissinger, Nobel Peace Laureate, then the US Secretary of State.

After the coup President Allende was found dead inside the presidential palace. Whether he was killed or whether he killed himself, we'll never know. In the regime of terror that ensued, thousands of people were killed. Many more simply 'disappeared'. Firing squads conducted public executions. Concentration camps and torture chambers were opened across the country. The dead were buried in mine shafts and unmarked graves. For seventeen years the people of Chile lived in dread of the midnight knock, of routine 'disappearances', of sudden arrest and torture. Chileans tell the story of how the musician Victor Jara had his hands cut off in front of a crowd in the Santiago stadium. Before they shot him, Pinochet's soldiers threw his guitar at him and mockingly ordered him to play.

In 1999, following the arrest of General Pinochet in Britain, thousands of secret documents were declassified by the US government. They contain unequivocal evidence of the CIA's involvement in the coup as well as the fact that the US Government had detailed information about the situation in Chile during General Pinochet's reign. Yet Kissinger assured the general of his support: *'In the United States as you know, we are sympathetic to what you are trying to do,'* he said. *'We wish your government well.'*

Those of us who have only ever known life in a democracy, however flawed, would find it hard to imagine what living in a dictatorship and enduring the absolute loss of freedom really means. It isn't just those who Pinochet murdered, but the lives he stole from the living that must be accounted for too.

Sadly, Chile was not the only country in South America to be singled out for the US Government's attentions. Guatemala, Costa Rica, Ecuador, Brazil, Peru, the Dominican Republic, Bolivia, Nicaragua, Honduras, Panama, El Salvador, Peru, Mexico and Colombia—they've all been the playground for covert—and overt—operations by the CIA. Hundreds of thousands of Latin Americans have been killed, tortured or have simply disappeared under the despotic regimes and tin-pot dictators, drug runners and arms dealers that were propped up in their countries. (Many of them learned their craft in the infamous US government funded School of Americas in Fort Benning, Georgia, which has produced 60,000 graduates.) If this were not humiliation enough, the people of South America have had to bear the cross of being branded as a people who are incapable of democracy—as if coups and massacres are somehow encrypted in their genes.

This list does not of course include countries in Africa or Asia that suffered US military interventions—Vietnam,

Korea, Indonesia, Laos, and Cambodia. For how many Septembers for decades together have millions of Asian people been bombed, burned, and slaughtered? How many Septembers have gone by since August 1945, when hundreds of thousands of ordinary Japanese people were obliterated by the nuclear strikes of Hiroshima and Nagasaki? For how many Septembers have the thousands who had the misfortune of surviving those strikes endured the living hell that was visited on them, their unborn children, their children's children, on the earth, the sky, the wind, the water, and all the creatures that swim and walk and crawl and fly? Not far from here, in Albuquerque, is the National Atomic Museum where Fat Men and Little Boy (the affectionate nicknames for the bombs that were dropped on Hiroshima and Nagasaki) were available as souvenir earrings. Funky young people wore them. A massacre dangling in each ear. But I am straying from my theme. It's September that we're talking about, not August.

September 11th has a tragic resonance in the Middle East too. On the 11th of September 1922, ignoring Arab outrage, the British government proclaimed a mandate in Palestine, a follow up to the 1917 Balfour Declaration, which Imperial Britain issued, with its army massed outside the gates of the city of Gaza. The Balfour Declaration promised European Zionists a national home for Jewish people. (At the time, the Empire on which the Sun Never

Set was free to snatch and bequeath national homes like the school bully distributes marbles.) Two years after the declaration, Lord Balfour, the British foreign secretary said, '*In Palestine we do not propose to go through the form of consulting the wishes of the present inhabitants of the country. Zionism, be it right or wrong, good or bad, is rooted in age old traditions, in present needs, in future hopes of far profounder import than the desires or prejudices of the 700,000 Arabs who now inhabit this ancient land.*'

How carelessly imperial power decreed whose needs were profound and whose were not. How carelessly it vivisected ancient civilizations. Palestine and Kashmir are Imperial Britain's festering, blood-drenched gift to the modern world. Both are fault-lines in the raging international conflicts of today.

In 1937 Winston Churchill said of the Palestinians: '*I do not agree that the dog in a manger has the final right to the manger even though he may have lain there for a very long time. I do not admit that right. I do not admit for instance that a great wrong has been done to the Red Indians of America or the black people of Australia. I do not admit that a wrong has been done to these people by the fact that a stronger race, a higher grade race, a more worldly wise race to put it that way, has come in and taken their place.*' That set the trend for the Israeli State's attitude towards Palestinians. In 1969, Israeli Prime Minister Golda Meir said, '*Palestinians do not exist.*' Her successor, Prime

Minister Levi Eshkol said, '*What are Palestinians? When I came here [to Palestine] there were 250,000 non-Jews, mainly Arabs and Bedouins. It was desert, more than underdeveloped. Nothing.*' Prime Minister Menachem Begin called Palestinians '*two-legged beasts*'. Prime Minister Yitzhak Shamir called them '*grasshoppers*' who could be crushed. This is the language of Heads of State, not the words of ordinary people.

In 1947 the UN formally partitioned Palestine and allotted 55 per cent of Palestine's land to the Zionists. Within a year they had captured 76 per cent. On the 14th of May 1948 the State of Israel was declared. Minutes after the declaration, the United States recognized Israel. The West Bank was annexed by Jordan. The Gaza strip came under Egyptian military control. Formally, Palestine ceased to exist except in the minds and hearts of the hundreds of thousands of Palestinian people who became refugees.

In the summer of 1967, Israel occupied the West Bank and the Gaza Strip. Settlers were offered state subsidies and development aid to move into the occupied territories. Almost every day more Palestinian families are forced off their lands and driven into refugee camps. Palestinians who continue to live in Israel do not have the same rights as Israelis and live as second class citizens in their former homeland.

Over the decades there have been uprisings, wars, *intifadas*. Tens of thousands have lost their lives. Accords and treaties have been signed. Cease-fires declared and violated. But the bloodshed doesn't end. Palestine still remains illegally occupied. Its people live in inhuman conditions, in virtual Bantustans, where they are subjected to collective punishments, twenty-four hour curfews, where they are humiliated and brutalized on a daily basis. They never know when their homes will be demolished, when their children will be shot, when their precious trees will be cut, when their roads will be closed, when they will be allowed to walk down to the market to buy food and medicine. And when they will not. They live with no semblance of dignity. With not much hope in sight. They have no control over their lands, their security, their movement, their communication, their water supply. So when accords are signed and words like 'autonomy' and even 'statehood' are bandied about, it's always worth asking: What sort of autonomy? What sort of State? What sort of rights will its citizens have?

Young Palestinians who cannot contain their anger turn themselves into human bombs and haunt Israel's streets and public places, blowing themselves up, killing ordinary people, injecting terror into daily life, and eventually hardening both societies' suspicion and mutual hatred of each other. Each bombing invites merciless reprisals and even more hardship on Palestinian people. But then suicide bombing is an act of individual despair, not a revolutionary tactic. Although Palestinian attacks strike terror into Israeli civilians, they provide the perfect cover for the Israeli government's daily incursions into Palestinian territory, the perfect excuse for old-fashioned, nineteenth-century colonialism, dressed up as a new-fashioned, twenty-first century 'war.'

Israel's staunchest political and military ally is and always has been the US Government. The US government has blocked, along with Israel, almost every UN resolution that sought a peaceful, equitable solution to the conflict. It has supported almost every war that Israel has fought. When Israel attacks Palestine, it is American missiles that smash through Palestinian homes. And every year Israel receives several billion dollars from the United States.

What lessons should we draw from this tragic conflict? Is it really impossible for Jewish people who suffered so cruelly themselves—more cruelly perhaps than any other people in history—to understand the vulnerability and the yearning of those whom they have displaced? Does extreme suffering always kindle cruelty? What hope does this leave the human race with? What will happen to the Palestinian people in the event of a victory? When a nation without a state eventually proclaims a state, what kind of state will it be? What horrors will be perpetrated under its flag? Is it a separate state that we should be fighting for, or the rights the rights to a life of liberty and dignity for everyone regardless of their ethnicity or religion?

Palestine was once a secular bulwark in the Middle East. But now the weak, undemocratic, by all accounts corrupt but avowedly non-sectarian PLO, is losing ground to Hamas, which espouses an overtly sectarian ideology and fights in the name of Islam. To quote from their manifesto: *'we will be its soldiers, and the firewood of its fire, which will burn the enemies.'*

The world is called upon to condemn suicide bombers. But can we ignore the long road they have journeyed on before they arrived at this destination? September 11th 1922 to September 11th 2002—eighty years is a long, long time to have been waging war. Is there some advice the world can give the people of Palestine? Some scrap of hope we can hold out? Should they just settle for the crumbs that are thrown their way and behave like the grasshoppers or two-legged beasts they've been described as? Should they just take Golda Meir's suggestion and make a real effort to not exist?

In another part of the Middle East, September 11th strikes a more recent chord. It was on the 11th of September

1990 that George W. Bush Sr., then President of the US, made a speech to a joint session of Congress announcing his Government's decision to go to war against Iraq.

The US Government says that Saddam Hussein is a war criminal, a cruel military despot who has committed genocide against his own people. That's a fairly accurate description of the man. In 1988 he razed hundreds of villages in northern Iraq and used chemical weapons and machine-guns to kill thousands of Kurdish people. Today we know that that same year the US government provided him with 500 million dollars in subsidies to buy American farm products. The next year, after he had successfully completed his genocidal campaign, the US government doubled its subsidy to 1 billion dollars. It also provided him with high quality germ seed for anthrax, as well as helicopters and dual-use material that could be used to manufacture chemical and biological weapons.

So it turns out that while Saddam Hussein was carrying out his worth atrocities, the US and the UK governments were his close allies. Even today, the Government of Turkey which has one of the most appalling human rights records in the world is one of the US government's closest allies. The fact that the Turkish government has oppressed and murdered Kurdish people for years has not prevented the US government from plying Turkey with weapons and Development Aid. Clearly it was not concern for the Kurdish people what provoked President Bush's speech to Congress.

What changed? In August 1990, Saddam Hussein invaded Kuwait. His sin was not so much that he had a committed an act of war, but that he acted independently, without orders from his masters. This display of independence was enough to upset the power equation in the Gulf. So it was decided that Saddam Hussein be exterminated, like a pet that has outlived its owner's affection.

The first Allied attack on Iraq took place in January 1991. The world watched the prime-time war as it was played out on TV. (In India those days, you had to go to a five star hotel lobby to watch CNN.) Tens of thousands of people were killed in a month of devastating bombing. What many do not know is that the war did not end then. The initial fury simmered down into the longest sustained air attack on a country since the Vietnam War. Over the last decade American and British forces have fired thousands of missiles and bombs on Iraq. Iraq's fields and farmlands have been shelled with 300 tons of depleted uranium. In countries like Britain and American depleted uranium shells are test-fired into specially constructed concrete tunnels. The radioactive residue is washed off, sealed in cement and disposed off in the ocean (which is bad enough). In Iraq it's aimed—deliberately, with malicious intent—at people's food and water supply. In their bombing sorties, the Allies specifically targeted and destroyed water treatment plants, fully aware of the fact that they could not be repaired without foreign assistance. In southern Iraq there has been a fourfold increase in cancer among children. In the decade of economic sanctions that followed the war, Iraqi civilians have been denied food, medicine, hospital equipment, ambulances, clean water—the basic essentials.

About half a million Iraqi children have died as a result of the sanctions. Of them, Madeleine Albright, then US Ambassador to the United Nations, famously said, '*It's a very hard choice, but we think the price is worth it.*' 'Moral equivalence' was the term that was used to denounce those who criticized the war on Afghanistan. Madeleine Albright cannot be accused moral equivalence. What she said was just straight forward algebra.

A decade of bombing has not managed to dislodge Saddam Hussein, the 'Beast of Baghdad'. Now, almost twelve years on, President George Bush Jr. has ratcheted up the rhetoric once again. He's proposing an all out war whose goal is nothing short of a regime change. The *New York Times* says that the Bush administration is '*following a meticulously planned strategy to persuade the public, the Congress and the allies of the need to confront the threat of Saddam Hussein.*' Andrew H. Card, Jr., the White House chief of staff, described how the administration was stepping up its war plans for the fall: '*From a marketing point of view,*' he said, '*you don't introduce new products in August.*' This time the catchphrase for Washington's 'new product' is not the plight of Kuwaiti people but the assertion that Iraq has weapons of mass destruction. '*Forget the feckless moralizing of the peace lobbies,*' wrote Richard Perle, a former advisor to President Bush, '*We need to get him before he gets us.*'

Weapons inspectors have conflicting reports about the status of Iraq's Weapons of Mass Destruction, and many have said clearly that its arsenal has been dismantled and that it does not have the capacity to build one. However, there is no confusion over the extent and range of America's arsenal of nuclear and chemical weapons. Would the US Government welcome weapons inspectors? Would the UK? Or Israel?

What if Iraq *does* have a nuclear weapon, does that justify a pre-emptive US strike? The US has the largest arsenal of nuclear weapons in the world. It's the only country in the world to have actually used them on civilian populations. If the US is justified in launching a pre-emptive attack on Iraq, why, then any nuclear power is justified in carrying out a pre-emptive attack on any other. India could attack Pakistan, or the other way around. If the US government develops a distaste for the Indian Prime Minister, can it just 'take him out' with a pre-emptive strike?

Recently the United States played an important part in forcing India and Pakistan back from the brink of war. Is it so hard for it take its own advice? Who is guilty of feckless moralizing? Of preaching peace while it wages war? The US, which George Bush has called '*the most peaceful nation on earth,*' has been at war with one country or another every year for the last fifty years.

Wars are never fought for altruistic reasons. They're usually fought for hegemony, for business. And then of course there's the business of war. Protecting its control of the world's oil is fundamental to US foreign policy. The US government's recent military interventions in the Balkans and Central Asia have to do with oil. Hamid Karzai, the puppet president of Afghanistan installed by the US, is said to be a former employee of Unocal, the American-based oil company. The US government's paranoid patrolling of the Middle East is because it has two-thirds of the world's oil reserves. Oil keeps American's engines purring sweetly. Oil keeps the Free Market rolling. Whoever controls the world's oil controls the world's market. And how do you control the oil?

Nobody puts it more elegantly than the *New York Times*' columnist Thomas Friedman. In an article called 'Craziness Pays' he says '*the US has to make it clear to Iraq and US allies that . . . America will use force without negotiation, hesitation or UN approval.*' His advice was well taken. In the wars against Iraq and Afghanistan as well as in the almost daily humiliation the US government heaps on the UN. In his book on globalization, *The Lexus and the Olive Tree*, Friedman says, '*The hidden hand of the market will never work without the hidden fist. McDonald's cannot flourish without McDonnell Douglas . . . and the hidden fist that keeps the world safe for Silicon Valley's technologies to flourish is called the US Army, Air Force, Navy and Marine Corp.*' Perhaps this was written in a moment of vulnerability, but it's certainly the most succinct, accurate description of the project of Corporate Globalization that I have read.

After September 11th 2001 and the War Against Terror, the hidden hand and fist have had their cover blown—and we have a clear view now of America's other weapon— the Free Market—bearing down on the Developing World, with a clenched unsmiling smile. The Task That Never Ends is America's perfect war, the perfect vehicle for the endless expansion of American Imperialism. In Urdu, the word for Profit is *fayda*. Al Qaida means The Word, The Word of God, The Law. So, in India some of us call the War Against Terror, *Al Qaida* Vs *Al Fayda*— The Word Vs The Profit (no pun intended).

For the moment it looks as though *Al Fayda* will carry the day. But then you never know . . .

In the last ten years of unbridled Corporate Globalization, the world's total income has increased by an average of 2.5 per cent a year. And yet the numbers of the poor in the world has increased by 100 million. Of the top hundred biggest economies, 51 are corporations, not countries. The top 1 per cent of the world has the same combined income as the bottom 57 per cent and the disparity is growing. Now, under the spreading canopy of the War Against Terror, this process is being hustled along. The men in suits are in an unseemly hurry. While bombs rain down on us, and cruise missiles skid across the skies, while nuclear weapons are stockpiled to make the world a safer place, contracts are being signed, patents are being registered, oil pipelines are being laid, natural resources are being plundered, water is being privatized and democracies are being undermined.

In a country like India, the 'structural adjustment' end of the Corporate Globalization project is ripping through people's lives. 'Development' projects, massive privatization, and labor 'reforms' are pushing people off their lands and out of their jobs, resulting in a kind of barbaric dispossession that has few parallels in history. Across the world as the 'Free Market' brazenly protects Western markets and forces developing countries to lift their trade barriers, the poor are getting poorer and the rich richer. Civil unrest has begun to erupt in the global village. In countries like Argentina, Brazil, Mexico, Bolivia, India, the resistance movements against Corporate Globalization are growing. To contain them, governments are tightening their control. Protestors are being labeled 'terrorists' and then being deal with as such. But civil unrest does not only mean marches and demonstrations and protests against globalization. Unfortunately, it also means a desperate downward spiral into crime and chaos and all kinds of despair and disillusionment which, as we know from history (and from what we see unspooling before our eyes), gradually becomes a fertile breeding ground for terrible things—cultural nationalism, religious bigotry, fascism and of course, terrorism.

All these march arm in arm with corporate globalization.

There is a notion gaining credence that the Free Market breaks down national barriers, and that Corporate Globalizations' ultimate destination is a hippie paradise where the heart is the only passport and we all live together happily inside a John Lennon song. This is a canard.

What the Free Market undermines is not national sovereignty, but *democracy*. As the disparity between the rich and poor grows, the hidden fist has its work cut out for it. Multinational corporations on the prowl for 'sweetheart deals' that yield enormous profits cannot push through those deals and administer those projects in developing countries without the active connivance of State machinery—the police, the courts, sometimes even the army. Today Corporate Globalization, needs an international confederation of loyal, corrupt, preferably authoritarian governments in poorer countries, to push through unpopular reforms and quell the mutinies. It needs a press that pretends to be free. It needs courts that pretend to dispense justice. It needs nuclear bombs, standing armies, sterner immigration laws, and watchful coastal patrols to make sure that its only money, goods, patents and services that are globalized—not the free movement of people, not a respect for human rights, not international treaties on racial discrimination or chemical and nuclear weapons, or greenhouse gas emissions, climate change, or god forbid, justice. It's as though even a *gesture* towards international accountability would wreck the whole enterprise.

Close to one year after the War Against Terror was officially flagged off in the ruins of Afghanistan, in country after country freedoms are being curtailed in the name of protecting freedom, civil liberties are being suspended in the name of protecting democracy. All kinds of dissent is being defined as 'terrorism'. All kinds of laws are being passed to deal with it. Osama Bin Laden seems to have vanished into thin air. Mullah Omar is said to have made his escape on a motor-bike (They could have sent Tin-Tin after him). The Taliban may have disappeared but their spirit, and their system of summary justice is surfacing in the unlikeliest of places. In India, in Pakistan, in Nigeria, in America, in all the Central Asian Republics run by all manner of despots, and of course in Afghanistan under the US-backed Northern Alliance.

Meanwhile down at the Mall there's a mid-season sale. Everything's discounted—oceans, rivers, oil, gene pools, fig wasps, flowers, childhoods, aluminum factories, phone companies, wisdom, wilderness, civil rights, ecosystems, air—all 4,600 million years of evolution. It's packed, sealed, tagged, valued and available off the rack. (No returns). As for justice—I'm told it's on offer too. You can get the best that money can buy.

Donald Rumsfeld said that his mission in the War Against Terror was to persuade the world that Americans must be allowed to continue their way of life. When the maddened King stamps his foot, slaves tremble in their quarters. So, standing here today, it's hard for me to say this, but 'The American Way of Life' is simply not sustainable. Because it doesn't acknowledge that there is a world beyond America.

Fortunately power has a shelf life. When the time comes, maybe this mighty empire will, like others before it, over-reach itself and implode from within. It looks as though structural cracks have already appeared. As the War Against Terror casts its net wider and wider, America's corporate heart is hemorrhaging. For all the endless empty chatter about democracy, today the world is run by three of the most secretive institutions in the world: The International Monetary Fund, the World Bank, and the World Trade Organization, all three of which, in turn, are dominated by the US. Their decisions are made in secret. The people who head them are appointed behind closed doors. Nobody really knows anything about them, their politics, their beliefs, their intentions. Nobody elected them. Nobody said they could make decisions on our behalf. A world run by a handful of greedy bankers and CEOs who nobody elected can't possibly last.

Soviet-style communism failed, not because it was intrinsically evil but because it was flawed. It allowed too few people to usurp too much power. Twenty-first century market-capitalism, American-style, will fail for the same reasons. Both are edifices constructed by human intelligence, undone by human nature.

The time has come, the Walrus said. Perhaps things will get worse and then better. Perhaps there's a small god up in heaven readying herself for us. Another world is not only possible, she's on her way. Maybe many of us won't be here to greet her, but on a quiet day, if I listen very carefully, I can hear her breathing.

September 2002

the end of imagination

1. Raj Chengappa, 'The Bomb Makers', *India Today*, 22 June 1998.

2. Pradeep Thakur, 'India Protected Against Nuclear War', *The Pioneer*, 24 April 1998, interview with the Head of the Health, Environment and Safety Group, Bhabha Atomic Research Centre (BARC), Bombay.

3. See Chandan Mitra, 'Explosion of Self-esteem', *The Pioneer*, 12 May 1998; Shekhar Gupta, 'Road to Resurgence', *The Indian Express*, 12 May 1998; and 'A Moment of Pride', *The Hindustan Times*, Editorial, 12 May 1998.

4. Bal Thackeray quoted in 'Voices', *India Today*, 25 May 1998.

5. Remarks of George Fernandes, Indian Minister for Defence, in an interview with Home TV, quoted in 'Pakistan Lags in Number and Potency: George', *The Pioneer*, 1 June 1998; and 'Pakistan Tests No Match for Ours: Fernandes', *The Hindu*, 1 June 1998.

6. Kaveree Bamzai, 'Pakistan TV Will be Banned, Says Naqvi', *The Indian Express*, 3 July 1998.

7. 'Delhi Government Wants Churches Struck Off List of Religious Places', *The Indian Express*, 3 July 1998; and 'High on Hubris', *Times of India*, 4 July 1998.

8. 'Text of Vajpayee's Letter to Clinton', *The Hindu*, 14 May 1998.
9. 'HDI Ranking for Developing Countries', *Human Development Report 1997*, Oxford University Press and United Nations Development Programme, New York, 1997, p. 45.

the greater common good

1. C.V.J. Sharma (ed.), *Modern Temples of India: Selected Speeches of Jawaharlal Nehru at Irrigation and Power Projects,* Central Board of Irrigation and Power, 1989, pp. 40–49.
2. Patrick McCully, *Silenced Rivers: The Ecology and Politics of Large Dams,* Orient Longman, Hyderabad, 1998, p. 80.
3. From (uncut) film footage of Bargi dam oustees, 1995. Anurag Singh and Jharana Jhaveri, Jan Madhyam, New Delhi.
4. C.V.J. Sharma (ed.), *Modern Temples of India* (Note 1 above), pp. 52–6. In a speech given before the 29th Annual Meeting of the Central Board of Irrigation and Power (17 November 1958) Nehru said, 'For some time past, however, I have been beginning to think that we are suffering from what we may call "the disease of gigantism". We want to show that we can build big dams and do big things. This is a dangerous outlook developing in India . . . the idea of big—having big undertakings and doing big things for the sake of showing that we can do big things—is not a good outlook at all.' And 'It is . . . the small irrigation projects, the small industries and the small plants for electric power, which will change the face of the country far more than half-a-dozen big projects in half-a-dozen places.'
5. Centre for Science and Environment (CSE), *Dying Wisdom: Rise, Fall and Potential of India's Traditional Water Harvesting Systems,* CSE, New Delhi, 1997, p. 399; and Madhav Gadgil and Ramachandra Guha, *Ecology and Equity*, Penguin India, New Delhi, 1995, p. 39.
6. Indian Water Resources Society, *Five Decades of Water Resources Development in India*, 1998, p. 7.

7. World Resource Institute, *World Resources 1998–99*, OUP, Oxford, 1998, p. 251.

8. McCully, *Silenced Rivers* (Note 2 above), pp. 26–9. See also *The Ecologist Asia*, Vol. 6, No. 5 (Sept.–Oct. 1998), pp. 50–51 for excerpts of speech by Bruce Babbit, US Interior Secretary, in August 1998.

9. Besides McCully, *Silenced Rivers* (Note 2 above), see also the CSE's *State of India's Environment*, 1982, 1985 and 1999; Nicholas Hildyard and Edward Goldsmith, *The Social and Environmental Impacts of Large Dams*, Wadebridge Ecological Centre, Cornwall, UK, 1984; Satyajit Singh, *Taming the Waters: The Political Economy of Large Dams*, OUP, New Delhi, 1997; World Bank, *India: Irrigation Sector Review of the World Bank*, 1991; and IUCN et al., *Large Dams: Learning from the Past, Looking to the Future*, 1997.

10. Mihir Shah et al., *India's Drylands: Tribal Societies and Development through Environmental Regeneration*, OUP, New Delhi, 1998, pp. 51–103.

11. Ann Danaiya Usher, *Dams as Aid: A Political Anatomy of Nordic Development Thinking*, Routledge, London and New York, 1997.

12. At current prices; €41,100,000,000, at constant 1996–97 prices.

13. GoI, *Ninth Five Year Plan 1997–2002*, Vol. 2, Planning Commission, New Delhi, 1999, p. 478.

14. D.K. Mishra and R. Rangachari, *The Embankment Trap and Some Disturbing Questions*, Seminar 478 (June 1999), pp. 40–48 and 62–3; and CSE, *Floods, Floodplains and Environmental Myths*, CSE, New Delhi, 1991.

15. Mihir Shah et al., *India's Drylands* (Note 10 above), pp. 51–103.

16. Satyajit Singh, *Taming the Waters* (Note 9 above), pp. 188–90; also, GoI figures for actual displacement.

17. At a meeting in New Delhi on 21 January 1999 organized by

the Union Ministry of Rural Areas and Employment, for discussions on the draft National Resettlement and Rehabilitation Policy and the Amendment to the draft Land Acquisition Act.

18. The WCD Report published in November 1999 estimates the number of people displaced by Big Dams in India at 25 million. The India Country Study, which is part of the WCD Report, says it could be as high as 56 million (online at www.dams.org/global/india.htm).

19. Bradford Morse and Thomas Berger, *Sardar Sarovar: The Report of the Independent Review,* originally published by Resource Futures International (RFI) Inc., Ottawa, 1992, p. 62.

20. GoI, 28th and 29th *Report of the Commissioner for Scheduled Castes and Scheduled Tribes,* New Delhi, 1988–89.

21. *The Indian Express,* New Delhi, 10 April 1999.

22. GoI, *Ninth Five-Year Plan* (Note 13 above), p. 437.

23. India Country Study of the WCD Report (1999) says 10 per cent.

24. Siddharth Dube, *Words Like Freedom,* HarperCollins (India), New Delhi, 1998; CMIE (Centre for Monitoring the Indian Economy), 1996; see also *World Bank Poverty Update,* quoted in *Business Line,* 4 June 1999.

25. Refer to starvation deaths in Orissa, 2001.

26. National Human Rights Commission, *Report of the Visit of the Official Team of the NHRC to the Scarcity-affected Areas of Orissa,* December 1996.

27. GoI, *Award of the Narmada Water Disputes Tribunal,* 1978–79.

28. GoI, *Report of the FMG-2 on SSP,* 1995; cf. various affidavits of the Government of India and Government of Madhya Pradesh before the Supreme Court of India, 1991–98.

29. CWC, *Monthly Observed Flows of the Narmada at Garudeshwar,* Hydrology Studies Organization, Central Water Commission, New Delhi, 1992.

30. *Written Submission on Behalf of Union of India,* February 1999, p. 7, clause 1.7.

31. *Tigerlink News,* Vol. 5, No. 2 (June 1999), p. 28.

32. *World Bank Annual Reports 1993–98.*

33. McCully, *Silenced Rivers* (Note 2 above), p. 274.

34. McCully, *Silenced Rivers* (Note 2 above), p. 21. The World Bank started funding dams in China in 1984. Since then, it has lent around $3.4 billion (not adjusted for inflation) to finance thirteen Big Dams that will cause the displacement of 360,000 people. The centrepiece of the World Bank's dam financing in China is the Xiaolangdi dam on the Yellow River, which will single-handedly displace 181,000 people.

35. McCully, *Silenced Rivers* (Note 2 above), p. 278.

36. J. Vidal and N. Cumming-Bruce, 'The Curse of Pergau', *The Economist,* 5 March 1994; 'Dam Price Jumped 81 Million Pounds Days After Deal', *Guardian,* London, 19 January 1994; 'Whitehall Must Not Escape Scot Free', *Guardian,* London, 12 February 1994; quoted in McCully, *Silenced Rivers* (Note 2 above), p. 291.

37. McCully, *Silenced Rivers* (Note 2 above), p. 62.

38. For example, see Sardar Sarovar Narmada Nigam Ltd, *Planning for Prosperity,* 1989; Babubhai J. Patel, *SSP: Progressing Amidst Challenges,* Sardar Sarovar Narmada Nigam Ltd, Gandhinagar, 1992; C.C. Patel, *SSP: What It Is and What It Is Not,* Sardar Sarovar Narmada Nigam Ltd, Gandhinagar, 1991; P.A. Raj, *Facts: Sardar Sarovar Project,* Sardar Sarovar Narmada Nigam Ltd, Gandhinagar, 1989, 1990 and 1991.

39. Ibid.; also Rahul Ram, *Muddy Waters: A Critical Assessment of the Benefits of the Sardar Sarovar Project,* Kalpavriksh, New Delhi, 1993.

40. Morse and Berger, *Sardar Sarovar* (Note 19 above), p. 319. According to official statistics (Narmada Control Authority, *Benefits to Saurashtra and Kutch Areas in Gujarat,* NCA, Indore,

1992), 948 villages in Kutch and 4,877 villages in Saurashtra are to get drinking water from the SSP. However, according to the 1981 Census, there are only 887 inhabited villages in Kutch and 4,727 villages in the whole of Saurashtra. The planners had simply hoovered up the names of villages from a map, thereby including the names of 211 deserted villages! Cited in Rahul Ram, *Muddy Waters* (Note 39 above).

41. For example, the minutes of the various meetings of the Rehabilitation and Resettlement Sub-Groups of the Narmada Control Authority, 1998–99. Also, Morse and Berger, *Sardar Sarovar* (Note 19 above), p. 51.

42. Rahul Ram, *Muddy Waters* (Note 39 above), p. 34.

43. See, for example, the petition filed by the NBA in the Supreme Court, 1994.

44. SSNNL, *Planning for Prosperity,* Government of Gujarat, 1989.

45. S. Dharmadhikary, 'Hydropower at Sardar Sarovar: Is It Necessary, Justified and Affordable?', in W. F. Fisher (ed.), *Towards Sustainable Development? Struggling Over India's Narmada River,* M.F. Sharpe, Armonk, New York, 1995, p. 141.

46. McCully, *Silenced Rivers* (Note 2 above), p. 87.

47. Ibid. (Note 2 above), p. 185.

48. World Bank, *Resettlement and Development: The Bankwide Review of Projects Involving Resettlement 1986–1993,* 1994.

49. World Bank, *Resettlement and Rehabilitation of India: A Status Update of Projects Involving Involuntary Resettlement,* 1994.

50. World Bank, *Resettlement and Development* (Note 48 above).

51. Morse and Berger, *Sardar Sarovar* (Note 19 above), Letter to the President, pp. xii, xxiv and xxv.

52. Morse and Berger, *Sardar Sarovar* (Note 19 above), p. xxv.

53. Minimum conditions included unfinished appraisal of social and environmental impacts. For details, see Lori Udall, 'The International Narmada Campaign: A Case of Sustained Advocacy', in William Fisher (ed.), *Towards Sustainable Development,* M.E. Sharpe, London, 1995; McCully, *Silenced Rivers* (Note 2

above); and 'Cracks in the Dam: The World Bank in India', *Multinational Monitor*, December 1992.

54. See the letter from the GoI to the World Bank, 29 March 1993; press release of the World Bank dated 30 March 1993, a copy of which can be found in Campaign Information Package of International Rivers Network, Narmada Valley Development Project, Vol. 1, August 1998.

55. The date was 14 November 1992. Venue: outside the Taj Mahal Hotel, Bombay, where Lewis Preston, President of the World Bank, was staying. See Lawyers Committee for Human Rights, *Unacceptable Means: India's Sardar Sarovar Project and Violations of Human Rights: Oct. 1992–Feb. 1993*, April 1993, pp. 10–12.

56. On the night of 20 March 1994, the NBA Office at Baroda was attacked by hoodlums simply because of a (baseless) rumour that one member of the Five Member Group Committee was sitting inside with members of the NBA. Some NBA activists were manhandled, and a large collection of NBA documents was burnt and destroyed.

57. GoI, *Report of the Five Member Group on Sardar Sarovar Project*, Ministry of Water Resources, New Delhi, 1994.

58. Writ Petition 319 of 1994 argued that the Sardar Sarovar Project violated the fundamental rights of those affected by the project, and that the project was not viable on social, environmental, technical (including seismic and hydrological), financial or economic grounds. The writ petition asked for a comprehensive review of the project, pending which construction on the project should cease.

59. *Frontline,* 27 January 1995; *Sunday,* 21 January 1995.

60. In January 1995, the Supreme Court took on record the statement of the Counsel for the Union of India that no further work on the Sardar Sarovar dam would be done without informing the Court in advance. On 4 May 1995, the Court allowed construction of 'humps' on the dam, on the plea of

the Union of India that they were required for reasons of safety. The Court, however, reiterated its order of January 1995 that no further construction will be done without the express permission of the Court.

61. *Report of the Narmada Water Disputes Tribunal with Its Decision,* Vol. II, 1979, p. 102; cited in Morse and Berger, *Sardar Sarovar* (Note 19 above), p. 250.

62. Morse and Berger, *Sardar Sarovar* (Note 19 above), pp. 323–9.

63. P.A. Raj, *Facts* (Note 38 above).

64. Medha Patkar, 'The Struggle for Participation and Justice: A Historical Narrative', in William Fisher (ed.), *Toward Sustainable Development: Struggling Over India's Narmada River,* M. Sharpe, Inc., London, 1995, pp. 159–78; S. Parasuraman, 'The Anti-Dam Movement and Rehabilitation Policy', in Jean Dreze et al., *The Dam and the Nation,* OUP, New Delhi, 1997, pp. 26–65; and minutes of various meetings of the R&R sub-group of the Narmada Control Authority.

65. On my visit to the valley in March 1999, I was told this by villagers at Mokhdi who had returned from their resettlement colonies.

66. *Kaise Jeebo Re,* documentary film by Anurag Singh and Jharana Jhaveri, Jan Madhyam, 1997; also, unedited footage in the NBA archives.

67. Letter to the Independent Review from a resident of Parveta Resettlement Colony, cited in Morse and Berger, *Sardar Sarovar* (Note 19 above), pp. 159–60.

68. *Narmada Manavadhikar Yatra* that travelled from the Narmada valley to Delhi via Bombay. It reached Delhi on 7 April 1999.

69. Told to me by Mohan Bhai Tadvi, in Kevadia Colony, March 1999.

70. Morse and Berger, *Sardar Sarovar* (Note 19 above), pp. 89–94; and NBA interviews, March 1999.

71. NBA interviews, March 1999.

72. Morse and Berger, *Sardar Sarovar* (Note 19 above), pp. 277–94.

73. McCully, *Silenced Rivers* (Note 2 above), pp. 46–9.

74. For a discussion on the subject, see the World Bank, *India Irrigation Sector Review*, 1991; A. Vaidyanathan, *Food, Agriculture and Water*, MIDS, Madras, 1994; and McCully, *Silenced Rivers* (Note 2 above), pp. 182–207.

75. The World Bank, *India Irrigation Sector Review*, 1991, Vol. 2, p. 7.

76. Cited in McCully, *Silenced Rivers* (Note 2 above), p. 187.

77. Shaheen Rafi Khan, *The Kalabagh Controversy*, Sustainable Development Policy Institute, Pakistan, 1998; E. Goldsmith, 1998, 'Learning to Live with Nature: The Lessons of Traditional Irrigation', *The Ecologist*, Vol. 6, No. 5 (Sept.–Oct. 1998).

78. Mihir Shah et al., *India's Drylands* (Note 10 above), p. 51; also in Goldsmith, 'Learning to Live with Nature' (Note 77 above).

79. Operations Research Group, *Critical Zones in Narmada Command—Problems and Prospects*, ORG, Baroda, 1981; ORG, *Regionalization of Narmada Command*, ORG, Gandhinagar, 1982; World Bank, *Staff Appraisal Report, India, Narmada River Development—Gujarat, Water Delivery and Drainage Project*, Report No. 5108–IN, 1985; and Core Consultants, *Main Report: Narmada Mahi Doab Drainage Study*, commissioned by Narmada Planning Group, Government of Gujarat, 1982.

80. Robert Wade, 'Greening the Bank: The Struggle over the Environment, 1970–1995', in Devesh Kapur et al. (eds), *The World Bank: Its First Half Century*, Brookings Institution Press, Washington, DC, 1997, pp. 661–2.

81. Shaheen Rafi Khan, *The Kalabagh Controversy* (Note 77 above).

82. CES, *Pre-Feasibility Level Drainage Study for SSP Command Beyond River Mahi*, CES Water Resources Development and Management Consultancy Pvt Ltd, New Delhi, for Government of Gujarat, 1992.

83. Rahul Ram, 'The Best-laid Plans . . .', *Frontline*, 14 July 1995, p. 78.
84. Core Consultants, *Main Report* (Note 79 above), p. 66.
85. Ibid.
86. For example, see GoI, *Report of the FMG* (Note 57 above); and Rahul Ram, *Muddy Waters* (Note 39 above).
87. Called the 'Economic Regeneration Programme', formulated to generate funds for the cash-strapped Sardar Sarovar Narmada Nigam Ltd. Under the programme, land along the main canal of the Narmada Project will be acquired and sold for tourist facilities, hotels, water parks, fun world sites, garden restaurants, etc. Cf. *The Times of India*, Ahmedabad, 17 May 1998.
88. World Bank, *India Irrigation Sector Review* (Note 74 above).
89. Written submissions on behalf of the petitioners (NBA) in the Supreme Court, January 1999, p. 63; and *The Times of India*, Ahmedabad, 23 May 1999.
90. Ismail Serageldin, *Water Supply, Sanitation and Environmental Sustainability*, The World Bank, Washington, DC, 1994, p. 4.
91. Morse and Berger, *Sardar Sarovar* (Note 19 above), p. xxiii.
92. Ibid., pp. 317–19.
93. McCully, *Silenced Rivers* (Note 2 above), p. 167.

power politics

1. 'US-India Agreement,' *New York Times*, 11 January 2000, p. 4.
2. 'US, India Announce Deals of Dollars 4bn,' *Financial Times*, 25 March 2000, p. 10.
3. A Memorandum of Intent signed by the Ogden Energy Group and S. Kumars: Peter Popham, 'Clinton's Visit Seals Future for Controversial Indian Dam', *The Independent*, 28 March 2000, p. 16; and 'S Kumars Ties Up with Ogden for MP Project', *Economic Times of India*, 14 December 1999.

4. See WCD Report, p. 117; Steven A. Brandt and Fekri Hassan, 'Dams and Cultural Heritage Management: Final Report—August 2000', WCD Working Paper (online at http://www.dams.org/docs/html/contrib/soc212.htm); and WCD, 'Flooded Fortunes: Dams and Cultural Heritage Management', Press Release, 26 September 2000 (online at http://www.dams.org/press/pressrelease_61.htm). See also 'Do or Die: The People Versus Development in the Narmada Valley', *New Internationalist*, 336 (July 2001) (online at http://www.oneworld.org/ni/issue336/title336.htm) and documentation Friends of the River Narmada (online at http://www.narmada.org/nvdp.dams/).

5. Second World Water Forum: From Vision to Action, 17–22 March 2000, The Hague. See online report at http://www.worldwaterforum.net/.

6. UNDP, *Human Development Report 2000: Human Rights and Human Development*, Oxford University Press, New York, 2000, p. 4.

7. UNDP, *Human Development Report* (Note 6 above), p. 225.

8. See 'Bolivian Water Plan Dropped After Protests Turn Into Melees', *New York Times*, 11 April 2000.

9. 'Develop Infrastructure to Cope With Digital Revolution: Jack Welch', *The Hindu*, 17 September 2000; and 'Welch Makes a Power Point', *The Economic Times of India*, 17 September 2000. Webcast of Jack Welch's 16 September 2000 speech online at http://www.ge.com/in/webcast.html.

10. Peter Marsh, 'Big Four Lead the Field in Power Stakes: The Main Players', *Financial Times*, 4 June 2001, p. 2.

11. US Department of Energy, Energy Information Administration, *International Energy Outlook 1998*, Electricity Report (DOE/EIA-0484 [98]). Online at http://www.eia.doe.gov/oiaf/archive/ieo98/elec.html.

12. See 'India: Bharat Heavy Electricals–GE's Refurbishment Centre', *The Hindu*, 17 March 2001; and 'BHEL Net Rises

10% to Rs 599 Crore', *The Economic Times of India*, 30 September 2000.

13. Abhay Mehta, *Power Play: A Study of the Enron Project*, Orient Longman, Hyderabad, 2000, p. 15; Irfan Aziz, 'The Supreme Court Upheld the Ruling that the Jain Diary Constituted Insufficient Evidence', Rediff.com, 22 July 2000 (online at http://www.rediff.com/news/2000/jul/22spec.htm); and Ritu Sarin, 'Ex–CBI Official Accuses Vijaya Rama Rao', *Financial Express*, 11 May 1997.

14. See figures on 'Clinton's India Sojourn: Industry Hopes Doubling of FDI, Better Access to US Markets', 27 March 2000, DHAN.com News Track (online at http://www.india-world.co.in/home/dhan/news/y2k0327–news.html); and George Pickart, 'Address to the Network of South Asian Professionals', Washington, DC, 9 August 1997 (online at http://www.indiainc.org.in/h0809971.htm).

15. P.R. Kumaramangalam, speech at the Conference of the Power Ministers of India, 2 March 2000. See also 'India: Power Problems', *Business Line*, 21 June 2000.

16. Ritu Sarin, 'Disappearing Power', *The Indian Express*, 28 March 2000 (online at http://www.expressindia.com/ie/daily/20000328/ian28048.html).

17. See Neeraj Mishra, 'Megawatt Thieves', *Outlook*, 31 July 2000, p. 54; Sarin, 'Disappearing Power' (Note 16 above); 'India: Power Problems', *Business Line*, 21 June 2000; Louise Lucas, 'Survey—India: Delays and Bureaucracy Force Investors to Flee: Power', *Financial Times*, 6 November 2000; and 'India's Power Generation to Increase Over Next 3 Years: Minister', *Asia Pulse*, 27 April 2001.

18. Sarin, 'Disappearing Power' (Note 16 above); 'Red Tape and Blue Sparks: A Survey of India's Economy', *The Economist*, 359/8224, 2–8 June 2001, pp. 9–10; and Sunil Saraf, 'At Last, The Sell-off Gets Underway', *Financial Times*, 16 September 1996, p. 5.

19. See Abhay Mehta, *Power Play* (Note 13 above); Human Rights Watch, *The Enron Corporation: Corporate Complicity in Human Rights Violations*, Human Rights Watch, New York, 1995 (online at http://www.hrw.org/reports/1999/enron/enron-toc.htm); Tony Allison, 'Enron's Eight-Year Power Struggle in India', *Asia Times Online*, 18 January 2001 (online at http://www. atimes.com/reports/CA13Ai01.html); Scott Baldauf, 'Plug Pulled on Investment in India', *Christian Science Monitor*, 9 July 2001, p. 9; S.N. Vasuki, 'The Search for a Middle Ground', *Business Times* (Singapore), 6 August 1993; Agence France-Presse, 'Work to Start in December on India's Largest Power Plant', 14 September 1993; and Agence France-Presse, 'Work on Enron Power Project to Resume on May 1', 23 February 1996.

20. Scott Neuman, 'More Power Reviews Likely in India', United Press International, 5 August 1995. See also Abhay Mehta, *Power Play* (Note 13 above).

21. Agence France-Presse, 'India, Enron Deny Payoff Charges Over Axed Project', 7 August 1995, which acknowledges 'a remark by an Enron official that the company spent 20 million dollars on "educating Indians" about the controversial deal'.

22. See 'Former US Amabassdor to India Joins Enron Oil Board', *Asia Pulse*, 30 October 1997; Girish Kuber, 'US Delegation to Meet Ministers on Enron Row', *The Economic Times of India*, 23 January 2001; and Vijay Prashad, 'The Power Elite: Enron and Frank Wisner', *People's Democracy*, 16 November 1997 (online at http://www.igc.org/trac/feature/india/profiles/enron/enronwisner.html).

23. See Mark Nicholson, 'Elections Cloud Investment in India: Opening the Economy Has Wide Support Despite Recent Events', *Financial Times*, 21 August 1995; Agence France-Presse, 'Hindu Leader Ready for Talks on Scrapped Enron Project', 31 August 1995; BBC Summary of World Broadcasts, 'Maharashtra Government Might Consider New Enron

Proposal', 2 September 1995; Suzanne Goldenberg, 'India Calls on Left Bloc as BJP Cedes Power', *The Guardian*, 29 May 1996; Mark Nicholson, 'Delhi Clears Way for $2.5bn Dabhol Power Plant', *Financial Times,* 10 July 1996, p. 4; and Associated Press, 'Enron Can Resume Big Indian Power Project', *New York Times,* 10 July 1996, p. D19.

24. See Abhay Mehta, *Power Play* (Note 13 above), pp. xv, 20–21 and 151–8; Agence France-Presse, 'Massive US-Backed Power Project Awaits Indian Court Ruling', 25 August 1996; Kenneth J. Cooper, 'Foreign Power Plant Blooms; Low-Key India Venture Avoids Enron's Woes', *International Herald Tribune,* 11 September 1996; Praful Bidwai, 'Enron Judgment: Blow to Energy Independence', *The Times of India,* 22 May 1997; and Praful Bidwai, 'The Enron Deal Must Go: Albatross Round Public's Neck', *The Times of India,* 4 May 1995.

25. Agence France-Presse, 'Enron Power Project Survives Court Challenge', 3 May 1997.

26. See 'The Dabhol Backlash', *Business Line,* 5 December 2000; Sucheta Dalal, 'No Power May End Up Being Better Than That High Cost Power', *The Indian Express,* 3 December 2000 (online at http://www.indian-express.com/ie/daily/20001207/sucheta.htm); Soma Banerjee, 'State Plans to Move Court on Tariff Revision Proposal', *Economic Times of India,* 26 May 2000; Madhu Nainan, 'Indian State Says It Has No Money to Pay Enron for Power', Agence France-Presse, 8 January 2001; Khozem Merchant, 'Enron Invokes Guarantee to Retrieve Fees from Local Unit', *Financial Times,* 31 January 2001, p. 7; S.N. Roy, 'The Shocking Truth About Power Reforms', *The Indian Express,* 28 February 2000; and Anthony Spaeth, 'Bright Lights, Big Bill', *Time* (Asian edition), 157: 8, 26 February 2001 (online at http://www.time.com/time/asia/biz/magazine/0,9754,99899,00.html).

27. 'India: Maharashtra State Electricity Board Stops Buying Power', *The Hindu,* 30 May 2001; Celia W. Dugger, 'High-

Stakes Showdown: Enron's Fight Over Power Plant Reverberates Beyond India', *New York Times,* 20 March 2001, p. C1.

28. See Abhay Mehta, *Power Play* (Note 13 above), p. 3; Celia Dugger, 'High-Stakes Showdown' (Note 27 above); 'Red Tape and Blue Sparks' (Note 18 above), pp. 9–10; Government of India, *Ninth Five Year Plan, 1997–2002* (online at http://www.nic.in/ninthplan/); and Government of India, Press Information Bureau, Fact Sheet (online at http://pib.nic.in/archive/factsheet/fs2000/planning.html).

29. See S. Balakrishnan, 'FIs in US Press Panic Button as MSEB Fails to Pay Enron', *The Times of India,* 7 January 2001; Madhu Nainan, 'Indian State Says It Has No Money' (Note 26 above); and Khozem Merchant, 'Enron Invokes Guarantee' (Note 26 above).

30. See Pratap Chatterjee, 'Meet Enron, Bush's Biggest Contributor', *The Progressive*, 64: 9, September 2000 (online at http://www.theprogressive.org/pc0900.htm). See also Celia Dugger, 'High-Stakes Showdown' (Note 27 above).

31. Celia Dugger, 'High-Stakes Showdown' (Note 27 above); and Praful Bidwai, 'Congentrix = Bullying Tricks', *Kashmir Times,* 27 December 1999.

32. Centre for Science and Environment, *State of India's Environment: The Citizens' Fifth Report: Part II: Statistical Database,* Centre for Science and Environment, New Delhi, 1999, p. 203; Union Power Minister Suresh Prabhu, Press Conference, Hyderabad, cited in *Business Line,* 21 July 2001; and Abusaleh Shariff, *India: Human Development Report: A Profile of Indian States in the 1990s,* National Council of Applied Economic Research/Oxford University Press, New Delhi, 1999, p. 238.

33. See 'The Maheshwar Dam: A Brief Introduction' and related links online at http://www.narmada.org/maheshwar.html; Meena Menon, 'Damned by the People: The Maheshwar

Hydro-Electricity Project in Madhya Pradesh', *Business Line*, 15 June 1998; Sanjay Sangvai, *The River and Life: People's Struggle in the Narmada Valley*, Earthcare Books, Mumbai, 2000, pp. 81–4; and Richard E. Bissell, Shekhar Singh and Hermann Warth, *Maheshwar Hydroelectric Project: Resettlement and Rehabilitation: An Independent Review Conducted for the Ministry of Economic Cooperation and Development (BMZ), Government of Germany*, 15 June 2000 (online at http://www.bmz. de/medien/misc/maheshwar_report.pdf).

34. See 'Mardana Resolution' online at http://www.narmada.org/maheshwar/mardana.declaration.html; NBA Press Note, 'Hundreds of Maheshwar Dam Affected People Demonstrate at IFCI, Delhi', 16 November 2000 (online at http://www.narmada.org/nba-press-releases/november-2000/ifci.demo.html); and Sangvai, *The River and Life* (Note 33 above), Annexure 4, pp. 194–7 and Annexure 6, pp. 200–201.

35. See Heffa Schücking, 'The Maheshwar Dam in India', March 1999 (online at http://www.narmada.org/urg990421.3.html).

36. See Meena Menon, 'Damned by the People' (Note 33 above).

37. See 'S. Kumars Forays into Ready-to-Wear Apparel', *India Info*, 10 December 2000; and 'S Kumars Ups Ads-Spend by 66% with Kapil Dev on Board', *The Indian Express*, 8 July 1999.

38. See Meena Menon, 'Damned by the People' (Note 33 above).

39. See 'German Firms Pull Out of MP Dam Project', *The Statesman*, 21 April 1999. See also Desikan Thirunarayanapuram, 'Siemens Role in Dam Project Doubtful', *The Statesman*, 30 June 2000.

40. See Bissell et al., *Maheshwar Hydroelectric Project* (Note 33 above).

41. See 'Leaked Letter Shows German Company Quits Bid for Dam Credit', *Deutsche Presse-Agentur*, 25 August 2000; and

'US Firm Pulls Out of Narmada Hydel Project', *The States-man*, 13 December 2000.

42. 'PM's is Going to Be a "Power Trip"', *The Indian Express*, 4 September 2000.

43. See Mark Landler, 'Hi, I'm in Bangalore (But I Can't Say So)', *New York Times*, 21 March 2001, p. A1.

44. See David Gardiner, 'Impossible India's Improbable Chance', *The World in 2001, The Economist*, London, 2000, p. 46.

45. See Prabhakar Sinha, 'Tatas Plan Foray Into Call Centre Business', *The Times of India*, 7 October 2000.

the ladies have feelings, so . . .

1. Roger Cohen, 'Germans Seek Foreign Labor for New Era of Computers', *New York Times*, 9 April 2000, p. 1.

2. See report at Rediff.com (online at http://www.rediff.com/news/2001/may/26pic3.htm).

3. For data on poverty and illiteracy in India, see United Nations Development Program, *Human Development Report 2000: Human Rights and Human Development*, Oxford University Press, New York, 2000, Table 1: Human Development Index, p. 159, Table 4: Human Poverty in Developing Countries, p. 170, and Table 19: Demographic Trends, p. 225. Reports also available online at http://www.undp.org and at the site of the UNDP Programme in India, online at http://www.undp.org.in/.

4. See UNDP, *Human Development Report* (Note 3 above), p. 225.

5. Ashok Gulati, 'Overflowing Granaries, Empty Stomachs', *The Economic Times of India*, 27 April 2000.

6. Joseph Kahn, 'US-India Agreement', *New York Times*, 11 January 2000, p. 4.

7. See Dev Raj, 'Land Acquisition Bill Worse than Colonial Law', Inter Press Service, 3 December 1998; and S.

Gopikrishna Warrier, 'India: NGOs for Including Relief, Rehab Provisions in Land Act', *Business Line,* 13 February 2001.

8. See 'Indian Govt to Protest World Commission on Dams Report', *Asia Pulse,* 5 February 2001; Kalpana Sharma, 'Misconceptions about Dams Commission', *The Hindu,* 11 September 1998; 'Keshubhai Warns Dam Inspection Team May Be Held', *The Indian Express,* 9 September 1998; 'Gujarat Bans Visit of "Anti-Dam" Body', *The Hindu,* 5 September 1998; and Kalpana Sharma, 'Damning all Dissent', *The Hindu,* 21 September 1998.

9. See the WCD website at http://www.dams.org/ and 'Medium and Large Dams Damned', *The Business Standard,* 23 September 2000.

10. 'SC Wants Time Limit on Closure of Polluting Units', *The Times of India,* 25 January 2001. Additional information supplied to the author by Sukumar Muralidharan, *Frontline* magazine's Chief of Bureau in New Delhi, India, based on research from news reports, the Finance Department, and the Delhi Lokatantrik Adhikar Manch.

11. See Peter Popham, 'Squalid, Disgusting, Toxic: Is This the Dirtiest City on the Planet?', *The Independent,* 27 October 1997, p. E9; and World Bank, 'World Bank Says World's Worst Slums Can Be Transformed', Press Release, 3 June 1996 (online at http://www.worldbank.org/html/extdr/extme/slumspr.htm).

12. On 5 September 2001, the Supreme Court of India issued a *suo moto* notice to Arundhati Roy for contempt of court.

13. GoI, *White Paper on Pollution in Delhi: With an Action Plan*, Ministry of Environment and Forests, New Delhi, 1997 (online at http://envfor.nic.in/divisions/cpoll/delpolln.html).

14. See WCD Report, p. 11 and Table 1.2.

the algebra of infinite justice

1. Fox News, 17 September 2001.
2. Marc Levine, 'New Suspect Arrested, But Doubts Grow Over Terrorists' Identities', Agence France-Presse, 21 September 2001.
3. President George W. Bush, Address to Joint Session of Congress, 'The 11 September 2001 Terrorist Attacks on the United States', Federal News Service, 20 September 2001.
4. See Elsa Brenner, 'Hoping to Fill the Need for Office Space', *New York Times* (Westchester Weekly Edition), 23 September 2001, p. 3.
5. Leslie Stahl, 'Punishing Saddam', produced by Catherine Olian, CBS, *60 Minutes*, 12 May 1996.
6. See Tamim Ansary, 'Bomb Afghanistan Back to Stone Age? It's Been Done', *Providence Journal*, 22 September 2001, p. B7.
7. Thomas E. Ricks, 'Land Mines, Aging Missiles Pose Threat', *Washington Post*, 25 September 2001, p. A15. See also Danna Harman, 'Digging up Angola's Deadly Litter', *Christian Science Monitor*, 27 July 2001, p. 6.
8. See Barry Bearak, 'Misery Hangs Over Afghanistan After Years of War and Drought', *New York Times*, 24 September 2001, p. B3; Rajiv Chandrasekaran and Pamela Constable, 'Panicked Afghans Flee to Border Area', *Washington Post*, 23 September 2001, p. A30; Catherine Solyom, 'Exhibit a Glimpse Into Refugee Life', *The Gazette* (Montreal), 21 September 2001, p. A13; and Raymond Whitaker, 'Pakistan Fears for Seven Million Refugees as Winter Looms', *The Independent* (London), 27 September 2001, p. 4.
9. BBC, 'Aid Shortage Adds to Afghan Woes', 22 September 2001 (online at http://news.bbc.co.uk/hi/english/world/south_asia/newsid_1556000/1556117.stm).
10. See Tamim Ansary, 'Bomb Afghanistan Back to Stone Age?' (Note 6 above).

11. See Paul Leavitt, 'Maps of Afghanistan Now in Short Supply', *USA Today*, 18 September 2001, p. 13A.

12. *Washington Post*, 7 February 1985, quoted in Raja Anwar, *The Tragedy of Afghanistan: A First-Hand Account*, trans. Khalid Hasan, Verso, New York and London, 1988, p. 232; 'Inside the Taliban: US Helped Cultivate the Repressive Regime Sheltering bin Laden', *Seattle Times*, 19 September 2001, p. A3; and Andrew Duffy, 'Geographic Warriors', *Ottawa Citizen*, 23 September 2001, p. C4.

13. On the CIA connection, see Steve Coll, 'Anatomy of a Victory: CIA's Covert Afghan War', *Washington Post*, 19 July 1992, p. A1; Steve Coll, 'In CIA's Covert Afghan War, Where to Draw the Line Was Key', *Washington Post*, 20 July 1992, p. A1; Tim Weiner, 'Blowback from the Afghan Battlefield', *New York Times Magazine*, 13 March 1994, p. 6: 53; and Ahmed Rashid, 'The Making of a Terrorist', *Straits Times* (Singapore), 23 September 2001, p. 26.

14. See Scott Baldauf, 'Afghans Try Opium-Free Economy', *Christian Science Monitor*, 3 April 2001, p. 1.

15. See David Kline, 'Asia's "Golden Crescent" Heroin Floods the West', *Christian Science Monitor*, 9 November 1982, p. 1; David Kline, 'Heroin's Trail from Poppy Fields to the West', *Christian Science Monitor*, 10 November 1982, p. 1; and Rahul Bedi, 'The Assassins and Drug Dealers Now Helping US Intelligence', *Daily Telegraph* (London), 26 September 2001, p. 10.

16. See Peter Popham, 'Taliban Monster That Was Launched by the US', *The Independent* (London), 17 September 2001, p. 4.

17. See Suzanne Goldenberg, 'Mullah Keeps Taliban on a Narrow Path', *Guardian* (London), 17 August 1998, p. 12.

18. See David K. Willis, 'Pakistan Seeks Help from Abroad to Stem Heroin Flow', *Christian Science Monitor*, 28 February 1984, p. 11.

19. See Farhan Bokhari, 'Pakistan: Living in Shadow of Debt Mountain', *Financial Times* (London), 6 March 2001, p. 4.

20. See Douglas Frantz, 'Sentiment in Pakistani Town Is Ardently Pro-Taliban', *New York Times*, 27 September 2001, p. B1; and Rahul Bedi, 'The Assassins and Drug Dealers Now Helping US Intelligence', *Daily Telegraph* (London), 26 September 2001, p. 10.

21. See Edward Luce, 'Pakistan Nervousness Grows as Action Nears', *Financial Times* (London), 27 September 2001, p. 6.

22. See Angus Donald and Khozem Merchant, 'Concern at India's Support for US', *Financial Times* (London), 21 September 2001, p. 14.

23. See Jeff Greenfield and David Ensor, 'America's New War: Weapons of Terror', CNN, *Greenfield at Large*, 24 September 2001.

24. Jim Drinkard, 'Bush Vows to "Rid the World of Evildoers"', *USA Today*, 17 September 2001, p. 1A.

25. Secretary of Defense Donald Rumsfeld, Special Defense Briefing, 'Developments Concerning Attacks on the Pentagon and the World Trade Center Last Week', Federal News Service, 20 September 2001.

26. See Robert Fisk, 'This is Not a War on Terror, It's a Fight Against America's Enemies', *The Independent* (London), 25 September 2001, p. 4.

27. George Monbiot, 'The Need for Dissent', *Guardian* (London), 18 September 2001, p. 17.

28. See Michael Slackman, 'Terrorism Case Illustrates Difficulty of Drawing Tangible Ties to Al Qaeda', *Los Angeles Times*, 22 September 2001, p. A1.

29. See Tim Russert, 'Secretary of State Colin Powell Discusses America's Preparedness for the War on Terrorism', NBC, *Meet the Press*, 23 September 2001.

30. See T. Christian Miller, 'A Growing Global Chorus Calls for Proof', *Los Angeles Times*, 24 September 2001, p. A10; and

Dan Rather, 'President Bush's Address to Congress and the Nation', CBS, CBS *News Special Report*, 20 September 2001.

31. See Nityanand Jayaraman and Peter Popham, 'Work Halts at Indian Unilever Factory After Poisoning Alert', *The Independent* (London), 11 March 2001, p. 19.

32. See Jack Hitt, 'Battlefield: Space', *New York Times Magazine*, 5 August 2001, p. 6: 30.

33. See Colin Nickerson and Indira A.R. Lakshmanan, 'America Prepares the Global Dimension', *Boston Globe*, 27 September 2001, p. A1; Barbara Crossette, 'Taliban's Ban on Poppy a Success, US Aides Say', *New York Times*, 20 May 2001, p. 1: 7; and Christopher Hitchens, 'Against Rationalization', *The Nation*, 273: 10, 8 October 2001, p. 8.

34. President George W. Bush, Address to Joint Session of Congress (Note 3 above).

war is peace

1. See Alexander Nicoll, 'US Warplanes Can Attack at All Times, Says Forces Chief', *Financial Times* (London), 10 October 2001, p. 2.

2. See Noam Chomsky, 'US Iraq Policy: Motives and Consequences', in *Iraq Under Siege: The Deadly Impact of Sanctions and War*, Pluto Press, London, 2000, p. 54.

3. See Michael Slackman, 'Terrorism Case Illustrates Difficulty of Drawing Tangible Ties to Al Qaeda', *Los Angeles Times*, 22 September 2001, p. A1.

4. 'Bush's Remarks on US Military Strikes on Afghanistan', *New York Times*, 8 October 2001, p. B6; and Ellen Hale, '"To Safeguard Peace, We Have to Fight" Blair Emphasizes to Britons', *USA Today*, 8 October 2001, p. 6A.

5. George W. Bush, 'Remarks by President George W. Bush at an Anti-Terrorism Event', Washington, DC, Federal News Service, 10 October 2001.

6. See Tom Pelton, 'A Graveyard for Many Armies', *Baltimore Sun*, 18 September 2001, p. 2A.

7. See Dave Newbart, 'Nowhere to Go But Up', *Chicago Sun-Times*, 18 September 2001, p. 10.

8. See Edward Epstein, 'US Seizes Skies Over Afghanistan', *San Francisco Chronicle*, 10 October 2001, p. A1.

9. See Steven Mufson, 'For Bush's Veteran Team, What Lessons to Apply?', *Washington Post*, 15 September 2001, p. A5.

10. Donald H. Rumsfeld, 'Defense Department Special Briefing Re: Update on US Military Campaign in Afghanistan', Arlington, Virginia, Federal News Service, 9 October 2001.

11. Edward Epstein, 'US Seizes Skies Over Afghanistan', *San Francisco Chronicle*, 10 October 2001, p. A1.

12. Human Rights Watch, 'Military Assistance to the Afghan Opposition', Human Rights Watch Backgrounder, October 2001. Available online at http://www.hrw.org/backgrounder/asia/afghan-bck1005.htm. See also Gregg Zoroya, 'Northern Alliance has Bloody Past, Critics Warn', *USA Today*, 12 October 2001, p. 1A.

13. See David Rohde, 'Visit to Town Where 2 Linked to bin Laden Killed Afghan Rebel', *New York Times*, 26 September 2001, p. B4.

14. See Zahid Hussain and Stephen Farrell, 'Tribal Chiefs See Chance to Be Rid of Taliban', *The Times* (London), 2 October 2001.

15. See Alan Cowell, 'Afghan King Is Courted and Says, "I Am Ready"', *New York Times*, 26 September 2001, p. A4.

16. See Said Mohammad Azam, 'Civilian Toll Mounts as Bush Signals Switch to Ground Assault', Agence-France Presse, 19 October 2001; Indira A.R. Lakshmanan, 'UN's Peaceful Mission Loses 4 to War', *Boston Globe*, 10 October 2001, p. A1; and Steven Lee Myers and Thom Shanker, 'Pilots Told to Fire at Will in Some Zones', *New York Times*, 17 October 2001, p. B2.

17. See United Nations documents and reports summarized in Center for Economic and Social Rights, 'Afghanistan Fact Sheet #3: Key Human Vulnerabilities'. Available online at http://www.cesr.org.

18. See David Rising, 'US Military Defends Its Food Drops in Afghanistan from Criticism by Aid Organizations', Associated Press, 10 October 2001; Luke Harding, 'Taliban Say Locals Burn Food Parcels', *Guardian* (London), 11 October 2001, p. 9; and Tyler Marshall and Megan Garvey, 'Relief Efforts Trumped by Air War', *Los Angeles Times*, 17 October 2001, p. A1.

19. Martin Merzer and Jonathan S. Landay, Knight Ridder News Service, 'Second Phase of Strikes Begins', *Milwaukee Journal Sentinel*, 10 October 2001, p. 1A.

20. Jennifer Steinhauer, 'Citing Comments on Attack, Giuliani Rejects Saudi's Gift', *New York Times*, 12 October 2001, p. B13.

21. See Robert Pear, 'Arming Afghan Guerrillas: A Huge Effort Led by US', *New York Times*, 18 April 1988, p. A1. See also Steve Coll, 'Anatomy of a Victory: CIA's Covert Afghan War; $2 Billion Program Reversed Tide for Rebels', *Washington Post*, 19 July 1992, p. A1; Steve Coll, 'In CIA's Covert Afghan War, Where to Draw the Line Was Key', *Washington Post*, 20 July 1992, p. A1; and Tim Weiner, 'Blowback From the Afghan Battlefield', *New York Times*, 13 March 1994, p. 6: 53.

22. See 'Voices of Dissent and Police Action', *The Hindu*, 13 October 2001.

23. 'Vajpayee Gets Tough, Says No Compromise with Terrorism', *Economic Times of India*, 15 October 2001.

24. Howard Fineman, 'A President Finds His True Voice', *Newsweek*, 24 September 2001. p. 50.

25. Aaron Pressman, 'Former FCC Head Follows the Money', The Industry Standard.com, 2 May 2001.

26. Alice Cherbonnier, 'Republican-Controlled Carlyle Group

Poses Serious Ethical Questions for Bush Presidents, but Baltimore Sun Ignores It', *Baltimore Chronicle and Sentinel.* Available online at http://www.charm.net/~marc/chronicle/media3_oct01.shtml. See also Leslie Wayne, 'Elder Bush in Big GOP Cast Toiling for Top Equity Firm', *New York Times*, 5 March 2001, p. A1.

27. 'America, Oil and Afghanistan', *The Hindu*, Editorial, 13 October 2001.

28. Tyler Marshall, 'The New Oil Rush: High Stakes in the Caspian', *Los Angeles Times*, 23 February 1998, p. A1.

29. See Ahmed Rashid, 2001, *Taliban: Militant Islam, Oil and Fundamentalism in Central Asia*, Yale Nota Bene/Yale University Press, New Haven, pp. 143–82.

democracy

1. Name changed.

2. Violence was directed especially at women. See, for example, the following report by Laxmi Murthy: 'A doctor in rural Vadodara said that the wounded who started pouring in from the 28th of February had injuries of a kind he had never witnessed before even in earlier situations of communal violence. In a grave challenge to the Hippocratic oath, doctors have been threatened for treating Muslim patients, and pressurised to use the blood donated by RSS volunteers only to treat Hindu patients. Sword injuries, mutilated breasts and burns of varying intensity characterised the early days of the massacre. Doctors conducted post-mortems on a number of women who had been gang raped, many of whom had been burnt subsequently. A woman from Kheda district who was gang-raped had her head shaved and 'Om' cut into her head with a knife by the rapists. She died after a few days in the hospital. There were other instances of 'Om' engraved with a knife on women's backs and buttocks.' From Laxmi Murthy, 'In the

Name of Honour', CorpWatch India, 23 April 2002. Available on-line at http://www.corpwatchindia.org/issues/PID.jsp?articleid=1283.

3. See 'Stray Incidents Take Gujarat Toll to 544,' the *Times of India,* 5 March 2002.

4. Edna Fernandes, 'India Pushes Through Anti-Terror Law,' *Financial Times* (London), 27 March 2002, p. 11; 'Terror Law Gets President's Nod', the *Times of India,* 3 April 2002; Scott Baldauf, 'As Spring Arrives, Kashmir Braces for Fresh Fighting', *Christian Science Monitor,* 9 April 2002, p. 7; Howard W. French and Raymond Bonner, 'At Tense Time, Pakistan Starts to Test Missiles', 25 May 2002, p. A1; Edward Luce, 'The Saffron Revolution', *Financial Times* (London), 4 May 2002, p. 1; Martin Regg Cohn, 'India's 'Saffron' Curriculum', *Toronto Star,* 14 April 2002, p. B4. Pankaj Mishra, 'Holy Lies', the *Guardian* (London), 6 April 2002, p. 24.

5. See Edward Luce, 'Battle Over Ayodhya Temple Looms', *Financial Times* (London), 2 February 2002, p. 7.

6. 'Gujarat's Tale of Sorrow: 846 Dead', the *Economic Times of India,* 18 April 2002. See also Celia W. Dugger, 'Religious Riots Loom Over Indian Politics', *New York Times,* 27 July 2002, p. A1; Edna Fernandes, 'Gujarat Violence Backed by State, Says EU Report', *Financial Times* (London), 30 April 2002, p. 12. See also Human Rights Watch, "We Have No Orders To Save You": State Participation and Complicity in Communal Violence in Gujarat', Vol. 14, No. 3(C), April 2002 [hereafter: 'HRW Report']. Available on-line at http://www.hrw.org/reports/2002/india/ and in PDF format at http://hrw.org/reports/2002/india/gujarat.pdf. See also Human Rights Watch, Press Release, 'India: Gujarat Officials Took Part in Anti-Muslim Violence', New York, 30 April 2002.

7. 'A Tainted Election', *Indian Express,* 17 April 2002; Meena Menon, 'A Divided Gujarat Not Ready for Snap Poll', Inter Press Service, 21 July 2002.

8. See HRW Report, pp. 27–31; Dugger, 'Religious Riots Loom Over Indian Politics', p. A1; 'Women Relive the Horrors of Gujarat', *The Hindu,* 18 May 2002; Harbaksh Singh Nanda, 'Muslim Survivors Speak in India', United Press International, 27 April 2002. 'Gujarat Carnage: The Aftermath: Impact of Violence on Women', Online Volunteers.org, 2002. Available on-line at http://www.onlinevolunteers.org/gujarat/women/index.htm.

9. HRW Report, pp. 15–16, 31; Justice A.P. Ravani, Submission to the National Human Rights Commission, New Delhi, 21 March 2002, Appendix 4. Available on-line at: http://www.secularindia.com/13new.htm. See also Dugger, 'Religious Riots Loom Over Indian Politics', p. A1.

10. HRW Report, p. 31. 'Artists Protest Destruction of Cultural Landmarks', Press Trust of India, 13 April 2002.

11. HRW Report, pp. 7, 45; Rama Lakshmi, 'Sectarian Violence Haunts Indian City: Hindu Militants Bar Muslims from Work', *Washington Post,* 8 April 2002, p. A12.

12. *Communalism Combat* (March–April 2002) recounted Jaffri's final moments: 'Ehsan Jaffri is pulled out of his house, brutally treated for 45 minutes, stripped, paraded naked, and asked to say, "Vande Maataram!" and "Jai Shri Ram!" He refuses. His fingers are chopped off, he is paraded around in the locality, badly injured. Next, his hands and feet are chopped off. He is then dragged, a fork-like instrument clutching his neck, down the road before being thrown into the fire.' See also '50 Killed in Communal Violence in Gujarat, 30 of Them Burnt', Press Trust of India, 28 February 2002.

13. HRW Report, p. 5. See also Dugger, 'Religious Riots Loom Over Indian Politics', p. A1.

14. 'ML Launches Frontal Attack on Sangh Parivar,' the *Times of India,* 8 May 2002.

15. HRW Report, pp. 21–7. See also the remarks of Kamal Mitra Chenoy of Jawaharlal Nehru University, who led an

independent fact-finding mission to Gujarat, 'Can India End Religious Revenge?' CNN International, 'Q&A with Zain Verjee', 4 April 2002.

16. See Tavleen Sigh, 'Out of Tune', *India Today,* 15 April 2002, p. 21. See also Sharad Gupta, 'BJP: His Excellency', *India Today,* 28 January 2002, p. 18.

17. Khozem Merchant, 'Gujarat Vajpayee Visits Scene of Communal Clashes', *Financial Times* (London), 5 April 2002, p. 10. See also Pushpesh Pant, 'Atal at the Helm, or Running on Auto?', the *Times of India,* 8 April 2002.

18. See Bharat Desai, 'Will Vajpayee See Through All the Window Dressing?', the *Economic Times,* 5 April 2002.

19. Agence France-Press, 'Singapore, India to Explore Closer Economic Ties', 8 April 2002.

20. See 'Medha Files Charges Against BJP Leaders,' the *Economic Times,* 13 April 2002.

21. HRW Report, p. 30. See also Burhan Wazir, 'Militants Seek Muslim-Free India', the *Observer* (London), 21 July 2002, p. 20.

22. See Mishra, 'Holy Lies', p. 24.

23. The Home Minister, L.K. Advani, made a public statement claiming that the burning of the train was a plot by Pakistan's Inter Services Intelligence (ISI). Months later, the police have not found a shred of evidence to support that claim. The Gujarat government's forensic report says that 60 litres of petrol was poured onto the floor by someone who was inside the carriage. The doors were locked, possibly from the inside. The burned bodies of the passengers were found in a heap in the middle of the carriage. So far, nobody really knows who started the fire. There are theories to suit every political position: It was a Pakistani plot. It was Muslim extremists who managed to get into the train. It was the angry mob. It was a VHP/Bajrang Dal plot staged to set off the horror that followed. No one really knows. See HRW Report,

pp. 13–14; Siddharth Srivastava, 'No Proof Yet on ISI Link with Sabarmati Attack: Officials', the *Times of India,* 6 March 2002, 'ISI Behind Godhra Killings, Says BJP', the *Times of India,* 18 March 2002; Uday Mahurkar, 'Gujarat: Fuelling The Fire', *India Today,* 22 July 2002, p. 38; 'Bloodstained Memories', *Indian Express*, 12 April 2002; Celia W. Dugger, 'After Deadly Firestorm, India Officials Ask Why', *New York Times,* 6 March 2002, p. A3.

24. 'Blame it on Newton's Law: Modi', the *Times of India,* 3 March 2002. See also Fernandes, 'Gujarat Violence Backed by State', p. 12.

25. 'RSS Cautions Muslims', The Press Trust of India, 17 March 2002. See also Sanghamitra Chakraborty, 'Minority Guide to Good Behaviour', *The Times of India,* 25 March 2002. The full text of the resolution ('Resolution 3: Godhra and After') is available on-line at http://www.rss.org/reso2002.htm.

26. 'Modi Offers to Quit as Gujarat CM', the *Economic Times,* 13 April 2002; 'Modi Asked to Seek Mandate', the *Statesman* (India), 13 April 2002.

27. See 'Gujarat Events a Turning Point: Modi', *The Economic Times,* 23 April 2002.

28. See M.S. Golwalkar, *We, Or Our Nationhood Defined*, Bharat Publications, Nagpur, 1939; and Vinayak Damodar Savarkar, *Hindutva*, Bharti Sadan, New Delhi, 1989. See also Editorial, 'Saffron Is Thicker Than . . .', *The Hindu,* 22 October 2000; David Gardner, 'Hindu Revivalists Raise the Question of Who Governs India', *Financial Times* (London), 13 July 2000, p. 12.

29. See Arundhati Roy, 'Power Politics', p. 147 above.

30. See Noam Chomsky, 'Militarizing Space "To Protect US Interests and Investment"', *International Socialist Review*, 19 (July–August 2001). Available on-line at: http://www.isreview.org/issues/19/NoamChomsky.shtml.

31. Pankaj Mishra, 'A Mediocre Goddess', *New Statesman,* 9 April

2001, a review of Katherine Frank, *Indira: A Life of Indira Nehru Gandhi*, HarperCollins, London, 2001.

32. William Claiborne, 'Gandhi Urges Indians to Strengthen Union', *Washington Post*, 20 November 1984, p. A9. See also Tavleen Singh, 'Yesterday, Today, Tomorrow', *India Today*, 30 March 1998, p. 24.

33. HRW Report, pp. 39–44.

34. President George W. Bush, Address to Joint Session of Congress, 'September 11, 2001, Terrorist Attacks on the United States', Federal News Service, 20 September 2001.

35. See John Pilger, 'Pakistan and India on Brink', *The Mirror* (London), 27 May 2002, p. 4.

36. Alison Leigh Cowan, Kurt Eichenwald and Michael Moss, 'Bin Laden Family, With Deep Western Ties, Strives to Re-establish a Name', *New York Times*, 28 October 2001, p. 1: 9.

37. Peter Popham, 'Profile: Atal Behari Vajpayee', the *Independent* (London), 25 May 2002, p. 17.

38. 'Either Govern or Just Go', *Indian Express*, 1 April 2002. HFDC is the Housing Development Finance Corporation Limited.

39. 'It's War in Drawing Rooms', *Indian Express*, 19 May 2002.

40. Ranjit Devraj, 'Pro-Hindu Ruling Party Back to Hardline Politics', Inter Press Service, 1 July 2002; 'An Unholy Alliance', *Indian Express*, 6 May 2002.

41. Nilanjana Bhaduri Jha, 'Congress [Party] Begins Oust-Modi Campaign', *The Economic Times*, 12 April 2002.

42. Richard Benedetto, 'Confidence in War on Terror Wanes', *USA Today*, 25 June 2002, p. 19A; David Lamb, 'Israel's Invasions, 20 Years Apart, Look Eerily Alike', *Los Angeles Times*, 20 April 2002, p. A5.

43. See Arundhati Roy, 'The End of Imagination', p. 3ff. above.

44. 'I would say it is a weapon of peace guarantee, a peace guarantor,' said Abdul Qadeer Khan of Pakistan's nuclear bomb. See Imtiaz Gul, 'Father of Pakistani Bomb Says Nuclear Weapons

Guarantee Peace', Deutsche Presse-Agentur, 29 May 1998. See also Raj Chengappa, *Weapons of Peace: The Secret Story of India's Quest to Be a Nuclear Power* HarperCollins, New Delhi, 2000.

45. The 1999 Kargil war between India and Pakistan claimed hundreds of lives. See Edward Luce, 'Fernandes Hit by India's Coffin Scandal', *Financial Times* (London), 13 December 2001, p. 12.

46. See 'Arrested Growth', the *Times of India,* 2 February 2000.

47. Dugger, 'Religious Riots Loom Over Indian Politics', p. A1.

48. Edna Fernandes, 'EU Tells India of Concern Over Violence in Gujarat', *Financial Times* (London), 3 May 2002, p. 12 Alex Spillius, 'Please Don't Say This Was a Riot. It Was Genocide, Pure and Simple', the *Daily Telegraph* (London), 18 June 2002, p. 13.

49. 'Gujarat is an internal matter and the situation is under control,' said Jaswant Singh, India's foreign affairs minister. See Shishir Gupta, 'The Foreign Hand', *India Today,* 6 May 2002, p. 42, and sidebar.

50. See 'Laloo Wants Use of POTO [Prevention of Terrorism Act] Against VHP, RSS', the *Times of India,* 7 March 2002.

war talk

1. *Prophecy*. 16 mm, Nagasaki Publishing Committee, Nagasaki, Japan, 1982

2. See Aruna Roy and Nikhil Dey, 'Words and Deeds', *India Together,* June 2002, and 'Stand-Off at Maan River: Dispossession Continues to Stalk the Narmada Valley', *India Together,* May 2002. Available online at: http://www.indiatogether.org/campaigns/narmada/. See also 'Maan Dam', Friends of River Narmada. Available on-line at: http://narmada.org/nvdp.dams/maan/.

3. 'Nobel laureate Amartya Sen may think that health and

education are the reasons why India has lagged behind in development in the past 50 years, but I think it is because of defence,' said Home Minister L.K. Advani. See 'Quote of the Week, Other Voices', *India Today*, 17 June 2002, p. 13.

4. See Human Rights Watch, 'Behind the Kashmir Conflict: Abuses by Indian Security Forces and Militant Groups Continue', 1999. Available on-line at http://www.hrw.org/reports/1999/kashmir/summary.htm.

5. See John Pilger, 'Pakistan and India on Brink', the *Mirror* (London), 27 May 2002, p. 4; Neil Mackay, 'Cash from Chaos: How Britain Arms Both Sides', the *Sunday Herald* (Scotland), 2 June 2002, p. 12.

6. See Richard Norton-Taylor, 'UK Is Selling Arms to India', the *Guardian* (London), 20 June 2002, p. 1; Tom Baldwin, Philip Webster and Michael Evans, 'Arms Export Row Damages Peace Mission', the *Times* (London), 28 May 2002; Agence France-Presse, 'Blair Peace Shuttle Moves from India to Pakistan', 7 January 2002.

7. Pilger, 'Pakistan and India on Brink', p. 4.

publisher's note

The eight essays in *The Algebra of Infinite Justice* were written between July 1998 and October 2001. They have all been specially revised for this volume, where they appear together for the first time.

'the ladies have feelings, so . . .' is based on a talk given as the Third Annual Eqbal Ahmad Lecture, 15 February 2001, at Hampshire College, Amherst, Massachusetts.

'the end of imagination', 'the greater common good', 'power politics', 'the algebra of infinite justice' and 'war is peace' first appeared in *Outlook* and *Frontline* magazines. They have also been published in several languages worldwide in the following newspapers and magazines:

'the end of imagination' in the *Guardian* (UK), *Politikens Forlag* (Denmark), *Dagens Nyheter* (Sweden), *El Pais* (Spain), *Ode Magazine* (the Netherlands), *Helsingen Sanomat* (Finland), *Tidens Tegn* (Norway), *Internazionale*

(Italy), *De Groener Amsterdammer* (the Netherlands), *TransEuropéennes* (France);

'the greater common good' in the *Guardian* (UK; under the title 'Lies, Dam Lies and Statistics'), *Dagens Nyheter* (Sweden), *Ode Magazine* (the Netherlands), *Internazionale* (Italy), *Marie-Claire* (UK), *Die Weltwoche* (Switzerland; German language), *Femina* (Denmark; an adapted article drawn from 'the end of imagination' and 'the greater common good', as taken from *Frontline*);

'the algebra of infinite justice' in the *Guardian* (UK), *Frankfurter Allgemeine* (Germany), *Le Monde* (France), *Internazionale* (Italy), *Vrij Nederland* (the Netherlands), *The Spokesman* (UK), *La Stampa* (Italy), *El Mundo* (Spain), *Emma Verlag* (Germany), *TMM Magazine* (Iceland), *Sekai* (Japan), *Kurve* (Germany), *Norskensflamman* (Sweden), *Ruminator Review* (USA);

'war is peace' in the *Guardian* (UK), *El Mundo* (Spain), *Der Spiegel* (Germany), *The Spokesman* (UK), *Internazionale* (Italy), *Ordfront Magasin* (Sweden), *De Standaard* (Belgium), *Hufvudstadtsbladet* (Finland; Swedish language), MSNBC (USA; Internet rights), *In These Times* (USA).

'the end of imagination' was first published in book form by IBD in India. 'the end of imagination' and 'the greater common good' were published together in book form as

The Cost of Living by HarperCollins Publishers. *The Cost of Living* was also translated and published by Prometheus (Dutch), Gallimard (French), Bertelsmann (German), Psichogios (Greek), Zmora Bitan-Dvir (Hebrew), Guanda (Italian), Tsukiji Shokan (Japanese), Moonhak Kwa Jisung Sa (Korean) and Pax Forlag (Norwegian).

'the end of imagination' was published in book form in Catalan and Spanish by Anagrama, in Portuguese by ASA and in Danish by Munksgaard Rosinante. 'the greater common good' was published in book form in Portuguese by ASA and in Spanish by Anagrama.

'the ladies have feelings, so . . .' and 'power politics' were published together in book form as *Power Politics* by South End Press.

'democracy' was first published by *Outlook India* magazine. 'war talk' is based on a piece first broadcast in June 2002 by BBC Radio 4 on the *Today* programme, entitled 'Under the Nuclear Shadow'. 'come September' was presented in Santa Fe, New Mexico at the Lensic Performing Arts Center on September 18, 2002. This is the first time they have been published in book form.

All the essays have also been published in India in Gujarati, Hindi, Marathi, Malayalam, Urdu, Tamil, Bengali and Assamese.